Hero of Hispaniola

Hero of Hispaniola

America's First Black Diplomat, Ebenezer D. Bassett

Christopher Teal

Westport, Connecticut
London

Library of Congress Cataloging-in-Publication Data

Teal, Christopher, 1971–

   Hero of Hispaniola: America's first black diplomat, Ebenezer D. Bassett / Christopher Teal
      p. cm.
   Includes bibliographical references and index.
   ISBN-13: 978-0-313-35195-2 (alk. paper)
   1. Bassett, Ebenezer D., 1833–1908. 2. African Americans—Biography. 3. Ambassadors—
United States—Biography. 4. African American diplomats—Biography. 5. United
States—Foreign relations—Haiti. 6. Haiti—Foreign relations—United States. 7. African
Americans—Segregation—History—19th century. 8. United States—Race relations—
History—19th century. 9. African American educators—Biography. 10. African American
abolitionists—Biography. I. Title.
   E185.97.B27T43 2008
   327.2092—dc22
   [B]   2008009956

British Library Cataloguing in Publication Data is available.

Library of Congress Catalog Card Number: 2008009956
ISBN-13: 978–0–313–35195–2

First published in 2008

Praeger Publishers, 88 Post Road West, Westport, CT 06881
An imprint of Greenwood Publishing Group, Inc.
www.praeger.com

Printed in the United States of America

The paper used in this book complies with the
Permanent Paper Standard issued by the National
Information Standards Organization (Z39.48-1984).

10 9 8 7 6 5 4 3 2 1

The author is a Foreign Service Officer at the Department of State. Any views expressed
herein are solely those of the author, and not necessarily those of the United States
Government or the U.S. Department of State.

In memory of my grandfather Eldon Phyllis (1921–2008).

To all those courageous diplomats who have lost their lives in the service of their country; we still seek to make this a better world.

The American Foreign Service Association (AFSA) is the professional organization that represents U.S. diplomats and promotes greater understanding of the critical role that the Foreign Service plays in American foreign policy. They have created a fund supporting higher education, including several perpetual scholarships established in memory of those who lost their lives while serving overseas. If you would like more information about AFSA, or if you want to contribute to the AFSA Scholarship fund, please see their Web page at http://www.afsa.org/scholar.

Contents

a photo essay follows page 102

Acknowledgments

I wish to acknowledge the following people for their assistance in my research for this book: Angela Ajayi, Jeffrey Bassett, James and Charlotte Brown, Karen Burress, Dorothy A. DeBisschop, Brian Foster, Frank Gagliardi from Central Connecticut State University; the staff of the Ralph J. Bunche Library at the State Department, Jean Dietz, Glenn LaChapelle, and the staff at the Wilbraham-Monson Academy; Lisbeth Keefe, Jill Legner, Marian O'Keefe, and the staff at the Derby Historical Society; Steve Honley and Susan Maitra of the *Foreign Service Journal;* Alice and Eldon Phillis, Gayle Potter, R. C. Potter, Gail Ross, Avery Teal, Brook Teal, Simira Tobias, Susie Yaters, Juan Williams, and my wonderful colleagues at the Foreign Press Center.

Ebenezer D. Bassett Genealogy

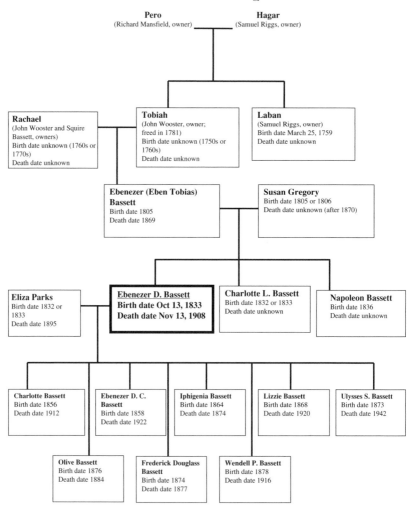

Pero
(Richard Mansfield, owner)

Hagar
(Samuel Riggs, owner)

Rachael
(John Wooster and Squire
Bassett, owners)
Birth date unknown (1760s or
1770s)
Death date unknown

Tobiah
(John Wooster, owner;
freed in 1781)
Birth date unknown (1750s or
1760s)
Death date unknown

Laban
(Samuel Riggs, owner)
Birth date March 25, 1759
Death date unknown

**Ebenezer (Eben Tobias)
Bassett**
Birth date 1805
Death date 1869

Susan Gregory
Birth date 1805 or 1806
Death date unknown (after 1870)

Eliza Parks
Birth date 1832 or
1833
Death date 1895

Ebenezer D. Bassett
Birth date Oct 13, 1833
Death date Nov 13, 1908

Charlotte L. Bassett
Birth date 1832 or 1833
Death date unknown

Napoleon Bassett
Birth date 1836
Death date unknown

Charlotte Bassett
Birth date 1856
Death date 1912

**Ebenezer D. C.
Bassett**
Birth date 1858
Death date 1922

Iphigenia Bassett
Birth date 1864
Death date 1874

Lizzie Bassett
Birth date 1868
Death date 1920

Ulysses S. Bassett
Birth date 1873
Death date 1942

Olive Bassett
Birth date 1876
Death date 1884

**Frederick Douglass
Bassett**
Birth date 1874
Death date 1877

Wendell P. Bassett
Birth date 1878
Death date 1916

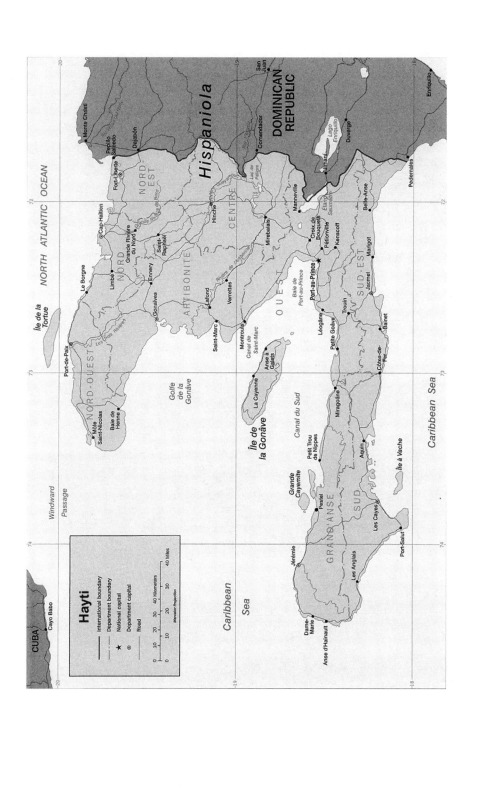

1

Under Siege

A stillness finally settled into the air by late evening. Though it was muggy, the sweltering heat of summer had not yet fallen with its full force upon Port-au-Prince. As an eerie quiet enveloped the houses, darkness cloaked the blood that still covered the roads throughout the city.

For days Haytian President Michel Domingue had boldly declared open warfare against any perceived enemy. Homes were shelled; children were shot down in the street; even the American diplomat himself had come under attack.

Now, with the hoped-for end of hostilities apparently in sight, Ebenezer D. Bassett attempted to drift into a full night of sleep. He had served in Hayti for six years, since 1869, and had sadly grown used to the frequent outbreaks of violence. He had witnessed civil wars and coups d'état that were as frequent in Hayti as the hurricanes that menaced the Caribbean. As the first black man ever to serve as chief diplomatic envoy representing the United States, Bassett thought that by now he had seen, and could handle, most anything. Surely this latest round would soon pass as well.

At 3:00 a.m. Bassett awoke with a start. Downstairs, the loud banging on his official residence door had stirred the entire family and household staff. The Minister Resident, his official diplomatic title, could hear muffled voices outside speaking in the native French Creole. Moments later one of his staff knocked gently on his bedroom door and announced that he had better come downstairs right away.

Opening the wide front door, Bassett had no time to even utter a word before three large men rushed past him. A mulatto, tall and handsome, with broad shoulders, led the group and spoke first to the American diplomat.

"I am Boisrond Canal. These two young men are my relatives."

Bassett was stunned. He of course knew Pierre Boisrond Canal and knew of the integrity of the former general in the Haytian Army. Canal was certainly not a personal friend, was not a drunkard, and was not known to drop by unannounced. What could this man be doing at his doorstep? Half asleep, Bassett impatiently replied: "What in the world are you doing here at this time of night?"

Standing in candlelight before a nervous audience of Bassett's family and staff, the General rose to his full stature, as if in a theatrical perform-ance. Despite having narrowly escaped the guns of Haytian troops, he mustered the strength to look Bassett directly in the eye and explain his ordeal over the previous two days:

"We have been ruthlessly, without shadow of law, attacked by a whole army," Canal calmly told him. "Five of us held them at bay for thirty-six hours, drove them back, evaded them, and fought our way here, intend-ing to keep on to town. Two of our number fell in our contests. We are not in arms against the government; we are not enemies of society. We are fleeing for our lives before merciless pursuers acting outside the law. We seek the protection of your flag," Canal dramatically concluded.

The American diplomat was in a quandary. Bassett had previously dealt with numerous Haytian figures requesting amnesty and protection. Given the violent unrest that had marked most of the previous seven decades of Haytian independence, recriminations against political foes were common. With almost every new administration in Hayti, opposi-tion forces sought refuge in the embassies and foreign missions of the American or European powers. Though controversial, this tradition had continued through Bassett's tenure. In earlier circumstances, Washington had been adamant in responding to their envoy that this right to accept those seeking asylum was to be used only in extreme cases and, in fact, preferably not at all. Bassett knew that his boss, Secretary of State Hamilton Fish (and in turn perhaps President U. S. Grant), would not be pleased. However, he had no choice.

"They would be slaughtered," Bassett thought to himself, if he turned Canal away at this late hour with Haytian troops on their heels. No mat-ter how reluctant he was to take on this burden, Ebenezer Bassett led them inside his home, offering whatever slim protection international treaties and law afforded him.

It did not take long for President Domingue's forces to find the where-abouts of their prey. Rushing his soldiers toward the official residence, Domingue ordered the grounds surrounded. Though they did not imme-diately enter the gates, the military held the road and offered no means of escape for the general. Bassett reminded the authorities of his protected status as an accredited diplomat, and in the morning he proceeded into town to meet with the Foreign Minister himself.

The U.S. envoy's house lay in the hillsides, overlooking the capital. The majestic French colonial architecture could still be seen in some of the remaining homes that had not been destroyed through years of fighting. As he did most mornings, Bassett saddled his horse and made his way through the dusty roads toward his offices at the U.S. Legation to the Republic of Hayti. Only this morning things were very different.

By now Bassett estimated that several hundred armed men lingered around his fifteen-acre compound. Dark-skinned for the most part, they gave the lighter-skinned Bassett menacing looks as he passed. While Bassett was traveling along about a mile from his house, some of those soldiers grew emboldened, rushed him with drawn swords, and grabbed the reigns of his horse. A commanding officer closed in on Bassett and ordered him to go no farther. Protests about diplomatic immunity from detention or arrest were cut off, and the swords rose again.

"Obey the military authority," the commander shouted menacingly. But Bassett's years of negotiations, calm demeanor, and mastery of the local language and customs placated the commander, who reluctantly allowed him to continue toward the city.

As soon as he arrived in Port-au-Prince, Bassett complained to the Foreign Minister about this unacceptable treatment. The response from him and from every other Haytian official was simple—Canal had been in the process of instigating a coup against the legitimate and democratic government of the Republic. He was to be turned over immediately for trial. Bassett politely demurred, citing earlier occasions when others had requested his protection.

By now, the entire city was abuzz with rumors of Canal's escape. Visitors inundated Bassett's office, begging for the latest gossip. He refused to discuss the matter openly, and he quietly continued to press the government for a negotiation on Canal. He knew that to simply turn over the general would mean a summary execution. It would take all of his skills as a diplomat and negotiator to avoid such an outcome. Given the heated state of affairs, however, he was not sure how much longer that he could hold back the Haytian military.

Bassett returned home and found the situation deteriorating; the Haytian army had laid in for a siege of his house. His wife Eliza and their five children were on the verge of tears, as he frantically began thinking about ways to end this crisis. By nightfall, everyone was exhausted, but the noise outside only intensified. Looking out his second story window, he could see the number of troops growing in the distance. To his disbelief and horror he watched as this mass of soldiers, by this point fired on by rum, began yelling, singing, and banging metal drums to create as loud a racket as possible. If Bassett would not voluntarily turn over their prisoners, these soldiers would ratchet up the situation to force them out. Night after night this scene continued. Pleas to Washington would take days by boat for any answer or support. He stood alone as the defender of someone he was not even sure deserved defending, and he was now a target himself.[1]

*****

Ebenezer Bassett's life lay at the crossroads of integrity and diplomacy—where one man found himself defying the odds, trying to pursue what was right, while protecting the national interests of the country and upholding the directives of the President he was there to serve.

It has often been said that diplomats are America's first line of defense. They are the U.S. government's eyes and ears, seeking to understand events in distant lands, and assessing their repercussions for those of us at home. But they are also literally the face of America, showing other nations and cultures who we are.

However, for most of the early history of the Republic, that face was Anglo, wealthy, and even slaveholding.

With the Civil War, race relations within the United States began a radical transformation. Black slaves were freed, and black men were given presumptive equal protection and voting rights with the Fourteenth and Fifteenth Amendments. The Congress embarked upon a Reconstruction period that brought dramatic changes to the body politic. The most profound among these would be the fact that blacks would hold public office in the old Confederacy and would be given unprecedented freedoms and protections by the federal government. Though America would continue to struggle with its internal demons of racism, it slowly embarked on another transformation—that of sending blacks abroad as official representatives of a more fully democratic United States.

Bassett's work as a politically appointed diplomat forever altered U.S. foreign policy. For the first time, a nation founded on the principle that "all men are created equal" would have as the President's foreign representative someone who had previously been less than equal under the law. This movement toward equality and democratization of international affairs would be neither quick nor perfect. But it proved to be a force that was impossible to turn back, and it had implications for both domestic and foreign policy in the years ahead.

Though much has been written about the politics of race within America, far too little attention has been placed on how those same politics shaped relationships with other countries, including support for having a black American represent the United States abroad. This book seeks to fill that gap and pay deserving tribute to a man who helped change the way the world saw the United States and reflected how the United States saw itself.

Only one question remained. In spite of Bassett's accomplishments and connections, and the symbolism of his position, would he be able to negotiate the safety of his refugees, his own family, and himself to survive until the break of day?

2

Horns of a Dilemma

Christopher Columbus reeled upon the island in 1492 during his first quest for a western trade route to India. Naming it Hispaniola, Columbus claimed it, as well as everything else he found, for the Spanish monarchy. The island was inhabited by Native Americans of the Taino and Caribe cultures, who referred to their home as Hayti, meaning *high land*. The eastern portion of the island was known as Quisqueya or *motherland*, and the west, Babeque or *golden land*. They were rich tropical zones with fertile soil and a warm climate.

Based on the promise of his discoveries on this maiden voyage, the explorer greedily returned with seventeen ships and over 1,500 people to begin the conquest of the New World in earnest. Settlements grew in various parts of the island over the next two centuries in support of a mining and plantation system in the burgeoning Spanish empire. The port of Santo Domingo blossomed, serving as the capital and seat of the Viceroy for the Spanish crown.

The Spaniards attempted to enslave the local natives, but after a brutal campaign of warfare and rapidly spreading European disease, they found the natives ill-suited and of insufficient numbers for the forced labor the colonizers required. Thus as early as 1510, they began a program of importing massive numbers of enslaved Africans to the island. As the productivity of the land increased, so did the number of slaves.

Spain was not alone in its efforts to conquer territory and take riches from the New World. Soon Portugal, England, and others followed suit throughout the Caribbean. The French in particular, had their eye on this Spanish island, and after years of assault by British and other pirates, they found much of the western part uninhabited and undefended.

Starting in the early 1600s from a base on the island of Tortuga, off the northwestern coast of Hispaniola, French pirates, hunters, and adventurers gradually established a tenuous foothold. Eventually the Treaty of Ryswick in 1697 brought peace between Spain and France with the arrival of Filipe V to the Spanish throne. Filipe, the grandson of French king Louis XIV, split the island and proclaimed "leave to the French the land they occupied."[1]

The French referred to their new colony as *Saint Domingue,* and over the next hundred years it became one of the most profitable of all the colonies in the hemisphere. The exportation of minerals, sugar, coffee, and tobacco would enrich thousands of merchants and supply the Monarchy with the wherewithal to expand their empire throughout the globe. Only thirty years after formally gaining control of the western third of the island, the French had already imported over 50,000 African slaves for the plantation system that produced these riches.[2] That number grew exponentially through the following decades of the eighteenth century. By 1789, whereas some 30,000 slaves were recorded across the border in Spanish Santo Domingo, a population of over 500,000 filled French-controlled Saint Domingue.

The system of slavery was not much different in French-controlled St. Domingue from what it had been in the days of the Spanish reign. The sheer number of slaves, however, a sixteen-to-one ratio of blacks to whites, made the nature of slavery perhaps more brutal out of the necessity of control. Just as the native tribes had been decimated by their first exposure to European diseases, the Europeans would also find themselves battling for survival against local illnesses such as dengue fever and malaria. The frontier conditions, constant battles against sickness, and occasional hurricanes would ensure that life on St. Domingue would never be easy, especially for the slaves themselves.

Slaves were subjugated to the cruelest forms of humiliation, even when working. From contemporary accounts, slaves would be fitted with manacles, and masks were used over their faces to prevent them from eating any of the sugarcane they harvested. Bodily mutilations were carried out to keep the slaves compliant: acts ranging from nailing them by the ears to posts to cutting off limbs and genitalia. Also, salt, ashes, and lemon were rubbed into their wounds to increase their pain. Even worse, slaves were thrown into boiling cauldrons, buried alive, or fed to packs of hungry dogs if they disobeyed.

The 1789 revolution that exploded in France would strain the status quo in St. Domingue as well. The passage of the liberal "Rights of Man" by the French assembly, the independence of the United States from Britain, and efforts by white Haytian planters to maintain their hegemony all made for a combustible mix as the repressed slaves began to expect better treatment at the hands of their owners.

Finally in 1791, at plantations near the northern coast of Cap Francais, slaves rose up and killed most of their white owners. The fever spread with the rapidity and force of a tropical storm, and soon a full-scale rebellion was underway.

From accounts of the insurrection, the first two months of the revolt saw that "upwards of two thousands whites had been massacred, one hundred and eight sugar plantations and about nine hundred coffee, cotton, and indigo settlements had been destroyed." According to that same account, an incredible estimate of ten thousand slaves also died "by the sword or famine and some hundreds by the hand of the executioner, many of these on the wheel," a hideous torture device used to stretch out the victims, ripping ligaments, tearing muscle, and pulling apart bones.[3]

The white planters, who gained little support from the revolutionary fires of France, turned to the newly independent United States. The leadership controlling the new country, President George Washington, Secretary of State Thomas Jefferson, and many others who had fought against British rule, were themselves plantation owners, and they were sympathetic to the pleas of neighboring slaveholders.

In a blistering critique of the racial aspects of early U.S. foreign policy, a later historian would write: "Nowhere has racism been more apparent in American foreign relations than in U.S. relations with Hayti. . . . The first president formulated a proslavery policy toward the Haytian revolution that left a legacy of racism and white supremacy in the White House, the State Department, and the halls of Congress."[4]

In fact, George Washington did provide support when asked by French colonialists for arms to put down the rebellion. In 1791, the American President wrote to the French Minister, Jean de Ternant, "I am happy . . . that the United States are to render every aid in their power to quell 'the alarming insurrection of the negroes of Hispaniola.'"[5] Moreover, because the United States still owed France a considerable war debt, the shipment of arms to a steadfast ally was seen as the least America could do. Washington instructed Secretary of the Treasury Alexander Hamilton to release $40,000 to aid St. Domingue.[6]

Thomas Jefferson authored the noble words in the Declaration of Independence that all men were created equal, but the reality could not have been starker. No equality would exist for millions of Africans exported in a thriving trade of human property, least of all for Jefferson's own slaves. They and their descendants lived under the yoke of seemingly perpetual dependence. They owed their very lives to the whims of their masters. And the southern slaveholders whom Jefferson and Washington represented anxiously sought to prevent the spread of the slave revolt north into their fledgling nation.

But the arms proved of little use when the white plantation owners of St. Domingue were so vastly outnumbered, and the former slaveholders now found their resources in the hands of people who had formerly been their abused property.

Whites continued to flee the French colony, and a struggle ensued between blacks and free mulattoes (many of whom had themselves been slaveholders) over the balance of power in what was still nominally a French possession. In 1794 the French National Convention issued a decree of emancipation, freeing all slaves in every French territory, including St. Domingue. Adding to the confusion, England and Spain both made grabs for possession of disputed territory on the island, and both gained control of large segments as civil war spread. It was amid this chaos that the black military leader Toussaint l'Ouverture rose to gain control over the disparate forces remaining in St. Domingue and assisted the French to restore order. Together the French and Toussaint's forces were successful in driving out both the Spanish and British, restoring a degree of self-rule to St. Domingue, while maintaining the freedom of the formerly enslaved masses.

With Toussaint eventually able to consolidate power, few whites remained on the island by 1800. Meanwhile his subordinate, Jean Jacques Dessalines, managed to force out or kill thousands of the mulattoes as well. A constitution was drafted, and Toussaint was soon declared governor general. St. Domingue appeared only a small step from formal independence until the rise of Napoleon Bonaparte, who jealously set his eyes on regaining control of this once rich colony.

The French Emperor sent an army of twenty thousand troops to take back its wayward child. Through deceit, French military commander Victor Leclerc captured Toussaint and sent him to a French prison, where he soon died. Meanwhile, the revolt grew more fearsome, particularly when they learned that Bonaparte had restored slavery in the nearby islands of Martinique and Guadeloupe. However, malaria, yellow fever, and dengue ravaged the French troops, and Toussaint's second in command, Dessalines, wiped out the survivors.

Finally, on January 1, 1804, Saint Domingue, with Dessalines as its undisputed leader, declared itself the independent Republic of Hayti, becoming the second colony in the Western Hemisphere to do so, and the world's first Black Republic. But immediately he incurred the ire of a potential ally when Dessalines declared "that a great number of native blacks and men of colour are suffering in the United States" and ordered that ship captains would be paid $40 per head for the return of slaves to

Hayti.[7] This decree, a direct threat to the American slaveholders' control over their slaves, hindered any chance at immediate support or recognition from the United States.

Europeans continued to see large chunks of their territory lost to the revolutionary fervor that began on Bunker Hill and flowed into Port-au-Prince. Only a few years after Hayti declared its independence, Argentina, Colombia, Mexico, and Central America would undertake their own struggles for freedom, and by the 1820s all had been recognized by the United States as new nations. The colonial powers were not willing to let their treasures slip so easily from their grasp, however, and they continued to wage warfare—both literally and figuratively—against the West.

In response to this continued conflict, President James Monroe established a new policy with regard to the Americas that sought to minimize outside interference, declaring to the Congress in 1823 "that the American continents, by the free and independent condition which they have assumed and maintain, are henceforth not to be considered as subjects for future colonization by any European powers." The Monroe Doctrine laid out a strong position that the United States would not tolerate efforts to recolonize the Western Hemisphere. Though he hinted that there would be no threat to existing colonies, President Monroe argued that those that had already severed their ties with the Old Continent should remain free and independent nations. For Europe to act against that, Monroe felt, would be a threat not simply against the former colony, but also against the United States itself.

Meanwhile on the island of Hispaniola, the Black Republic crumbled under the weight of revolution and civil war. Though Dessalines had been the one to take Toussaint's mantle and proclaim independence, his rule was bloody and brief. His assassination in 1806 did nothing to bring calm to the island. Hayti soon found itself split between two factions, as Henri Christophe gained control of the north, while Alexandre Petion held the south, effectively keeping the country divided until their deaths. Finally with Jean Pierre Boyer's consolidation of power in 1820, the nation would once again be unified. Soon thereafter, Boyer gained control of the eastern Spanish portion, and the whole island merged under one government, and developed a growing commercial importance for the United States.

With Hayti's new-found power under Boyer, France gradually and reluctantly acknowledged the reality that they would never again control their former colony. In 1825, French King Charles X accepted St. Domingue's liberty and formally recognized Hayti as a nation. In return, President Boyer's government would pay indemnities to France for its losses and would allow a reduction of duties for shipping and commerce.[8] Britain, soon after it had passed its abolition of slavery law in 1833, also came to recognize Hayti's independence. In the United States, however, the reaction to these moves was mixed and fraught with domestic politics over the brewing issue of slavery.

Free blacks in large East Coast cities watched with interest the unfolding drama in Hayti, and they urged greater interaction with their sister republic. New York's large free black population was home to the country's first black-owned newspaper, *Freedom's Journal,* which was founded in 1827 and regularly featured articles on the events in Hayti.

As home to the largest number of free blacks living in the country prior to the U.S. Civil War, Baltimore was also the center of a growing middle class of black businessmen, who admired the Haytian movement and sought to increase commerce with the Caribbean nation. *Niles Weekly Register,* one of the nation's most influential news magazines, observed events in Hayti with keen interest. Published by Quakers, strong supporters of abolition, it was natural for publications like *Niles* to pay special attention to events unfolding in Hayti. As early as 1823, *Niles* entered the public debate about the justification of recognizing Hayti's independence:

> It is strongly recommended by many, that the United Sties should officially acknowledge a fact which really exists, the independence of Hayti. Much may be said on both sides of the question; and, though, the general opinion is against the proceeding. . . . the people have a regular and enlightened government of the republican form—more liberal, perhaps, in its operation than any now existing in Europe, those of Great Britain and Spain only accepted. . . . The press is freer than in France, Russia, Austria or Prussia.

But when it came to making the radical push for full diplomatic recognition, even liberals such as *Niles* realized the societal hurdles of the day:

> It is admitted, and it is certainly true, that our present trade with Hayti is of greater importance to us than our trade with France, herself. It employs much more of our tonnage, and is, every way, more beneficial to us: But shall we, by, acknowledging the independence of the island, involve ourselves in a war with France? . . . But again, are we yet prepared to send and receive ministers to and from Hayti? Could the prejudices of some and the, perhaps just fears of others, be quieted? We think not. The time has not yet come for a surrender of our feelings about color, nor is it fitting at any time, that the public safety should be endangered. Hayti is, and will be, independent—we cannot prevent it if we would, nor are we so disposed. In looking into the vista, of futurity, great events may be anticipated—but we cannot wish to hurry them on. . . . We are on the horns of a dilemma, and how to get off, at some future period—we leave to that period to determine as well as it can.[9]

Indeed, the conflict only grew between southern planters and northern merchants. Southern intransigence grew more acute as the pressure to expand holdings through the recently acquired Louisiana Purchase led to greater debate about slavery. So severe was President Jefferson's dislike of Hayti that he even imposed a trade embargo against the country in 1806. Though he knew it would be difficult to choke Hayti economically in its infancy, he was compelled politically to represent the landed interests such as those of his old Virginia home. However, many began coalescing around another tactic less economically damaging to U.S. interests—colonization.

The idea of a recolonization effort to Africa had been around for several years. But with the independence of Hayti and a growing number of free blacks populating several states, the sense of urgency to handle this "problem" only grew.

The idea initially hatched was to send free blacks to the West Coast of Africa to start their own colony. Figures such as James Monroe, Francis Scott Key, Daniel Webster, and Henry Clay gathered in December of 1816 to develop this notion further, chartering the American Colonization Society. George Washington's nephew Bushrod was named its first president.

They raised money, and by 1819 they chartered a ship to carry over the first group to resettle the African homeland. This maiden effort was less than successful because yellow fever killed a quarter of the voyagers, and the remainder sought passage back to the United States. Undeterred, the American Colonization Society continued and would eventually move over 12,000 free blacks back to Africa.

But, given the difficulties involved in "repatriation" to Africa, others began to look for points of debarkation much closer, including Hispaniola. Thomas Jefferson himself was an advocate for this possibility: "Nature seems to have formed these islands to become the receptacles of the blacks transplanted to this hemisphere. . . . The most promising . . . is the island of St. Domingo, where the blacks are established into a sovereignty de facto. . . ."[10]

Seeing that money was being raised in the United States for migration to Africa, Haytian President Boyer thought that his nation could benefit from the skills of American freemen, and also saw it as an opportunity to continue the Haytian Revolution against the tyranny of slavery by encouraging migration to his country.

In 1824, Boyer notified his commercial contact in New York that he was sending a shipload of coffee to "facilitate the emigration of such individuals of the African race, who, groaning in the United States, under the weight of prejudice and misery, should be disposed to come to Hayti and partake with our citizens the benefits of a liberal constitution, and a paternal government."[11] African Americans were quite supportive of their "black brethren" in Hayti. An estimated 6,000 immigrated to Hayti during this time of the 1820s and 1830s.[12] However, many leading abolitionists, freed blacks, and escaped slaves opposed what appeared to them a "forced expulsion" from the United States.

Meanwhile the issue of Haytian recognition continued to simmer in the background. The divided nature of the United States, with over half the states allowing slavery, continued to make the recognition of a rebellious former slave colony anathema. Congressional debates at the time reveal the split in the discussion. Senator Thomas Hart Benton of Missouri said in 1825: "Our policy towards Hayti . . . has been fixed . . . for three and thirty years. We trade with her, but no diplomatic relations have been established between us. . . . We receive no mulatto consuls, or black ambassadors from her. And why? Because the peace of eleven states will not permit the fruits of a successful negro insurrection to be exhibited among them. It will not permit black ambassadors and consuls . . . to give their fellow blacks in the United States proof in hand of the honors that await them for a like successful effort on their part."[13]

Though this lack of recognition grated on the Haytians, lures of the commercial ties overcame even the prejudice of U.S. policy. American commercial agents had resided in Port-au-Prince since 1799, when Hayti was still a French colony. By 1827, however, Boyer told American officials that a U.S. commercial agent would no longer be recognized in the Haytian capital if official recognition of independence was not forthcoming. After the dismissal of the commercial agent, Hayti stepped up the pressure, imposing tariffs on U.S. vessels in Haytian ports. The race-conscious Americans refused to back down.[14]

By the 1840s, Hayti had lost its struggle to maintain control over the entire island. The former Spanish colony in the east had never been fully subdued, and it finally broke free of Hayti in 1844. Complaints about the brutal nature of the Haytian regime there are still discussed almost two centuries later. Hayti retreated to its former borders and again looked toward the United States for assistance.

The commercial ties between Hayti and the U.S. gradually gained strength with the reduction of tariffs in 1850. For the new Haytian president Faustin Soulouque, this was a far cry from the much-coveted recognition he craved, but it represented a thawing of the relationship, and it emphasized the growing dominance of the American North and their antislavery and business factions.

In response to the détente, Soulouque wanted to appoint a Haytian commercial agent in Boston, but Secretary of State Daniel Webster told him that only someone "not of African extraction" would be acceptable.[15] The United States and Hayti could not find a way around the issue of race. Though trade between the two had grown, it was clear that a normal, bilateral relationship could never form until America addressed its own racial issues.

3

Recognition at Last

President Abraham Lincoln had been in office for a just a few months. In that short time, he had witnessed the unimaginable, and he now had the dubious honor of being the American executive to preside over the dissolution of the Union.

His predecessors in the Oval Office had managed to hold together the disparate factions of an unholy match from the beginning of independence. Like a castle of sand facing the onrush of waves, however, the United States of America was finally overwhelmed by the force of conflict rolling across its shores. Lincoln manned those turrets, as an ocean raced around him and his deeply divided people.

Though some states were certainly worse for slaves than others were, the very existence of the institution of slavery offered little hope for any who were held in its bonds. Despite the fact that the majority of the nation's citizens did not themselves hold slaves, an uneasy balance had been struck to preserve the unity of the former British colonies. But this pact that the United States had made with itself would turn out to become a true Faustian bargain. Morally, economically, and by the mid-nineteenth century, even politically, slavery would be the one domestic issue that trumped all others. Presidents had treaded its waters lightly or not at all. That equilibrium reached a breaking point with the 1860 Presidential election and the victory of the Illinois attorney.

The ruinous conflict that began in the aftermath of Lincoln's election had lurched through its bloody beginnings by the end of 1861. A neophyte politician, Lincoln struggled through his first year in office as the body count grew and, along with it, public discontent.

During his first annual message to Congress on the state of affairs, Lincoln almost obliquely referred to the turmoil that had consumed the Union, calling the outbreak of the Civil War an "unprecedented political trouble." When he delivered his speech on December 3 of 1861, Lincoln did not need to create false images for political gain. He simply noted what everyone fully understood, that the "United" States was no more, and that eleven members of that Union had engaged in open warfare and rebellion against his government over one single issue: slavery.

Though fully absorbed in domestic affairs, Lincoln was keenly aware of the temptation that his fractious nation might present to European countries, like wounded prey before ruthless predators. The royal families of Europe were interested in gaining advantages by playing off both sides in the conflict. He even feared that some might be plotting to regain territory in the New World. At the very least, the President was sure that a failing nation-state was an easy victim for those wishing to establish alliances, and that the precarious situation could lead to permanent division of the country. Raising just such a specter, Lincoln warned Congress in his message of the power vacuum that eager Europeans might foresee: "A disloyal portion of the American people have during the whole year been engaged in an attempt to divide and destroy the Union. A nation which endures factious domestic divisions is exposed to disrespect abroad, and one party, if not both is sure sooner or later to invoke foreign intervention."

With this warning, Lincoln assured the legislature of his diplomatic efforts of "practiced prudence" toward Europe, "averting causes of irritation." The White House, with many more pressing concerns to confront, simply could not afford political differences to create diplomatic fissures with superpowers such as Great Britain, France, or Spain.

It was not surprising that the majority of his message was devoted to domestic battles, or that what he chose to present as a major foreign policy initiative would also be an extension of his domestic policy. In a move that shocked many, Lincoln called for the recognition of two "black" nations— Hayti and Liberia. Both had been troublesome partners of the United States for many decades. Since its independence in 1804, Hayti had represented the worst fears of the Southern plantation-holder—a full-scale rebellion and independence by slaves. Liberia was in many ways the opposite side of that coin. Declaring its independence in 1847 as an outgrowth of the American Colonization Society, Liberia continued to represent an effort by some of its supporters to rid the U.S. of its "black burden." For others, Liberia was an acknowledgment of the wrongs of slavery, and a remedy, no matter how feeble, to confront it.

Though both countries were developing their unique national courses, Hayti and Liberia were intimately tied together for several reasons. They were both virtually all-black nations, and each had strong bonds to the United States. Neither state had been officially recognized as independent by any American administration, and both for the same reason—their "blackness."

The impasse over recognition was broken with the secession of the southern States and the resulting absence from Congress of their voting members. Sympathizers from the North now looked to take advantage of this opening. Lincoln, quick to understand a way to curry favor among supporters of recognition, pushed the issue into the forefront of the political debate by the end of 1861.

"If any good reason exists why we should preserve longer in withholding our recognition of the independence and sovereignty of Hayti and Liberia," Lincoln wrote in his message to Congress, "I am unable to discern it."

"Unwilling, however, to inaugurate a novel policy in regard to them without the approbation of Congress, I submit for your consideration the expediency of an appropriation for maintaining a *charge d'affaires* near each of those new States."

With this opening salvo, Abraham Lincoln sought to shore up a political constituency in the North wanting to increase trade. He also had the advantage of giving the proverbial poke in the eye to southerners who would find any such recognition anathema. Lincoln, however, was not interested simply in scoring short-term political points. No doubt he understood that with a war unfolding in states with large slave populations, he would one day have to cope with potentially millions of poor and uneducated blacks who had been subjected to the most brutal system of humiliation and degradation imaginable.

Lincoln also saw Hayti and Liberia as safety valves. As a charter member of the American Colonization Society in Illinois, Lincoln had long advocated its policies. Now in the White House, he sought to use his power to allow for the emigration of hundreds of thousands of freed slaves whom the country would one day have as its burden. Surely many of these once abused farmhands would prefer to live in a country of their own, a country run by blacks. Cultural or language issues aside, Lincoln assumed that many would want to leave the land that had been responsible for their despicable treatment. Why not begin the process via this recognition?

A cruder political reading would be that Lincoln also feared the repercussions of the freedom of millions of black slaves. Even if the Union eventually regained control of these rebellious states, with a defeated white population and an empowered but angry black population, was he sure that fighting would not continue unabated? And what if the fighting spread? Had Hayti not once been controlled by white French landholders? A quick look at its history was not comforting. Lincoln could end up winning the war of southern rebellion, but losing political control of his entire country. It was a fate he would rather not face. Congress would quickly take the war president up on his request.

Just a few months after President Lincoln made his appeal for the recognition of Hayti, Senator Charles Sumner of Massachusetts spearheaded a resolution through the chamber calling for recognition and the appointment of a Minister Resident to Port-au-Prince.

Sumner, from a patrician family in Boston, was a successful lawyer and champion of many reform causes, including being an abolitionist. One of his early speeches in Congress, "Crime against Kansas," railed against the proslavery forces that had won flawed elections in that new territory; his price for the invective was to be beaten by a member of the House of Representatives from South Carolina. No stranger to controversy, it was not surprising that Sumner now took the lead for President Lincoln in the matter of Hayti's diplomatic recognition.

In Senate Bill 184, the Senator sought to "authorize the President of the United States to appoint diplomatic representatives to the republics of Hayti and Liberia respectively." Amid Congressional discussions of the alleged drunkenness of a Union general and the confiscation of property from rebels, a tense debate opened on the Senate floor on April 22 of 1862.

Sumner stood ready for battle. With limited southern voices of opposition (nominally representatives from the border states now took on that role) he assumed passage to be assured. But the level of bigotry would surprise even the radical abolitionists from the Northeast.

Sumner himself acknowledged the fact that Lincoln was not required to consult the legislature in this manner. The executive had long held power over which governments it saw fit to recognize, but Lincoln took the extra and unusual step of including Congress. In part it was an attempt to seek political cover for this hot potato of an issue. It was also an effort to increase the public discussion of Hayti, and perhaps to test the waters about the development of a colonization program for the island, or even annexation, allowing a freer movement of blacks off the mainland.

Sumner spoke in the well of the Senate in a hyperbolic manner, extolling the tropical paradise that was the western part of Hispaniola: "Hayti is one of the most beautiful and important islands in the world, possessing remarkable advantages in size, situation, climate, soil, productions, and mineral wealth."[1] The senator waxed poetic about mahogany trees, plentiful banana plants, fields of waving sugarcane, and hillsides covered with coffee. It truly seemed to offer everything, lacking only U.S. sanction.

As if that were not enough, Sumner continued, one need look no further than the cold, hard economic facts. Drawing on the Treasury Department's statistical information of 1860, the Senator pointed out that Hayti ranked number twenty-one out of more than seventy nations or entities with which the United State traded. "The exports to Hayti are $2,673,682; while those to Russia amount to $2,062,723."

Though not the most important trading partner for the U.S. (a position indisputably held by Britain), Hayti was certainly an economic source of many jobs, and Sumner felt it had the potential for much more trade with the United States. With its population of over 600,000, Hayti offered a skilled workforce and enough arable land to warrant strengthening ties via recognition. "Hayti, in this scale of commerce and navigation, stands above Sweden, Turkey, Central America, Portugal, the Papal States, Japan, Demark, Prussia, and Ecuador, where we are represented by minister residents," Sumner continued. [2]

Sumner recalled for his colleagues that the United Kingdom, Spain, and even the vanquished colonial power, France in 1825, had all recognized Hayti's independence and appointed diplomatic representatives.

The opponents of Haytian recognition and of the growing abolition movement within Congress leapt to strike a reactionary blow against the proposal. Though border states such as Maryland and Kentucky had remained in the Union, they and others were also home to a great many plantations and slave populations. Residents of those states feared that this move toward recognition was further proof that the proverbial camel's nose had entered the tent. They knew that it was only a matter of time before the whole beast would enter as well, and that meant the realization of their worst fears—full emancipation.

Senator Garrett Davis of Kentucky stood as a bulwark against this effort. He proposed an amendment to the Sumner bill that would allow for the appointment of a consul, rather than that of a higher-ranking diplomat to the island. Killing the effort entirely was a vain wish, but he thought that at least they could postpone the inevitable by not allowing black ambassadors or ministers to walk the corridors of power in the capital city.[3]

Senator Davis argued that there was nothing wrong with formalizing relations and even establishing treaties between the powers, but he was repulsed by the idea that if the United States sent an individual to represent America as a high-ranking diplomat, Hayti would obviously do the same. The Haytian representative would definitely be a black man.

"Well, a great big negro fellow, dressed out with his silver and gold lace clothes in the most fantastic and gaudy style, presented himself in the court of Louis Napoleon, and I admit was received. Now, sir, I want no such exhibition as that in our capital and in our government," Davis said, mocking his colleagues.[4]

To press his case, Davis relied on the racial populism of bigotry: "I do begin to nauseate the subject of slaves and slavery in debate in this Chamber," Davis continued, only days after Union general Ulysses S. Grant had won the particularly bloody, but important, Battle of Shiloh. "And it was only because this measure has been perseveringly and uniformly opposed from the slave States heretofore, and I know is distasteful, to a very considerable extent, to the people of those States." Davis hoped his appeal to the basest instincts of the voter and to his fellow politician would hold sway and prevent the vile picture of a black man being greeted by the President and being treated as the equal of whites from becoming a reality.

For two days, the debate held the Senate in suspense, but in the end Senator Davis failed to persuade his colleagues. Finally Sumner called for the vote on the Davis amendment, and by a count of 8 to 30, it was defeated. Recognition now inched one step closer to reality. Not to be gracious in defeat, Senator Willard Saulsbury of Delaware made this final dig at the effort: "I want the country, however, to know that according to the rules of the Senate, foreign ministers have a right upon this floor, and we have set apart a portion of the gallery for the ministers and their families. If this bill should pass both Houses of Congress and become a law, I predict that in twelve months some negro will walk upon the floor of the Senate of the United States. . . . If that is agreeable to the tastes and feeling of the people of this country, it is not to mine; and I only say that I will not be responsible for any such act." As soon as Saulsbury sat down, the final vote came. By a margin of 32 yeas and 7 nays, the Sumner bill passed.[5]

The border states hoped to rally support for their cause in the House of Representatives, killing the initiative there. The battle began on June 4, when Representative Daniel Gooch from Massachusetts introduced the House version of the bill.

But as subtexts for the deliberation, several themes arose speaking to larger issues of international balances of power. Representative Gooch made reference to the vacuum that Europe saw with the outbreak of fighting, making America the "sick man" of the Western Hemisphere: "Mr. Speaker, the experience of the last few months has taught us very forcibly that the Powers of Europe—I mean the Governments and rulers, not the mass of people—have little sympathy with us or our institutions, and that they will not hesitate to improve what seems to them a favorable opportunity to recover lost power and jurisdiction over American territory."

He alluded to the fact that Spain had recently regained control of its former colony, the Dominican Republic, "and is today seeking pretexts for a war with the Haytians, hoping thereby to establish her power over the whole island." Clearly Republican policymakers feared the prolongation of the Civil War and its implications for the primacy of the United States in the region. The once unchallenged Monroe Doctrine now came into doubt as the foundation of America's foreign policy discourse.

Gooch also touched upon another issue that Lincoln himself grappled with as fighting continued throughout the country. The fate of the millions of slaves and the implications of their eventual freedom would need resolution. "Again, sir, Hayti is willing, even desirous, to receive and furnish homes to the blacks of this country," the Congressman asserted optimistically as a means to resolve this problem for his party and the country.

Just as Senator Davis had proposed an amendment to downgrade representation in the Senate version, Representative Samuel Cox of Ohio, who had once worked at the U.S. diplomatic legation in Peru, made a similar push in the House. Cox lambasted the public argument that the administration made for recognition as a means to increase commerce. The Republicans had a more sinister intention, he asserted, saying: "It may be, the gentlemen on the other side intends to carry out their schemes of emancipation to that extent that they will raise the blacks to an equality in every respect with the white men of this country."

The House debate had taken an even nastier turn than that in the Senate. The discussion centered not only on whether Hayti and Liberia could serve as homes for freed slaves, but also on whether the American government ought to set as policy a forcible repatriation of sorts. "The free blacks ought to be transported from this country, as Jefferson said; when free, they are better away from whites," Cox continued.[6]

Despite long hours of bitter debate, the Cox amendment died on June 5, and the final House bill passed by a margin of 86 to 37. With President Lincoln's signature following, the United States of America finally bestowed official recognition upon the Republic of Hayti, fifty-eight years after it had gained independence from France.

Soon after this legislative victory, Lincoln swung into action. Inviting a small group of free black leaders to the White House, he laid out his plea that they begin the process of encouraging their "brethren" to emigrate: "There is an unwillingness on the part of our people, harsh as it may be, for you free colored people to remain with us." Lincoln told the gathering in August of 1862.

Though he expressed sympathies for the harsh treatment that blacks (both slave and free) had received in the United States, he clearly saw the cause of the war and its solution tied to racial separation: "We look to our condition, owing to the existence of the two races on this continent. I need not recount to you the effects upon white men, growing out of the institution of Slavery. I believe in its general evil effects on the white race. See our present condition—the country engaged in war!—our white men cutting one another's throats, none knowing how far it will extend; and then consider what we know to be the truth. But for your race among us there could not be war, although many men engaged on either side do not care for you one way or the other. Nevertheless, I repeat, without the institution of Slavery and the colored race as a basis, the war could not have an existence."[7]

The President quickly proposed Liberia and an undisclosed location in Central America as possible outlets for their resettlement. It was not clear how this "invitation" was received from the group, but prominent leaders who were not present, such as Frederick Douglass, were furious. Nonetheless, plans were pushed for increasing the outflow of blacks from American shores. Though Lincoln did not specifically mention Hayti as a location for them, clearly many leaders were considering just such an option. A newly "independent" Hayti was too tempting a target.

Lincoln appointed James Mitchell to be Commissioner of Emigration, charging him with oversight of colonization schemes. A fund of $600,000 had been appropriated by Congress for the endeavor, and the relative virtues of various locations were explored, including those of the Isle aux Vache off the southern coast of Hayti. It was there that 450 blacks were transported in 1863, only to have several die in a smallpox outbreak, and scores of others starve before the colony was finally abandoned.[8]

In spite of his victory authorizing the recognition of Hayti, Lincoln cautiously chose to appoint his first diplomat to Port-au-Prince at the lower rank of Consul General. Benjamin Whidden, a white New Hampshire Republican party official, would receive that post on July 12 of 1862. Lincoln remained wary, and though he might have found it politically advantageous to name someone black to the post, he had watched the debate in Congress and understood the feelings they reflected in the countryside. The outcome of the war was still far from certain, and Lincoln could take no further chances, particularly if doing so would jeopardize efforts toward the relocation of American blacks to the island. Lincoln had sealed a great victory, and he knew it was best not to overreach.

H. E. Peck, a white, abolitionist Oberlin professor, was Whidden's successor in 1865. Peck would later be promoted to Minister Resident, second in diplomatic rank only to a Minister Plenipotentiary (the title Ambassador was not used until 1893 for the United States), but he died of yellow fever in 1866 while serving in Port-au-Prince. Gideon Hollister, from Litchfield, Connecticut, would be the third white man to fill that position, which he held until 1869, when war hero U. S. Grant assumed the high office of Chief Executive and began looking for someone new.

With Grant's election, in the aftermath of the Northern victory in the Civil War and the beginnings of Reconstruction, the nation would prepare for a truly radical departure from the norm. Slaves had been emancipated, starting with President Lincoln's noble proclamation in 1863. But that decree did not see full freedom for most of the slaves throughout the country. Universal emancipation required further warfare, further acts of Congress, and a constitutional amendment to procure that final freedom. But Grant's victory was made possible in part because of the newly won freedom of black voters, and, as a result, racial politics took on new urgency. Not only were black men voting, they were also sending black representatives to Congress from districts in southern states with new black majorities.

Black demands for equality would not end at the ballot box. The worst fears of Senator Davis and Representative Cox would soon be realized. Blacks were not just walking as equals on the floor of the Congress. It was time for the most radical of ideas to become a reality—a black diplomat representing America abroad.

4

The Bassetts of Connecticut

In 1833, when Ebenezer D. Bassett was born, the town of Litchfield was at the height of its golden age. The small community in the northwestern hill country of Connecticut was home to an educated elite and boasted a unique mix of prosperous commercial and skilled craftsmen. It was these opportunities and a progressive attitude that attracted growing numbers of people like the Bassetts to Litchfield.

The town had been founded over a century earlier. During the American Revolution it served as a safe haven from the fighting in major cities and along the coast. After the war of independence, numerous artisans developed their businesses in the community, with blacksmiths, carpenters, and carriage makers populating the center of town. This prosperity led to a rise in the educational base of Litchfield. Local attorney Tapping Reeve began a law school there in 1784, educating men, such as Aaron Burr and John Calhoun, who would go on to lead the new nation.

Women were also included in the field of education with the establishment of the Litchfield Female Academy, which was one of the first schools in the country for women. By the beginning of the nineteenth century, the population had grown so much that Litchfield was Connecticut's fourth largest city.[1]

Though a growing number of free blacks were coming to communities like Litchfield, slavery was still legal in the state at the time of Ebenezer Bassett's birth. Both Africans and Native Americans were listed as property throughout the colonial period of Connecticut's history. Freed slaves had even been prohibited from owning land during the 1700s.

The enslaved population never reached the highs of the colonies in the South, but as many as five thousand slaves resided in Connecticut in the years prior to the Revolutionary War. After independence, the state legislature took a measured approach to break the shackles of the pernicious institution of slavery. In 1784 they passed the Gradual Emancipation Act, which held that any children of enslaved blacks were to be set free by their twenty-fifth birthday. Four years later, state leaders barred the sale of slaves and required that owners register any children born into slavery in the hopes of gaining compliance with earlier efforts toward gradual emancipation.

By the first national census of the United States, in 1790, the state population numbered 2,759 black slaves, but an even higher number of free blacks: 2,801. Slavery continued to dwindle, and in the decade before Bassett's birth, the population of African Americans enslaved in Connecticut had fallen to only 97 persons. It would not be until 1848, however, that the state finally outlawed the holding of all slaves.[2]

Despite the existence of slavery in the state, the strong tradition of blacks owning their own property, running their own businesses, and playing important roles in the community was one in which the Bassetts would be among the leaders.

According to Bassett family lore, Pero was the ancestral slave first captured and brought from Africa. Though it is unknown when Pero was enslaved, it is likely to have been no earlier than the mid-1740s. No records exist of him, his capture, or his eventual transport to Connecticut. Neither is it known from which African region Pero was brought, but a later history written in dialect describes the kidnapping and enslavement of the once proud African prince:

> He had plenty of wives, and heap of soldiers. My mammy she lived in a house in de bush; she had nice mat and calabash, and was one great lady. But one day, when my fader and his men was huntin', white man come and burnt all de houses. Den dey took my mammy and her two boys, one younger dan me, and drove us away to de ship. It was a bad time we had on de water. My poor little brother died, and dey trow him in de sea. Mammy cry and go crazy when dey takes him away from her, and when we got to Jamaica, she die too. I's a picka-ninny den, little feller, and I feel very bad to lose my mammy. But de new tings I see made me forgit, in little while. Dey sends me 'way to de sugar plantation, where I fared very well. Massa was kind to me, and I had little to do but lie in de sun, and suck de sugar-cane.[3]

It is hard to tell how much of this later telling by Pero's unnamed descendant is accurate, but certain facts can be found through Connecticut church records and oral history that indicate his later life. Pero married a slave named Hagar, whose owner was Rev. Richard Mansfield, the rector of St. James Church in Derby. Rev. Mansfield was a Yale graduate and, like many ministers of his day, held a number of slaves. Pero and Hagar had at least two children, Tobiah and another boy, Laban.

It is possible that at some point the family was broken up or perhaps sold in union to a neighbor, Samuel Riggs. Though the fate of Pero and Hagar are unknown, baptismal records from the First Congregational Church in Derby do indicate several servant children in the Riggs household, including one from March 25, 1759, that lists "Laban, the servant child of Samuel Riggs and Abigail." There is no such birth record for Tobiah, but later histories indicate Laban was his brother. (Riggs held other slave children who were also listed in baptismal records as Prince [1756], Jethro [1762], and Rose [1764], though it is uncertain if they bore any relation to Laban and Tobiah.) [4]

At some point in his young life, Pero's son Tobiah was sold to John Wooster, of nearby Oxford, CT. There, his skill and intelligence made Tobiah much more than just a simple servant. He became manager of Captain John Wooster's Tavern, and was also a frequent companion on hunting trips in Wooster's park, the one-hundred-acre enclosed forest that abounded in deer and other wildlife. Wooster restricted access to his park, but Tobiah was such an expert hunter that it was later commented: "Few men caught more foxes, and coons, and rabbits, and squirrels than he."[5]

Just days before the Revolutionary War broke out, Tobiah married another of Wooster's slaves, a girl named Rachel, on June 19, 1776.[6] Her father, Peter Hull, was described as an "aged negro" living in a nearby small hut. Hull had been an agricultural slave for the Woosters as well, but due to his advanced age and failing health, apparently he could no longer work when young Rachel and Tobiah married.

The wedding of these two slaves is incredibly recorded in later Connecticut history, undoubtedly passed along as oral tradition until it was published at the end of the 19th century by the author Israel Warren. Though embellished, it provides a wonderful narrative about the lives of two slaves who were clearly well-known and respected individuals in the community, in spite of their servitude:

> It was a great day at the tavern when Tobiah and Rachel were married. Peter, who had given his consent with tears running down his happy old face, had had a suit of new clothes given him by his master in honor of the occasion. It had been proposed to the bridegroom that the ceremony should be performed by Captain Wooster himself, who was a magistrate, and would do it for a less sum than Parson Mansfield, if he came up from Derby for that purpose. But Tobiah would not listen to this. He was able to pay, he said, and he was going to be married just like white folks. For slaves, as I have stated, were allowed to have property, and Tobiah, in the course of years, had laid up quite a little sum of his own. So one Saturday he borrowed the captain's mare, and rode down to the Landing to engage

the clergyman for that interesting service. Wants yer to come up to Cap'n Wooster's next Monday night, Massa parson, he said; gwine to be a wedding dar.

A wedding, Toby?

Yes, massa; and here's de publis'ment and de barns; Yo'll read 'em in de church to-morrow?

Oh, yes; I'll publish the banns; but who is it, Toby?

Me, parson, and Rachel. Wants yer ter come shuah. Bring yer book wid yer, and marry us just as you do white folks. What d'ye ax, Massa Mansfield, for marryin'?

Well, Tobiah, white folks usually give me about six shillings, said the doctor, highly amused, sometimes more, and if you are going to be married just as they are, it will be right that you pay the same fee won't it?

Yes, massa, dat's right; you come and marry us just like white folks, and I'll gib you just de same pay.

The "barns" were published according to law, and on the appointed evening, the good parson presented himself in Captain Wooster's kitchen for the performance of his official duty. Her mistress had given Rachel a white dress which had belonged to Miss Ruth, and if there was any lack of diamonds, it was fully compensated by the sparkle of the laughing black eyes, which could not be sober even in a time of so much importance as this. Tobiah was gorgeous in crimson small-clothes and white stockings, while his woolly head, powdered after the fashion of the times, towered a foot above the red and yellow handkerchief which did duty as a turban by his side.

The ceremonies were completed, the festivities of the occasion were over, the clergyman was about to depart. Tobiah had apparently forgotten the promise which he made, when the latter jocosely reminded him of it.

Come, Tobiah; you remember the bargain: I was to marry you like white folks, and you was to pay me like white folks.

Yis, massa, sartin. But you habn't dun it.

Haven't done it, you rogue? What do you mean?

I means, sar, just what I says. Yer no sing de psalm, and *yer no kiss de bride!*

Amid the loud laugh which followed this speech, the minister, somewhat disconcerted, replied: 'But, Tobiah, that's not part of the ceremony. You are married just the same whether the bride is kissed or not.'

Don't know about dat, sar; yer don't think it's 'nuff when yer hab purty white gals to marry. Yer said yer'd marry Rachel and me just de same way.[7]

Though the two were married with great honor and happiness, for the colonies it was a time of great bloodshed. As the Revolutionary War began weeks later, Tobiah was put in an awkward position, because his owner John Wooster was a known Tory sympathizer who opposed the colonial independence movement. In spite of this, Tobiah was a great supporter of independence, as were many leading black men of New England who felt that their enslavement was tied to England's control. In fact, Tobiah heroically even helped save a local white boy, Chauncey Judd, who had been kidnapped by Tory supporters. Though just a slave, Tobiah confronted the Tories at gunpoint and later helped track them down as they fled.

In fact, it appears that popular support for the war and for Tobiah (as well as suspicion of Wooster) was so strong that the community held a town meeting in January of 1781, voting in favor of the emancipation of any slaves that agreed to serve one year in the Revolutionary Army:

> Voted, that the authority and selectmen be empowered and directed to give certificates to Capt Daniel Holbrook and Capt John Wooster, to free and emancipate their servants, negro men, on the condition that the said negro men enlist into the state regiment to be raised for the defense of the state, for the term of one year. [8]

Along with the approximately 5,000 other black residents of the colonies, Toby took up military service in support of independence. Though Connecticut did form a segregated all-black company, the Fourth Regiment, many of black troops were simply integrated into other units. Toby fought with distinction and eventually won himself the freedom that he so greatly desired.[9]

Returning after the war as a free black, he did not always find things as they should have been for a victorious war hero. He lived for a period of time in the city of Woodbury. The white leaders of the town did not like the presence of a black man because they were unsure of his status as slave or free man. But Toby was a fighter, and he requested that the city of Derby send over an affirmation, telling the Woodbury city selectmen that he had gained his liberty by fighting in the war for independence.[10]

But soon Toby returned closer to home and began to lead his community in the proud tradition of so many other blacks in Connecticut. Though they were not allowed to vote or hold office, black citizens of the state would regularly select their "Negro" political leaders. In a practice that predated the Revolution, annual "Election Days" were held to proclaim a black governor in various locales. In the town of Derby, a voice vote proclaimed the winner, choosing a leading black man held in high esteem by the community. A military-style parade accompanied the ceremonies, and speeches were made by leading figures. A grand feast was prepared at Warner's Tavern, and blacks from the surrounding communities would join in the revelry.

Tobiah himself held that honor of being "governor" of Derby in 1815. Historians noted that the black leaders elected as governors were "men of ready wit and keen intelligence." These black governors would also act as informal judges, settling disputes within the black community and even imposing fines. White slave owners and former owners, were also proud of their black governors, and they paid for the festivities surrounding Election Day. Because it reflected well on them to have even one of their former slaves recognized as a black leader, whites were frequently supporters of this process.[11]

Though records are vague and incomplete, Tobiah and Rachel had at least one child, Ebenezer, who was more commonly referred to as "Eben Tobias," born on October 21, 1805. Though Toby was now free, it may have been that his wife Rachel was not, and that their son Eben Tobias was also born into servitude. A letter attributed to Ebenezer D. Bassett years later indicated that Eben Tobias "was a mulatto, born in the family of Squire Bassett of Derby."[12]

If "Squire" Bassett had indeed purchased Rachel and owned her young son as well, there is no other record of it. It was common for many slaves to take the surname of previous owners, but given the close ties that Tobiah had with Wooster, it seemed unusual he did not choose that family name. The white Woosters and Bassetts of Derby had intermarried, however, as John Bassett and Naomi Wooster had their own son named Ebenezer Bassett (born in Derby on December 12, 1760). This white Ebenezer would have been about the same age as Tobiah, and despite the color barrier, perhaps they were playmates and friends as they grew up. It is also true that John Bassett's brother, Amos, held at least one slave.[13] It was also certain that the Bassetts of Derby were a large and leading family, offering additional support to any newly freed slave, especially the Negro Governor. So in choosing to name his son Eben Tobias Bassett, Tobiah may have acted out of friendship and respect for the Bassetts.[14]

Derby was a unique town that offered recognition and some degree of prosperity, and it provided a real home for offspring of former slaves. "The advantage of common schools, free to all . . . and the gradual abatement of prejudice against the colored race, have opened to them possibilities which were formerly denied them," a later historian would write.[15]

Eben Tobias joined his father Tobiah in the traditional business of farming. Perhaps they had been given a plot of land for use by their former owners, or perhaps they had purchased it themselves. But given the expertise with which Tobiah and Eben Tobias thrived off the land, their family was clearly never at want. Eben Tobias was described as possessing "natural intelligence" and grew to be over six feet tall, making him an imposing figure of the time.[16]

Eben Tobias would eventually marry Susan Gregory, described in some histories as a Pequot Indian but later listed in census records as black.[17] Perhaps of mixed race herself, she would have been one of the few remaining Pequot in Connecticut by the early 1800s.

The Pequot had been one of the strongest and most feared tribes in the Hudson River Valley prior to the European arrival in the 1600s. Soon after their first contacts with the Dutch and the English, however, conflict broke out along the major trading routes of the region. By 1637 the Pequot War would be waged against these indigenous people. The war and a smallpox outbreak resulted in an almost total demise of the group, dropping their numbers from over 6,000 to less than 3,000. Many of the remainder were sold off as slaves, either to other Indian tribes or to Europeans.[18] Sadly, Susan was truly among the last of her kind.

After their marriage, Ebenezer and Susan struck out on their own and relocated to nearby Litchfield, some 40 miles north of Derby. Their first child, a daughter named Charlotte, was born in 1832 or early 1833.[19] A year later they had a son, Ebenezer D. Bassett, on October 16 of 1833.

The Bassetts had moved to a booming town filled with the promise of numerous opportunities. Litchfield boasted a literate elite and was even the birthplace of the prominent writer Harriet Beecher Stowe, whose *Uncle Tom's Cabin* ignited such fury around the nation before the Civil War.

Soon, however, Eben Tobias found that the economic growth he had hoped to find was ephemeral, as rail and other trade routes moved away from the northern Connecticut hills. Litchfield lacked a sufficient water supply for its growing population, and as westward expansion pushed the frontiers of America beyond the original colonies, the city receded from prominence. And with their third child, Napoleon, arriving in 1836, the family must have found it a struggle to continue in Litchfield. By the late 1830s the Bassetts began to look back toward their family home in Derby for economic stability and a social network.

Just as Litchfield was fading from view, Derby offered the Bassetts the prominence and embrace of a community in which they had long been leading members. It would come as no surprise then that upon their return, the black Bassett family came back to live with the white branch of the family now headed by Martin Bull Bassett, the son of Amos Bassett.[20] All the Bassetts remained prominent and continued farming the family property, and they were certainly held in high regard by the community.

Following in his father's footsteps, Eben Tobias, was elected "governor" in the traditional free black vote in 1840. As newly elected governor, Eben was described as "of the finest physical mold" and "admirably proportioned." He was clearly a leader, "ready of speech and considered quite witty." His remarks were quoted by blacks in the region even years after his death. Moreover, he appeared to take his job of governor very seriously, despite the mocking tone that many white writers would later have when describing the ceremonial events related to that position. His young son Ebenezer would later recall the importance of the position fondly: "I remember that he held the office two or three terms, and I remember, too, how Sundays and nights he used to pore over books on military tactics and study up the politics of the state."[21]

A later Derby historian would recount one such undated Election Day event:

> The chief marshal of the day, a tall and stately figure, the father of our Ex-haytian minister, E.D. Bassett, was mounted, with his corps of assistants armed with pistols, with no lack of 'fuss and feathers,' and the horses gaily caparisoned. No victorious general on the field of battle was more proud of his situation than Grand Marshall Bassett on that day. To show off, and as evidence of his military tactics, he drew up in regular line his men and stated that he was about to issue an important order as a test of their saltpeter grit. 'Now do as I do and show yourselves brave darkies—brave officers!' All assented to obey the word of command, which was given in a stentorian voice: 'Attention! All ready! Advance! Wheel! Fire and fall off! The chief marshal put spurs to his horse, wheeled, fired and fell to the ground, but his mounted comrades sat dumbfounded in their saddles and saved their powder.[22]

This nineteenth-century account, depicting the common trait of extravagantly dressed "soldiers" and their parades, offers a lighter side of the Bassett men, but it is tinged with the racially derogatory stereotypes commonly found at the time. Another account of the election of Ebenezer's father describes the contest less as a political campaign and more as a test of brute strength: "The formalities of the election have not come down to us, save in one instance, when it was by test of wind and muscle, the successful candidate being he who first climbed a steep and almost unscalable sand bank. Eben Tobias, decked in feathers and flying ribbons, won that day . . ."[23]

Certainly, the royal lineage of the Bassett family made a profound impression on Eben Tobias's young son. Equally impressive was his mixed racial background, coming from two ethnic groups that had been severely oppressed during the colonial period. Perhaps this provided him with an early sensitivity to the issues of race and an awareness that other free blacks might not have possessed.

Connecticut was also home to a growing movement, often backed by Quakers or other white religious leaders, who attempted to address racial inequality more directly. Since the time of independence, northern states were gradually moving away from the legal institution of slavery. Two early organizations in the abolitionist movement came from that state, the Connecticut Anti-Slavery Society, founded in 1790, and the New Haven Anti-Slavery Society, in 1833.

Many of these early abolitionists were also advocates of education for black youth, and Ebenezer stood to benefit from the public education system for free blacks. The earliest attempts at providing education for blacks, however, met with setbacks in other parts of Connecticut. In 1831, two years before Ebenezer's birth, a group of free blacks attempted to establish their own college in New Haven, modeled on the success of Yale. However, prejudiced city officials denounced the plan and helped undermine the project. Undoubtedly, the creation of the Anti-Slavery Society two years later in that same city was a response to the actions of those city officials.

In Canterbury, near the Rhode Island border, educator Prudence Crandall established a school for black girls the same year as Ebenezer was born. But after threats, violence, and legal action, the state legislature passed a law stating that "no person should set up a school for the instruction of colored persons . . . without the consent of a majority of the civil authority and selectmen in town . . ." The school closed after further violent damage by a mob in 1834.[24]

Although they taxed black families, many jurisdictions, even in the North, excluded blacks from the public education system. Derby, however, was different.[25] As Ebenezer grew up, he was able to attend a public school across the Housatonic River, in the adjoining community of Birmingham. The Birmingham Academy had opened in 1838, and despite being one of the few black students in town, young Ebenezer was apparently able to pursue a normal course of studies and graduate from the school.

Ebenezer did not simply study and work on the family farm, however. As he grew older, he worked in town for a local white doctor, Ambrose Beardsley.[26]

Dr. Beardsley was a graduate of the Medical College in Pittsfield, Massachusetts, and he had moved to Derby just after Ebenezer's birth. As one of the few physicians in town, Beardsley was a prominent member of the community, serving as the city's treasurer for over two decades. He was also an active member of his local church and an amateur historian. Beardsley took a special interest in the gifted young black student that he came to know and hired him to assist in the running of his office. Dr. Beardsley also had another connection to the white Bassetts of Derby: he had married a young woman named Mary, daughter of Samuel Bassett.[27]

Under the tutelage of such a renaissance man, Ebenezer was exposed to the wider world of the sciences, the Greco-Roman classics, and the advantages of a rigorous and formal schooling. Ebenezer Bassett would later recall Beardsley and others in the town with deep appreciation: "My success in life I owe greatly to that American sense of fairness which was tendered me in old Derby, and which exacts that every man whether white or black, shall have a fair chance to run his race in life and make the most of himself."[28]

The young Bassett was driven by the idea of formal education. Though they were literate, proper schooling was something that neither his parents nor grandparents possessed. Given the leadership role that his grandfather and father held in the community, tremendous things were expected from the oldest son. Though the community of Derby had been racially tolerant of this family of free blacks, the Bassetts understood that real barriers existed all across the country because of race, and they knew that only a good work ethic and education would potentially provide an avenue to overcome this prejudice.

Graduation from high school was no small affair even for white citizens at the time. So it was an unusual suggestion that the gifted young student continue his studies. Perhaps Dr. Beardsley himself recommended the location, a college preparatory program at the Wesleyan Academy of Wilbraham, Massachusetts. The academy was located just outside of Springfield and not far from where Beardsley had trained in medicine. Most importantly, the preparatory school offered the kind of education that the small town of Derby simply could never provide.

Wesleyan Academy was the first coeducation boarding school in the country and a bastion of the budding abolitionist movement. The Academy was radical not only in that it admitted both women and black men, but also because it was a stop on the famed "underground railroad" for escaped slaves moving north. In this fertile environment—with its excellent academics, Philo Debating Society, and an emphasis on social activism—Ebenezer blossomed. He pursued his studies with vigor, which eventually made possible his acceptance and transfer to the Connecticut State Normal College in August of 1853 as a junior.[29]

Ebenezer Bassett was a handsome boy when he entered the Normal School. His student picture from 1853 shows a determined and fair-skinned face. His hair was parted to the side and he grew a full mustache that curled up at the ends, as it was the style of the day. In his suit and bow tie, he looked the part of any college student in Connecticut, with one exception—his skin color.

The all-white State Normal College was founded in 1849, and it remains today, (as Central Connetcut State Univeristy) the oldest public university in Connecticut. It was established to train teachers, and it was only the sixth such normal school founded in the United States. The school boasted a library collection of over four thousand volumes, and all students were supplied with free textbooks for their course of studies. Most students at State Normal lived off campus, in New Britain, boarding with local families for nominal fees.

It was certainly very unusual for a black student to attend school with whites in Connecticut, especially at a coeducational facility such as the Normal School. But with his admission, Bassett became one of the earliest pioneers at school integration, enrolling during the college's fifth year of existence as its very first black student.

The prominence of Ebenezer's family in nearby Derby, only some forty miles away, would surely not have been enough even for him, a fine black student, to be admitted to the Normal School. Perhaps once again the guidance of Dr. Beardsley and the white Bassetts played some role in Ebenezer's acceptance there. The fact that there were neither legal fights nor violent protests at the Normal School—as with earlier cases that did not even include integrated education—was a remarkable accomplishment. Already a diplomat, with his ability and personality, Ebenezer paved the way for this smooth transition as much as any outside help. In the graduation program of 1855, Ebenezer was one of the few to address the audience, giving a speech titled "The True Teacher."[30]

Ebenezer had excelled in his mission to become an educator, completing his course of studies and graduating after just fifty weeks. A freshly minted degree in hand, he immediately took a job teaching in a black public grammar school in New Haven. That job, which paid around $300 per year, made him one of only four "Negro" teachers in town.[31]

While in New Haven, Bassett also attended classes at Yale, studying Greek, Latin, French, math, and literature. He was not the first black to study at the university, but his attendance at a largely white institution of higher education was a remarkable achievement.[32] Though he never obtained a degree from Yale, this entry into the wider world of elite white men would serve him well, as he learned how to maneuver through their sometime opaque and biased social circles at an early age.

Though slavery was no longer legal in the state of Connecticut, the legislature had refused to pass a law allowing free black men to vote. Many states of New England began organizing black conventions to address this issue. Ebenezer would take an early leadership role to address this inequity by joining the Convention of Colored Men of the State of Connecticut. The Convention began in 1849 at a meeting in New Haven with a strong plea to voters to consider the "political disabilities" of blacks without any right to vote. Their opening call asked that the words of the authors of the Declaration of Independence be true for all: "While you are unwilling to write hypocrite upon their tombs—we are unwilling longer to remain silent and disfranchised," they wrote.[33] Upon Bassett's relocation to New Haven, he quickly became involved in the political life of the organization, including the circulation of a petition asking the state to give black citizens the right to vote.[34]

Ebenezer received further encouragement in the person of Frederick Douglass. As the preeminent black American of his day, Douglass was the runaway slave who had become the leading black voice of abolition throughout the country and the world. Fifteen years his senior, Douglass was an awe-inspiring orator who also published his own newspaper. So great was Douglass's renown that when he came to town, it attracted the attention of the entire black community in New Haven. The eager young Bassett was keenly impressed by the presence of Douglass. With his deep, booming voice, his dark skin, and his thick head of graying hair, the abolitionist made a forceful and unrepentant advocate of full equality for blacks, supporting efforts like those the Convention of Colored Men were pushing. And no doubt he advocated something else to his young admirer: it was simply not enough to be black and educated. Ebenezer had a responsibility to better those younger blacks around the country with the opportunities of higher education. He challenged Bassett to give something back to his community.

But it was not all work and sacrifice for the young educator. Ebenezer also found time to meet and fall in love—with Eliza Park. She was a young black woman also from New Haven, and it was a whirlwind courtship. The Parks were another leading black family, and Eliza's father, Robert, ran a successful catering business. Just months after meeting, the two were married in 1855. But Bassett was not simply in a hurry to marry; he remained a restless young man, seeking new challenges outside his cocoon of Connecticut.

When Ebenezer was offered the chance to really make his mark (and a salary of $700) by teaching at a progressive new all-black high school in Philadelphia, he jumped at the opportunity. At the age of just twenty-two, he was bursting with enthusiasm and energy to make a positive difference in the lives of black citizens. With his new wife in tow, the two made their way south.

Black Activist in Philadelphia

Ebenezer and Eliza moved into a city bursting with an energy they had never witnessed in sleepy Connecticut. Antebellum Philadelphia rang out with the production of the Industrial Age. The port town was home to heavy industry and textile mills pumping out products at a frenzied pace. The coal and iron that the state produced were transported via Philadelphia's rails, which connected the city with the entire eastern seaboard. It was a booming capitalist center in the middle ground of a growing new country.

The city was also home to a large and prosperous free black population. Philadelphia native Francis Johnson was one of the most prominent composers and musicians in the country, and the first black American to have his works published. And though the bulk of the African American population was involved in semi-skilled industry or crafts, it was not uncommon to see black educators, small business owners, or even dentists. As a stop in the "underground railroad," the local community worked hard through hundreds of benefit societies to assist free newcomers. According to the 1860 census, over 20,000 blacks lived in the city, which was 3.7 percent of Philadelphia's total population.[1]

The abolitionist movement also had strong roots throughout the commonwealth. Even prior to the Revolutionary War, Quaker activists had founded the Pennsylvania Abolition Society, working not only to end the institution of slavery but also to promote education and employment opportunities for the burgeoning black population. By 1780, they had successfully lobbied the state legislature for passage of the Gradual Abolition of Slavery Act, and by the mid-1800s there were no slaves left in the state.

The Abolition Society embarked on an educational improvement quest with zeal, opening the first private school for black children in 1799 and pushing the Philadelphia Board of Education to establish a public school of "color" by 1822.[2] However, the organization remained one run by whites for the "benefit" of blacks.

Despite the growing number of black citizens and an increasingly vocal, white-led abolitionist movement, the legislature had refused blacks the right to vote in the new state constitution of 1837 (even though the earlier one had no such prohibition). Discrimination was all too common in the city of Philadelphia.

The city's black community, however, was a fighting one and would not let the racist mores of the white majority undermine their efforts for equality. The year that Ebenezer and Eliza moved to the city, a party of leading African Americans established a group of *Memorialists* for the disenfranchised black citizens of Philadelphia. In their meeting and subsequent letter to the legislature, they attacked the new state constitution, saying that it was illegal to determine "a man's rights by the curl of his hair—[or] his citizenship by the color of his skin." By taking away their right to vote on the government that oversaw their lives, the new law "struck down that safeguard so indispensable to the protection, prosperity, and happiness of every honest citizen; establishing a fearful precedent, by which any class of our citizens, white or colored, may be despoiled of their rights by an unprincipled majority." The effort to regain their franchise was fundamental to all else, and they would actively move to regain the one right, they wrote, that "can redeem us."[3]

Ebenezer felt the anger of his fellow black citizens, but he must have equally felt the thrill of the strong activist community, both black and white, which was arguing forcefully on behalf of equality for all.

His first call to action, however, was with his employer. The Institute for Colored Youth (ICY), which would later become Cheyney University of Pennsylvania, was one of the early schools dedicated to educating black youth in the country. In 1837 Quaker philanthropist and former slave owner Richard Humphreys bequeathed $10,000 to create the Institute. It received a charter from the Pennsylvania State Legislature in 1842, and it opened as a mere farm school with just five boys. By the time Ebenezer Bassett arrived, over a decade later, it was home to more than one hundred students. In addition to mechanic arts and agriculture, so common in the era, the Institute covered academic subjects ranging from Latin and Greek to geometry and trigonometry, all in an effort to train the students to become teachers.

Charles L. Reason was the principal who pushed the Institute from its vocational roots to the more traditional (Anglo) curriculum. A native of

Hayti, Reason helped the school expand, overseeing its move to Seventh and Lombard Streets, in the heart of the city. He also pushed to make the school coeducational and to have a library and reading room, which opened in 1853. But his most important achievement may have been his efforts to recruit top quality faculty. Reason was the person who found and brought Ebenezer Bassett to the school in 1855. And unlike every other private school in the state of Pennsylvania that taught black students, the ICY was the only one with an all-black faculty.[4]

Bassett's fellow teacher Fanny Jackson-Coppin described the newly arrived as a man of "unusual natural and acquired ability, and an accurate and ripe scholar." More than just intelligent, she also saw him as a person "of great modesty [and] of character earnest."[5] Ebenezer was perceived as very faithfully dedicated to his work and his students, and his knowledge of both math and the classics propelled him into early leadership positions there.

Though he had long been befriended by whites, Ebenezer was always quick to challenge the prejudices that many white Americans held. Professor Bassett decided to make a strong point when he heard that a white lecturer was touring Philadelphia after having written a book manuscript proving that blacks were not human. Bassett invited the man to see the school and determine whether his central thesis was correct.

"He brought a friend with him, better versed in algebra than himself," Jackson-Coppin would later write of her memories of the occasion, "and asked Mr. Bassett to bring out his highest class. There was in the class at that time Jesse Glasgow, a very black boy. All Glasgow asked for was a chance. Just as fast as they gave the problems, Jesse solved them on the board with the greatest ease. This decided the fate of the book, then in manuscript form, which, so far as we know, was never published."[6] Glasgow was also the first boy to complete all the credits and actually graduate from the ICY, in 1856. Later he attended the University of Edinburgh, in Scotland.[7]

To everyone's surprise, Charles Reason announced to the staff that he was leaving at the end of that year to return to New York. The white Quakers overseeing the school looked no farther than their new star teacher for leadership. Several months after his arrival, and just 23 years old, Ebenezer Bassett found himself appointed as the new principal of the Institute for Colored Youth.

Undeterred by his relative inexperience, Ebenezer pushed through a number of academic changes, determined to continue improving the quality of the school. His first act was to close the night program that trained youth holding day jobs. If the ICY was to be on par with white institutions of learning, it had to be full-time and a day school.

Before long, the ICY became known not only throughout Philadelphia but throughout the entire state for its academic excellence. And not content with simply a strong scientific and classical education, Bassett pushed his staff to include greater political awareness in the curriculum. He began inviting politicians and abolitionists—such as Frederick Douglass, Alexander Crummell, and Henry Highland Garnet—to give lectures when they were in town.[8] Bassett knew that he was doing more than just teaching young boys and girls the traditional reading, writing, and arithmetic. He was exposing those black boys and girls to the greatest minds of the day and to the radical idea that they were every bit as good as the white children down the street, but he was also opening their minds to the fact that real wrongs existed in the United States—wrongs that those same black children would one day be called upon to correct.

Life at home for the Bassetts was unique as well. They lived in an integrated neighborhood in the city's 7th Ward on Lombard Street, along-side European immigrants as well as white native-born families of grocers, police officers, shoemakers, and teachers. Eliza soon became pregnant with their first child, Charlotte, who was born in 1856. A son, Ebenezer Junior, followed, born in 1858.

The family was entrenched in the middle class, and their personal estate was valued at $400. With Ebenezer's new income as principal of the ICY, the Bassetts even had enough extra money to afford a live-in servant, an older black woman named Lilly Sullivan. In his census form of 1860, Ebenezer modestly listed himself as a simple "school teacher," but he was truly becoming a leader in the community.[9]

Bassett took this leadership role so seriously that he began to personally groom his best students for their own key positions in the community. Octavius Catto, son of a Presbyterian minister, was one of the early pupils whom Ebenezer quickly took under his tutelage. Catto and his family had moved to Philadelphia when the boy was only five, and he enrolled at ICY in 1854.

Bassett encouraged the loquacious Catto to join the Banneker Debating Society at the school and pushed him to excel academically. In 1858 he was valedictorian and only the fourth person to graduate from ICY. After being privately tutored in Greek and Latin for a year in Washington, DC, he returned to Philadelphia, and Bassett hired him to become one of his teachers at the Institute.[10]

The school continued to grow in population and prestige. A report by the Philadelphia Board of Education found that the ICY, of the dozens of black schools in the city, was without parallel: "The unpretending title of the 'Institute for Colored Youth,' does not convey an adequate idea of the relation it sustains to the other [colored] schools. It is, in fact, the pioneer High School, and on that account alone cannot be too highly appreciated."[11]

The successes of black Philadelphians and of the school that Bassett had helped grow were, however, of only limited importance, given the roiling political debate that was shaking the country at the very end of the decade.

Bassett remained active in abolitionist affairs, as his like-minded countrymen grappled with how to tackle the evil of slavery. His friend Frederick Douglass continued to speak out on the issue, but Bassett and Douglass were in for a surprise when they came across a true radical for the cause—John Brown.

Brown was a Connecticut native, and he may have known the Bassett family while they resided there. But Bassett certainly got to know the white abolitionist by the 1850s in Philadelphia. Brown had long been involved in the cause of freedom of slaves, having even fought in the new Kansas territory to help keep it from falling into the control of slaveholders.

The revolutionary abolitionist constantly toured the country, seeking financial and military support for his growing idea of an armed rebellion to free slaves. Brown hoped to gain enough support to eventually end the institution across the country. By 1859, he embarked on what would be his final push, leading an attack on the federal armory at Harpers Ferry, in Virginia. Brown stopped in Pennsylvania and New York in the weeks leading up to the raid, where he met with black leaders including Frederick Douglass and Ebenezer Bassett.

Though Bassett did not advocate the violent attack Brown unveiled to him, he shared a sympathy for the cause. Wishing him well, Bassett sent Brown on his way. During the attack—which took place on October 16, 1859—Brown and eighteen of his followers temporary took control of the armory. But he was quickly captured, tried, and hanged, and subsequent investigations rounded up coconspirators, with the spotlight quickly turning to Douglass and Bassett. Among the several letters on Brown at the time of his capture were those from the two men. Brown even specifically listed in his diary the "names of men to call for assistance," which included "E. D. Bassett 718 Lombard Street, Philadelphia."[12]

Ebenezer must have been mortified that his name was now associated with the convicted traitor. Arrests were increasing as the U.S. Senate convened a select committee to investigate the conspiracy. Robert Adger, an acquaintance of Bassett's from Philadelphia, recalled that Bassett had been aware of Brown's plans and now that his name was out there: "[he] remember[ed] the distressing position Bassett was in, but [Bassett] had at that time a lot of young fellows who stood together."[13] He also counted on the support of the Quakers who ran the ICY and on Frederick Douglass himself. Fortunately for Bassett, he was never questioned by the Senate committee, and the whole matter was quickly overtaken by larger events as the 1860 presidential campaign threatened the stability of the entire country. Soon, the North and the South began to chew one another apart over the long-unresolved issue of slavery.

With Abraham Lincoln's election and the domino-like fall of southern state secession, many Philadelphians were reluctant to be drawn into the battle. Moreover, economic interests of the large industrial complex that fueled the city's growth depended on markets or products from the South. But the strong abolitionist sentiment and the vociferous support of the African American community held the state's loyalties for the Union. The war remained far removed for most until the summer of 1863, when Confederate general Robert E. Lee brought his rebellious troops across the Mason-Dixon Line. Though the Battle of Gettysburg would end with Gen. Lee's crushing defeat, the threat for most white Pennsylvanians became existential, and support for the armed militias grew exponentially.

While many of these calls to arms came to white citizens of the state, black leaders hastened to remind everyone of their obligations and began to organize themselves for combat as well. Bassett saw the ICY, though primarily a center for the education of young students, as unable to stay on the sidelines of the conflict. Despite being supported by Quakers, who as a matter of principle eschewed violence, Bassett understood the urgency of the war and the role that African Americans had to play in it. After all, the Civil War centered on a single issue: the continued enslavement of the black race in half of the nation. If violence was abhorrent to Quaker thinking, what could be more abhorrent than the continued capture, murder, and torture of millions of blacks? It was an inconsistency that could not longer be justified with religious conviction.

President Lincoln issued the Emancipation Proclamation in January of 1863, and later that year he established the Bureau of Colored Troops to begin the enlistment of black soldiers. The time had come for Bassett and black Philadelphia to engage in the fight as well. In spite of the controversy, Ebenezer Bassett opened the doors of ICY for the recruitment of black soldiers in the city. He hastened to invite many of the national civil rights leaders who had now become his close contacts and they descended upon the city to call for further support of black troops.

Teacher Octavius Catto and several students from the ICY went to register to join the fight in the summer of 1863. But when the volunteers made their way to the Harrisburg, the state capital, Major General Darius N. Couch refused them, citing as an excuse the congressional approval only for black troops willing to serve for three years, not for a militia formed in an emergency. A subsequent notice from the secretary of the army required that General Couch "receive into the service any volunteer troops that may be offered, without regard to color." But it was too late for Catto's group, who had already gone home. Upon their return to Philadelphia, Bassett helped stage a mass rally to protest the treatment of these black recruits and eventually formed a committee to recruit others.[14]

Just days after the bloody battle in nearby Gettysburg, a massive crowd packed into the National Hall in downtown Philadelphia. The hot summer night did not deter those concerned from gathering. Black troops were being raised, but the federal government was offering to pay $10 per month, much less than white recruits were given, which had created additional controversy among Pennsylvania's civil rights community.

Despite this discriminatory action, black leaders organized to encourage support. The Rev. Stephen Smith was elected president of the recruitment committee, and Ebenezer Bassett was selected as one of the secretaries. Bassett had the honor of being the second speaker of the night, presenting the resolution and making a rousing speech immediately before Frederick Douglass. He was now 30 years old.

"Men of Color, to Arms! Now or Never! This is our golden moment," Bassett told the crowd.

> The Government of the United States calls for every able-bodied colored man to enter the army for the three years' service, and join in fighting the battles of liberty and the Union. A new era is open to us. For generations we have suffered under the horrors of slavery, outrage, and wrong; our manhood has been denied, our citizenship blotted out, our souls seared and burned, our spirits cowed and crushed, and the hopes of the future of our race involved in doubts and darkness. But how the whole aspect of our relations to the white race is changed! Now, therefore, is our most precious moment. Let us rush to arms! Fail now, and our race is doomed on this soil of our birth. We must now awake, arise, or be forever fallen. If we value liberty; if we wish to be free in this land; if we love our country; if we love our families, our children, our homes—we must strike now while the country calls; we must rise up in the dignity of our manhood, and show by our own right arms that we are worthy to be freemen. Our enemies have made the country believe that we are craven cowards, without soul, without manhood, without the spirit of soldiers. Shall we die with this stigma resting on our graves? Shall we leave this inheritance of shame to our children? No! a thousand times no! We will rise! The alternative is upon us; let us rather die freemen than live to be slaves. What is life without liberty? We say that we have manhood—now is the time to prove it. A nation or a people that cannot fight may be pitied, but cannot be respected. If we would be regarded men; if we would forever silence the tongue of calumny, of prejudice and hate, let us rise now and fly to arms! We have seen that valor and heroism our brothers displayed at Port Hudson and Milliken's Bend; though they are just from the galling,

poisoning grasp of slavery, they have startled the world by the most exalted heroism. If they have proved themselves heroes, cannot we prove ourselves men? Are freemen less brave than slaves? More than a million white men have left comfortable homes and joined the armies of the Union to save their country; cannot we leave ours, and swell the hosts of the Union, to save our liberties, vindicate our manhood, and deserve well of our country?

Men of color! All races of men—the Englishman, the Irishman, the Frenchman, the German, the American—have been called to assert their claim to freedom and a manly character by an appeal to the sword. The day that has seen an enslaved race in arms has, in all history, seen their last trial. We can now see that our last opportunity has come! If we are not lower in the scale of humanity than Englishmen, Irishmen, white Americans, and other races, we can show it now.

Men of color! brothers and fathers! we appeal to you!—by all your concern for yourselves and your liberties; by all your regard for God and humanity; by all your desire for citizenship and equality before the law; by all your love for the country—to stop at no subterfuge, listen to nothing that shall deter you from rallying for the army. Come forward and at once enroll your names for the three years' service. Strike now, and you are henceforth and forever freemen!

Moreover, we, the colored people of Philadelphia, in mass meeting assembled, do most emphatically and unitedly express our firm belief that we not only ought, but may and will raise a full regiment of ten companies of eighty men each, of colored volunteers for the United States service, within the next ten days, in our own city of Philadelphia.[15]

The true star of the evening, however, was the great Douglass. The enthusiastic crowd whipped into a frenzy when Douglass rose to speak. And he did not disappoint, as his remarks were met with outbursts of applause and shouts. Addressing the issue of unequal pay for colored troops, Douglass said that he was "content with nothing for the black man short of equal and exact justice." However, the issue of pay was not one that should prevent African Americans from joining the fight. He said to loud applause that "it would be the wisest and best thing for us to enlist," adding that their actions would bury the "rebellion and slavery in a common grave."

Douglass also mentioned the then recent diplomatic recognition of Hayti, which opened a channel of communication with the Black Republic, while noting the lengths that that country still had to go to improve racial relations. "The independence of Hayti is recognized," Douglass stated. "Her Minister sits beside our Prime Minister [sic], Mr. Seward, and dines at his table in Washington, while colored men are excluded from the cars in Philadelphia; showing that a black man's complexion in Washington, in the presence of the Federal government, is less offensive than in the city of brotherly love."

Drawing on the sustained applause of the crowd, Douglass concluded boldly, telling the young black men of the audience that they had no further excuses: "Remember that the musket—the United States musket with its bayonet of steel—is better than all mere parchment guarantees of liberty. In your hands that musket means liberty; and should your constitutional right at the close of this war be denied, which, in the nature of things, it cannot be, your brethren are safe while you have a Constitution which proclaims your right to keep and bear arms."[16]

As a result of such meetings, Pennsylvania added eleven new "colored regiments." And by the end of the Civil War, almost 200,000 African Americans had joined the Union forces.[17]

Fighting the battle to end slavery, while trying to gain the same pay as white soldiers for that service, just reminded black residents of Philadelphia of the daily discriminatory insults they faced in that city. For example, the city's horse-drawn streetcars were segregated, and this was a matter of such concern to blacks in Philadelphia that lawsuits were filed for integration of the transport system.

Besides organizing a committee to support black efforts, many white civic leaders signed petitions favoring integration. But black members of the community wanted more. In 1864, several prominent blacks, including Ebenezer Bassett, founded the Pennsylvania Equal Rights League, a branch of the national organization Frederick Douglass had created. Their goal was "to obtain by appeals to the mind and conscience of the American people or by legal process a recognition of the rights of the colored people."[18]

All members of the League were black, and they pushed for more aggressive action against the segregated streetcars. They even began non-violent protests against the transportation companies by having black women, some of whom were pregnant, attempt to climb aboard. Black men also attempted to board en masse, thus preventing others from boarding for lack of room.[19] Eventually, a suit was filed, and though the transportation companies lost, many of them refused to fully comply. Finally, in 1867 the state legislature voted to end segregation on streetcars.

These victories and the end of the southern rebellion made for heady days for Ebenezer Bassett. As the principal of the ICY, he was earning $1200 a year. And despite conflicts, he never lost focus on his primary mission: education. Not only did he continue to teach, he also offered evening lectures on scientific subjects such as "The Atmosphere" and "Chemical Action."[20]

Pushing his students to excel had always been of utmost importance to Ebenezer. He tested them in Greek (by requiring them to recite Homer), Latin (by having them translate Cicero and Virgil), mathematics, and "higher English." The graduation ceremonies were becoming larger events, as more students now had the ability to complete the rigorous course laid down by the principal. In 1864, as the Civil War was winding down, a class of nine students graduated, and Bassett was on hand to give out diplomas to these high achievers. He delivered an hour-and-a-half "alumni oration" to the students on the subject of "Elements of Permanent Governments and Societies," arguing that wealth and military greatness were not sufficient to create a noble society. Liberty, virtue, and high morals were the essential elements for that success.[21]

Undoubtedly, this drive to imbue morality and education pushed the ICY to become a leader, in the postwar era too. Bassett began training black students to become teachers at "freedom schools" in the old Confederacy.[22] Prior to the Civil War, very few southern states had developed a system of universal public education. This was particularly true when it came to black youth, as many jurisdictions made it a crime to even teach slaves to read or write. As a result, a major challenge for the new Reconstruction governments in those states was to set up from scratch a system of education.[23] Working with charitable organizations such as the Pennsylvania Abolition Society, Bassett's newly minted black teachers made their way south to establish these new schools.[24]

Interestingly, while Ebenezer both encouraged others to join in the battle for freedom during the Civil War and sent others south to help rebuild the country during Reconstruction, he himself never volunteered for such dangerous duties. As the father of another young child— daughter Iphigenia, born in 1864—Bassett felt more comfortable in the confines of Philadelphia's elitist black middle class. He continued to work for the expansion of the ICY, which had grown so much that they relocated to a new facility on Ninth and Bainbridge Streets in 1866. Bassett was moving in higher political and elite circles as well; getting his hands dirty did not appear to be of much interest to him.

Bassett was sought out as a speaker on the lecture circuit in Philadelphia and even in nearby Delaware. His prominent role in the call for equal rights led to invitations by such groups as the Delaware Association for the Moral Improvement and Education of the Colored People. Bassett was the keynote speaker at their 1868 annual convention. He told the crowd of black educators and activists that it was time for the country to embrace the full integration of the "negro." Being a member of that "despised and unfortunate race" himself, Bassett argued that it was not possible for colonization or any other scheme to rid the country of its black citizens. "He has grown with the country, he has suffered for its growth, and has fought for its flag," Bassett proudly proclaimed. He defied those who wanted to be rid of blacks and argued that no group was more patriotic than his own.

Showing the racial proclivities of the time, however, Bassett did not refrain from making discriminatory remarks about other racial groups.

He said that the growing Asian population on the West Coast "clings to [its] barbarous language and heathenish customs." Of the Native Americans Bassett said that they "steadily resist[ed] all attempts to improve [their] condition," and that they were guilty of "hating civilization and spurning Christianity." This remark was all the more ironic given that his own mother came from this ethnic background and that American Indians had been hunted to almost extinction by the encroaching white settlers. Clearly, Bassett was not above the petty prejudices of his day even as he trumpeted the value of tolerance and condemned bigotry.[25]

Meanwhile Bassett continued turning to patrons as he looked for opportunities in the political sphere, and there was no one better than Frederick Douglass, the mightiest voice of all. Douglass agreed that a diplomatic appointment would be most appropriate for his young protégé, adding that Hayti was the ideal location to help break the diplomatic color barrier.

"I am glad to know that you are making an effort to induce Hon. William H. Seward . . . to send some competent colored citizens to represent this country," Douglass wrote at the beginning of a letter to Bassett in 1867. "Its adoption would be scarcely less gratifying and assuring to Hayti than to the millions of colored citizens of the United States."

The stamp of approval from the preeminent black American of the day would surely be enough to overcome any prejudice from former Confederate sympathizers and slaveholders. Douglass wrote his friend that he was ready "to recommend yourself as a man whom I regard as every way fitted to discharge the duties of the position. Your education, manners, business talents, prudence, and general information are full equal to the dignity and duties of the office." Jokingly, Douglass added that he was certain of Bassett's success because of the latter's ability to work so well with the Quakers, who ran the ICY, since they tolerated "no sluggards," adding, "Were you other than industrious and painstaking, they would have dispensed with your service long ago."[26]

Bassett took the next step of formally requesting the position with President Andrew Johnson's Secretary of State, William Seward. In addition to Douglass's recommendation, he had drawn support also from John Mercer Langston (the Dean of Howard University), George Downing (who ran the House of Representative's restaurant and was chair of the Committee of Colored Men), as well as from former professors from Connecticut Normal and Yale, and even from governors and senators of Connecticut, Rhode Island, and Pennsylvania. Just as importantly to him, Dr. Ambrose Beardsley, his first mentor, wrote on behalf of the former gifted young apprentice.

Penning his own letter on November 22 of 1867, Bassett put himself forward as a "candidate" to become the Minister Resident in Port au Prince. He noted to Secretary of State Seward that his goal was to "uphold the honor of our country, [and] the glory and dignity of its flag."[27]

But the autumn of 1867 was a difficult one for President Andrew Johnson. He gradually became despised by the Republican leadership in Congress for showing sympathy toward the former rebels and for being a weak advocate of full civil rights for black Americans. Moreover, he never measured up to the hero status that Lincoln assumed after the latter's assassination. Republicans in Congress began impeachment proceedings against Johnson for the first time in November of that year, and when that failed, they took up the charge again in early 1868. Though ultimately the impeachment failed, it was simply impossible not to perceive Johnson as anything other than a lame duck. Undoubtedly disappointed, Bassett would have to bide his time and hope for the best after Johnson left office the following year. He had learned his first lesson in the world of politics: no amount of support from senators, professors, or even Frederick Douglass could overcome the political realities of his time. He knew he had to persevere to attain his dream. Now it was just a matter of time.

6

Minister Resident

Friends and allies continued to urge Ebenezer to use his connections with the Republican Party to help him onto the next rung of the political ladder. Despite failing at convincing President Johnson to appoint a black diplomat, Ebenezer felt a new spark when the campaign of 1868 brought victorious war general Ulysses S. Grant to 1600 Pennsylvania Avenue. Taking over the presidency from his anemic predecessor, Grant brought new hope that black voices would finally be heard in the corridors of power.

Article Two of the Constitution authorizes the president to appoint diplomats with the advice and consent of the Senate. The highest-ranking U.S. diplomats were referred to as ministers, as the term ambassador would not be used by Americans until 1893. But from the founding of the country, these ministers had been for the most part wealthy, politically connected individuals. This system of patronage remained the rule of the day, as the State Department bloomed from its humble beginnings of just 10 positions overseas in 1781 to 804 such positions when Grant took the oath of office.[1]

Though not a wealthy man himself, Bassett hoped the racial factor would now weigh in his favor as he renewed his lobbying effort with the new political powers that ruled Washington. And through the years of toiling away on issues of racial equality, he managed to once again gather the various Quaker, abolitionist, and black activists in Philadelphia and Connecticut to support his candidacy, as he had done when Andrew Johnson was president. Seven pages worth of signatures accompanied one such letter of support to President Grant. Bassett had even been awarded an honorary degree by Pennsylvania's Lincoln University, one of the first schools of higher education for black men.[2]

More importantly, he had Frederick Douglass once again in his corner. As Douglass would describe later, he himself could have taken the position as the first black diplomat, but instead Douglass "preferred to urge the claims of [his] friend, Ebenezer Bassett, a gentleman and a scholar, and a man well fitted by his good sense and amiable qualities to fill the position with credit to himself and his country."[3]

Buoyed by Douglass's encouragement, Bassett wrote to the president directly, saying he had been persuaded by both white and black citizens to seek the Haytian posting. He referred to their argument that he was "a representative Colored man," who possessed "an unchallenged character of probity and patriotism." As an active Republican, he also hinted at the political gains for Grant if he saw fit to take this step: "My appointment, or the appointment of some other proper person of my race, would be hailed by them, especially by recently enfranchised colored citizens, as a marked recognition of *our* new condition in the Republic and an auspicious token of our great future."[4] It was a strong argument from a political standpoint. Though Grant had just been elected to the highest of offices, he would no doubt want to run for reelection, and by assigning Bassett to the position in Hayti, he could count on the vote of black citizens across the country. Appointing leading African Americans to visible positions would ensure a gratitude that paid dividends at the election.

The man Bassett hoped to replace was Gideon Hollister, another native of Lichtfield, Connecticut. Hollister had been a state senator until appointed to Hayti by President Johnson in 1868. As minister resident, Hollister had come under great pressure from certain shipping interests because of his refusal to back the rebels fighting against the government of General Sylvain Salnave. A group of merchants in Boston had even petitioned the Secretary of State for Hollister's recall, citing Salnave's crimes against the Haytian people, and because a "feeling of hostility against the United States has been provoked in consequence of the support which Salnave receives from the United States minister at Port-au-Prince."[5]

Of course it was a stretch to think that a diplomatic envoy would be flagrantly violating official U.S. policy, but Hollister was a convenient target. In fact as minister resident, Hollister had become something of a liability for the Department of State. He sometimes failed to report on events, leaving the secretary to learn about them from other sources. And occasionally he did act in ways that put Washington in an awkward position. Even President Johnson himself had expressed his displeasure in Hollister. In retrospect, it came as little surprise that he was recalled by the new Grant administration.

Many interpreted Hollister's recall as a victory for the opponents of Salnave. However, as newspapers pointed out, the new appointee to

Hayti would be "accredited to the constitutional President, as proof that, despite what the Boston merchants stated in their petition, the Government of Washington recognizes Salnave as the only legitimate ruler in Hayti."[6] Pressure mounted from all sides on the new president: he would have to decide whether to support Salnave or not, and whom he would support as the new minister to the politically sensitive post.

After just a few weeks in office, Grant dropped the bombshell. Not only would Grant appoint the next envoy to the sinking Salnave government, but he would also nominate a black man to serve as the chief of mission in Port-au-Prince.

> I nominate Ebenezer D. Bassett, of Pennsylvania, to be minister resident and consul-general of the United States to the Republic of Haiti, vice Gideon H. Hollister, recalled.
>
> U. S. Grant.
>
> Washington, April 12, 1869.[7]

Newspaper reports at the time noted that Grant was "besieged by politicians and office seekers." Among those to whom foreign ambassadorships were being doled out were former military officials, veterans of the Civil War, and personal friends of Grant. But the significance of the Haytian appointment was immediately evident. The *New York Times* even featured it on their front page, noting that two "Colored Ambassadors" were being sent forward to the Senate for confirmation:

"J.R. Clay, who goes to Liberia, is a native of Louisiana, who has negro blood in his veins, and so has Ebenezer D. Bassett, the Principal of the Colored High School in Philadelphia, who goes to Hayti. The latter nomination was warmly pressed by the colored people of intelligence at the North."[8] Clay's name was subsequently pulled, however, leaving Bassett as the only, and first, black American nominated to hold a chief of mission posting.

The White House feared a backlash both from racists who did not want to see an African American as a foreign representative as well as from opponents of Salnave who preferred a more sympathetic figure. But the government was able to nimbly limit the damage through favorable media coverage and through patronage to former Confederate leaders. As the Chicago *Tribune* wrote:

> In nominating General Longstreet, formerly a rebel, but now a Republican, to be Collector of Customs in New Orleans and the colored Mr. Pinchback of Louisiana, to a minor office in the same state, as well as in the nomination of colored men for a leading Post Office in South Carolina, for Justice of the Peace at Washington, and for Ministers to Hayti and Liberia, President Grant

has shown that he desires to recognize neither color nor past participation in the rebellion if followed by earnest conversion to the principles of freedom, as any bar to office or preferment.[9]

Harper's Weekly, the nation's premiere news and cultural magazine, even featured a picture of Bassett and an article describing him as "very fitly a colored man of the highest eminence."[10]

Grant also asked the Senate to quickly approve the nomination, no doubt to minimize having to expend political capital against racist enemies and to promptly show his supporters in the newly enfranchised black community that his presidency was an ally. Just four days after the president sent Ebenezer Bassett's name up to the Hill, the Senate voted forty-eight to five to confirm him. Only Senators Eugene Casserly of California, John Stockton of New Jersey, Allen Thurman of Ohio, and Garrett Davis and Thomas McCreery of Kentucky voted against confirmation. Reconstructionist Republicans assisted by limiting debate and hurrying the vote to a conclusion.[11]

The position provided Bassett with a salary of $7,500 per year and additional expenses; this was by far the most money that Ebenezer Bassett had ever earned. Now the father of four children, his daughter Lizzie having been born just the year before, he was quickly becoming a premiere leader in "black society" throughout the country.

Preparing for the job would not be simple, as the civil war in Hayti had now spread throughout the entire republic. Bassett went down to Washington to pay a visit on his future boss, Secretary of State Hamilton Fish, and to get instructions on how to proceed. Sitting in Fish's private office, the secretary coldly greeted his new minister, not even rising from his seat to shake Bassett's hand. Sitting uncomfortably across from the secretary, he listened as Fish talked at length about the position. But what was striking to Ebenezer was that Fish rarely made eye contact, and he quietly wondered if Fish was behaving so awkwardly because of his race.

Despite his inelegant demeanor during the meeting, the Secretary of State told Bassett that the State Department had the greatest confidence in his intelligence and ability to look after the interests of the United States. His very presence, Fish told him, would be "eminently conducive to the harmony and friendly relations existing between the Governments of the two countries."[12] They concluded slightly more amicably with the secretary telling Bassett to go down the street for a courtesy call on President Grant at the White House.

Arriving for his meeting with the President, Bassett was full of dread. He wondered why he had bothered to accept this appointment, and given the reception thus far, he was unsure how he would be treated by Grant.

In those days, it was easy to simply drop in and make an appointment with the chief executive officer of the United States. As it turned out, Grant was just finishing up a late morning public reception and had time in his schedule to personally congratulate his newest envoy.

Unlike Fish, who received Bassett with a stiff formality, Ulysses Grant warmly greeted Bassett, putting him at ease right away. Facing Ebenezer, the president gazed in full attention, listening to what his nominee had to say. Emotionally describing his sense of responsibility at the task, Bassett told the president that his desire was to preserve the good name of both his race and his country. Grant agreed, telling him that Hayti would be "only too glad to receive one of their own race as American Minister." Taken with Grant's personal charm, Bassett made an impulsive request to return later that afternoon to continue the discussion. Grant obliged and told him to return after 2 p.m.

Entering the Oval Office again, Bassett found another warm reception that afternoon, and he was joined by the Postmaster General John Cresswell. Grant offered Bassett a cigar, and though the high school principal was not a smoker, he accepted and awkwardly attempted to light it. For over an hour the three sat talking and looking over maps of the Caribbean. Grant mentioned in passing that he might be looking at an annexation in the region, and he added that a naval base at Mole St. Nicolas, on the northern coast of Hayti, would be of value. The entire visit reenergized Bassett, and he returned to Philadelphia eager to embark.[13]

Upon his return, he found among the letters wishing him well one from his abolitionist idol, Frederick Douglass. "Let me congratulate you and rejoice with you," Douglass wrote from his home in Rochester. "Your appointment is a grand achievement for yourself and for our whole people." Looking at the historical significance for the nomination, Douglass admonished his long time protégé: "I have no doubt you see the importance of your position. As you shall acquit yourself in it—wisely or otherwise, we shall be affected favorably or unfavorably." He concluded asking to see the Bassetts before they departed for Port-au-Prince.[14]

Unfortunately, personal tragedy struck just as Ebenezer was about to leave. His father, Eben Tobias, died at the age of sixty-four. The former "Black Governor" of Derby—son of a slave, and a man who had struggled to see his own son integrate schools and receive the finest education available in the country—would not live to see Ebenezer assume the highest-ranking diplomatic position for a black man in U. S. history. It was a bittersweet moment for the Bassetts, and Ebenezer took time with his elderly mother, Susan, to grieve the loss of the man who had stood out as the earliest role model and example of success in life. Ebenezer was concerned about leaving his frail mother alone. Despite the pain caused by their loss, she insisted that Ebenezer go; this was what Eben Tobais wanted. Their son had a destiny to fulfill.

Since Haytian independence in 1801, not one of that country's leaders had left the palace peacefully; they either died in office or were run out in a coup. The Haytian president at the time of Bassett's appointment, Salnave, had himself violently seized power from Fabre Geffrard in 1867.

The current war, the so-called Guerre des Cacos, was particularly devastating, even by the standards of previous bloodletting on the island. British Consul General Spenser St. John, who spent almost two decades on the island, called 1869 "the most disastrous I have known in Haytian history."[15] American media reports during the sieges around Cap Hatien referred to fighting of "the most barbarous and inhumane manner . . . converting what claims to be a war into a savage butchery."[16] Though he lived through the great U.S. Civil War, Bassett himself had never witnessed combat, nor did he know its brutality up close. Despite his vast education, he must have wondered if he were truly prepared to face the horrors that awaited him.

Full of anticipation and a sense of duty, he headed to New York to set sail on the steamship *City of Port-au-Prince*. When he arrived in Manhattan on May 25, 1869, the black community of New York, buzzing with news of his arrival, decided to throw a celebratory fete in his honor. Gathering at the Shiloh Church, the preeminent black house of worship and center of activism in New York, a great crowd of friends, as well as the curious, came together to bear witness to history.

In attendance were abolitionist leaders, Quakers, and New York Republican figures—both black and white. Of special meaning to Bassett was to see once again his old friend and former boss at the Institute for Colored Youth, Charles Reason. Now a prominent teacher in the city's public school system, Reason had been one of the earliest supporters of young Ebenezer, plucking him from the obscurity of small-town Connecticut and endorsing him to take over the most important school for blacks in Philadelphia. Each of those events had helped set the stage for this very moment.

The Reverend Charles Ray introduced Bassett to the excited crowd saying, "I feel a deep sense of no ordinary pride and heartfelt gratification in being selected to preside over the deliberations of one of the most auspicious events with the history of American civilization. It is the acme of our highest ambition, and no less an important feature of our happiness." Ray praised President Grant for the foresight of this appointment as well as others he had given to leading black citizens. Despite the ongoing violent revolution in Hayti, he told those in attendance that Bassett would "contribute to a better state of feeling in that country." Ray walked across the stage to shake Bassett's hand, concluding: "Now sir, you go to a foreign land as the representative of the United States. You go as one of the colored race; you go as an American citizen," concluding dramatically as the whole audience burst into loud cheers and prolonged applause.

Overcome with emotion, Ebenezer Bassett had not seen such a massive gathering since his days recruiting black troops for the Civil War. Those crowds were drawn by the power of a cause and the prominence of speakers like Frederick Douglass. But today there was no Douglass and no eminent threat to the nation. There was only the hope of millions of a repressed but resilient people, a hope embodied in the presence of Bassett.

"I cannot find the words to express my hearty thanks for the kind interest in my welfare and your generous consideration for the success of my mission abroad," he said scanning the audience. "I feel myself unworthy. I believe there is not a colored man in the whole country who has not pledged to me his prayers for my success."

Bassett took great pains to praise President Grant as a hero to blacks and a savior of the Union. But he also acknowledged the risk of the appointment, hinting at the concerns of the uncharted waters that lie ahead for him. "Diplomacy was a new field to the colored race in this country. How they would succeed remained to be seen. But one thing he [President Grant] knew, he brought to work an honest heart, a generous purpose, and unflagging industry, and an elevated patriotism. It shall be my daily prayer," Bassett promised them.

When he was boarding *The City of Port-au-Prince* a few days later, on June 5, a great group of onlookers came to the port to see him off. His father-in-law, Robert Park, his old friend and fellow teacher from the ICY, Fanny Jackson, various academics from Pennsylvania and New York as well as Haytian Ambassador Alfred Box, and even the former president of Liberia Joseph Jenkins Roberts stood to wish him well. In bidding farewell, Bassett waved and pledged, "I shall bring no stain upon the glorious old flag of our country." Keenly aware of the pressure upon him, he added: "Ladies and gentlemen, I may fail in this mission, but I promise you this, an honest heart, a noble endeavor, and true patriotism."[17]

The trip south was not an easy one for the new diplomat. The journey lasted ten days, and he was seasick during much of the trip. First landing in Cap Hatien on the northern coast, he found what he described as a "deplorable condition," which was the result of the siege of the city and the ongoing civil war. People were starving, and it was blisteringly hot: "100 [degrees] in the shade." The U.S. consulate there had been under attack from rebel groups for weeks, and Salnave's supporters were seeking refuge in the home of the vice-consul. The misery and tension were too great, and passengers quickly reboarded the ship for the final leg of the journey. A day later, on the afternoon of June 14, Bassett approached the majestic Port-au-Prince.

"It seemed as if the city had come to meet us," he wrote later. Throngs gathered as news spread of his arrival. The dark faces of the Haytians, their strange customs, and the babble of French Creole that surrounded him were off-putting. He was also astonished to see both teenage boys and girls running around with little or no clothing. Though Bassett spoke some French (having studied it while at Yale), he was hardly fluent, and what the pushing crowds were saying was as mysterious to him as everything else about his new home.

Fortunately, from among the sea of bodies emerged J. T. Holly, a local missionary who brought him from the chaos of the docks to his home in the city. Immediately after stepping into his house, however, he was again besieged by a stream of neighbors and visitors who had come by to see this new black "Monsieur le Ministre Américain."

As if the heat of the tropical sun and the press of bodies upon him were not enough, Bassett now had to grow accustomed to the army of mosquitoes and gnats that swarmed the city. Dengue and malaria were common illnesses, and though the connection between these insects and the dreaded diseases was still uncertain, their constant buzzing could be maddening for someone used to the colder climates of New England.

Soon he went to meet the man he was to replace, Hollister, who warmly greeted the new minister. Because they were of different races and perhaps expecting some degree of anger or jealousy on Hollister's part at having to leave his post, Bassett was uncertain of what to expect. The only information he had about Hollister were those less-than-flattering press reports, but he found him to be quite charming and capable, quickly making Bassett feel welcome and comfortable. "I am truly sorry that he has been misrepresented at home," Bassett later wrote.

Having no experience internationally, it was daunting for the thirty-six-year-old to find himself as one of the most powerful figures in Hayti. Hollister did his best to describe the profession, but much of the work of diplomacy involved intangibles, as Bassett quickly came to realize. "I find the duties of my office not so onerous as delicate. Common sense and some little knowledge of law . . . will carry me through."

The wider society he had entered was one of extremes. Not simply torn apart by warfare, the country had no middle class to speak of; a small and refined elite prospered while the rest of the nation teemed in poverty and resentment. Despite all the difficulties he encountered, Ebenezer quickly became enamored with the country's natural beauty as well as with the flowers and fruits that perfumed the Caribbean air. Though he was in for the challenge of his life, he felt this was where he was meant to be. "This is truly a wonderful country," he optimistically concluded in a letter to his friend Frederick Douglass.[18]

Bassett was, however, unable to present his credentials to the Haytian president and to get started. Salnave remained with his troops, furiously attempting to defend his reign, which had increasingly come under attack since he declared himself "President for Life." Bassett stayed with Hollister and busied himself by taking an inventory of the U.S. Legation. The conditions were difficult and the office was sparse; a simple case with a few books on international law, files of letters from the State Department, and a desk were that all the office held. The only adornment was a map of North America on the wall.

But as the battles raged outside the capital, the diplomats soon found out that they were not immune to the violence either. In an argument with a carpenter working on his residence, Hollister was attacked with a hatchet. Though not fatally injured, his scalp wounds were enough to prompt media attention as far away as New York, causing wild speculation that the violence was political in nature, and that even Bassett himself had come under attack. This incident clearly demonstrated to the newcomer the treacherous waters of everyday life in the Caribbean as well as the vast potential for misinterpretation of events far away in the United States.[19]

In the days before cables or phone calls were used to transmit messages over wires, information passed between Washington and embassies the old-fashioned way. Handwritten letters, numbered sequentially for filing, were the only form of communication. And at a time when it took days for these "despatches" to reach their intended audience, two things were of utmost importance: accuracy in reporting and good handwriting. Bassett possessed both of these attributes, and his memos back to Washington displayed a quick grasp of the unfolding political situation on the island. His notes were written in the learned and preferred style of diplomacy, that is, in long sentences filled with complex ideas. Never failing in form, Bassett always signed the correspondence "Your obedient servant." But given the amount of time it required for Washington to receive reports, Bassett knew he had to act in a manner that was less than purely servile and he would be forced to subsequently explain his actions to the State Department.

On September 7, almost three months after he first set foot on the island, Ebenezer Bassett was finally able to present his credentials to President Salnave, thus officially becoming the first African American accredited to serve as a foreign chief diplomat. As the afternoon sun drew toward the horizon, Bassett entered the ornate wooden reception hall of the Haytian Presidential Palace dressed in his finest clothing.

Presenting his papers, he reminded Salnave and his entourage of military and cabinet officials that the United States and Hayti were the first two nations to break their chains of bondage from European dominance. But he also alluded to the conflict that now held the island in a state of tension—similar to the one that only four years earlier had torn apart his own country.

"It has sometimes happened in the history of nations that great and liberal principles of government incorporated into the Constitution have seemed to lie temporarily inoperative," Bassett told Salnave. "But I pray your Excellency to observe that I am sent here . . . partly to give assurance by my presence of the practical recognition of a great principle in the United States—the principle for which your ancestors were among the first in the New World to contend when they founded the Haytian Republic and by which all class of men under the broad shield of my government stand equal before the law."

This call for racial equality and rule of law had been precious commodities in the United States. These words, however, also served as a warning to Hayti, lest the civil war there slid into complete anarchy. Equality before the law and the protections offered by the legal system were the only way to maintain the principles upon which these nations were founded.[20]

As an honor guard escorted the esteemed guest toward the gates after the reception that evening, Bassett looked back to see the raising of the American flag. Shots rang out in a seventeen gun salute. He had achieved his long-sought dream.

Though ordinarily such official ceremonies are a moment to savor, Bassett could not do so. He was immediately pressed into action as the revolution bore down on Salnave's fragile hold on power. After Hollister left the island, Bassett stood alone, leading a delegation of ten American vice-consuls and commercial officials scattered in different parts of the war-ravaged country. The rest of the year would be spent dealing with a government increasingly on the defensive, while its control of Haytian territory shrank week after week.

President Salnave wasted no time to test the new American envoy, coming to see him just days later to seek assistance in quelling the insurgency. Careful not to commit to something he was unable to provide, Bassett noted that governments acted cautiously in such extreme circumstances, saying, "I cannot assure you of anything further than the same friendly sympathy which has heretofore been shown your government."[21]

Diplomacy was an art. As such, it was frequently noted that when a diplomat said "yes," it meant maybe; but when he said "no," then he was simply not a diplomat. Ebenezer was anything if not gracious and concerned about the effects of his words on the Haytian head of state. Though a novice in the nuances of diplomatic parlance, his years of experience as a political activist had taught him to be vigilant. And vigilant he was, especially as blood flowed, and communication and help from Washington lay several days away.

Ebenezer also had internal problems to manage. Many of the consular and commercial agents that he supervised in the country were little more than drunkards and opportunists, with some even acting as partisans in the civil war. Knowing he would need the best people during the crisis, he set about to replace several members of his staff. In addition, out of his own pocket he hired clerks for his Consular Office in Port-au-Prince, which cost him $1,200 that year. Bassett was determined that the presence and efficiency of the United States would no longer suffer compared to those of European powers.

The fighting worsened, and by the autumn the Haytian president controlled barely a tiny portion of his territory. After the northern city of Cap Hatien fell to the rebel leader Jean Nicholas Nissage Saget, Bassett had a difficult choice to make. Abraham Crosswell, his new vice-consul at the northern Cap, wrote that his "worst fears were realized" when he was flooded with refugees, including many of Salnave's family. Starvation in the city was common as supplies vanished during the yearlong siege. In the interest of humanity, Bassett decided that the refugees could remain inside the protection of the American consulate in Cap Hatien. But the rebels began threatening the vice-consul, demanding that he turn over Salnave's partisans. Because the vice-consul refused to do so, rebel troops rushed his doors. It was not until he appeared on the balcony, revolver in hand, that the troops backed down. Such an undiplomatic display was the only thing that prevented further violence, as Vice-Consul Crosswell later recounted: "Had I not shown a bold front, I would probably not have been able to have the honor of relating these details."[22]

As the situation deteriorated, Bassett felt compelled to call for help. Getting a message to Key West, Florida, where he was able to send a telegram to be forwarded to Washington, he pleaded with the Secretary of State: "'Gettysburg' disabled, no ship here. Please send one immediately and keep it constantly here."[23] The cry for a battleship was one he repeated numerous times throughout the year. With Washington turning a deaf ear to his appeal, he worked out an arrangement with the French and British legations, both of whom oversaw numerous warships in the harbor of Port-au-Prince. If American interests required protection, Bassett had convinced them to provide support. The American diplomat also rented a new office for the Legation, one in a fireproof building to prevent destruction of records in the event of the much-rumored looting and burning of the city.

Salnave grew more desperate and the U.S. media referred to him as a "caged lion" capable of any duplicity. Inflation had rendered Haytian currency useless, and the embattled president offered Bassett control of the Mole St. Nicolas in exchange for American money and support to prop up his regime. Though the American Secretary of State was interested in the Mole for use as a naval station in the northern part of the island, he also knew Salnave precariously clung to power. And as Bassett had reported, there was no popular support within Hayti for American control of "a single foot of her territory."[24]

Given this scenario, the secretary sent instructions to Bassett to remain as neutral as possible in hope of avoiding a backlash should the rebels gain full control: "The unhappy strife going on there partakes of the nature of a civil war, although it is not recognized as such by us . . . If the United States under such circumstances gives to the existing government the moral force of their recognition of it as the rightful ruler of the whole territory of the Republic, and withholds from the insurgents even the recognition of a state of war, all of which we are doing, that is the extent to which a neutral can be asked to go."[25]

Bassett had in fact taken great lengths to reach out to Salnave and develop personal relationships with his cabinet and advisors. The frequent dinners and visits of personal diplomacy, he hoped, would lead to changes in the regime's behavior. Bassett saw himself helping in the "adoption of liberal and humane measures," and as a voice of reason opposing Salnave's scorched-earth campaign against enemies.[26] He even took the extraordinary measure of marching up to the palace with the French and British consuls to negotiate the end of conflict and to ask Salnave to step down, but all these efforts were in vain.

In the end, there was little that could hold back the waves of discontentment, as rebel troops swarmed through the countryside. By December the capital itself was under siege, and rebels bombarded the Presidential Palace. From his residence overlooking the city, Bassett and his family saw the ships in the harbor and heard their cannons booming, as Saget's forces pounded the city. A few errant rounds even landed on Bassett's property. Salnave's supporters and family rushed for cover, many coming onto Bassett's fifteen-acre compound. Nonetheless, the minister resident, who at the time was very sick due to exposure to a tropical illness, continued working and reporting about the fighting to his boss in Washington. Now almost three thousand terrified refugee women and children filled the grounds of his home. Eliza Bassett and her young children attempted to assist as many as they could, but in the end, they were simply overwhelmed and at their wits end.

Secretary Fish replied rather bureaucratically, noting that Bassett's actions had not been sanctioned by the State Department, but that he personally understood: "While you are not required to expel those who may have sought refuge in the Legation, you will give them to understand that your government cannot on that account assume any responsibility for them."[27] Bassett was forced to balance a tricky series of negotiations to ensure that revenge was not brought against those unarmed targets. Later, he helped assure their safe passage out of harm's way. All of this he did without help from the State Department, which would only write approvingly of his actions weeks later. Despite all of his diligence to help broker this deal—and as a reminder of how distant and uncaring the bureaucracy could sometimes be—his simple request for supplies, stationery, a flag, and an iron safe were promptly denied. "It is not thought necessary to furnish you with an iron safe for the preservation of the archives," incredibly Fish wrote to him amid the burning warfare.[28]

Eventually the rebels struck the fatal blow, hitting the Palace and destroying it. Salnave, who had threatened to burn Port-au-Prince rather than surrender, was cornered by insurgent Generals Brice and Boisrond Canal. He fled across the Dominican border, vainly seeking help from his ally, President Buenaventura Baez, of Santo Domingo. But he was quickly captured by Dominican rebels allied to Saget and brought back to Hayti for quick "justice." He was charged with treason, found guilty, and executed in the very smoldering ruins of his former palace. Even in defeat, Bassett witnessed Salnave's defiance, writing that the former president "faced death in a bold and manly manner."[29]

Bassett negotiated with the new government for the release of thousands that still sat panic-stricken in his compound. Saget was reluctant, demanding a list of refugees so that he could determine who might actually be political enemies. Bassett refused, boldly writing: "You will pardon me for reminding that the holding of women and children as hostages is repugnant to modern civilization and especially to the government of the United States." He went on to express to the Haytian rebel leader that if he desired good bilateral relations, then he should simply allow the release of the refugees.

Saget finally gave in. With little regard for his personal safety and despite a continuing fever, the American Minister Resident personally escorted this army of refugees into the heart of the capital soon after sunset so that they might return to their homes. Some political opponents captured earlier did not fare as well as Bassett's group. Many were quickly killed, having their throats slit, because the new government did not want to waste time on trials.

Though unsettling for Ebenezer Bassett, it would be an early lesson in diplomacy for the fresh-faced minister resident: Hayti, born out of violent revolution and controlled by force ever since, would be no easy place to conduct international relations. He would have to choose wisely or perhaps suffer the same fate as some of Salvane's partisans.

After his victory, Saget called a national assembly, which of course elected him president in May of 1870. Conditions after the war, however, remained bleak. "There are no general means of education or communication, except for road ordinarily only for animals. . . . There is no general system of agriculture and absolutely no manufacture of any kind," a report of the situation later expressed.[30]

As the cannons stilled and some degree of peace returned to the city, Ebenezer Bassett found he survived the destruction that had laid waste to much of the country. Not only that, he had managed to thread the dangerous needle of negotiations between a collapsing dictator and his furious enemies. Even more impressively, he did so while European powers were parking their naval vessels in the harbor, ready to defend their national interests, whereas all Ebenezer possessed was his intellect. Bassett had not just survived, he had thrived, keeping the relations among all parties and the United States from becoming mired in rancor. With less than a year of assignment under his belt, he was accredited to his second government as American Minister Resident in Hayti. Now more sure of himself, he stood ready to help the Haytians rebuild their country with a new and more open sense of purpose.

Annexation Vexation

Amid all the chaos on the Haytian side of Hispaniola, there was tremendous interest in Washington in the annexation of Dominican side of the island. However, many newspaper opinions were brutal given the level of violence taking place in Hayti and the instability that raged east of the Dominican border. "We have to consider Hayti and St. Domingo as they are, with a population ignorant, treacherous, brutalized and lazy," one column scathingly laid out.[1]

Secretary of State William Seward had even visited both Hayti and the Dominican Republic in January of 1866, a rare foreign trip for a leading American official in those days.[2] But with such hostile opinions expressed in the American media, efforts to annex the Dominican Republic had gone down in flames before the U.S. Congress at the end of the Johnson administration.

Early in Grant's tenure, the White House became fixated on the idea of annexing the Dominican Republic, as the president had hinted to Ebenezer during their meeting in the Oval Office. Just months after taking office, Grant sent his personal secretary, General Orville Babcock, to determine yet again the suitability of making it a U.S. protectorate. American military leaders and several individuals with strong commercial interests quietly backed this effort.

Secretary of State Fish was disinclined to move on annexation, feeling that greed rather than national interest lay at the heart of these schemes. Nonetheless, when his boss sent Babcock to investigate, a move outside the boundaries of proper diplomatic channels, Fish knew there was nothing that could stop the momentum. Dominican President Baez was having difficulty holding on to power with the demise of his ally Salnave and he became an all-too eager partner in negotiating any treaty.

The year 1870 had brought not only a new government into Port-au-Prince with the victorious rebels but also a greater scrutiny from the United States into the internal affairs of the Black Republic. "Surrounded by enemies on all sides" was a cry that played into Haytian existential fears, and the light-skinned President Saget shrewdly used it to maintain control over his base of support, largely formed by dark-skinned rural people. As part of this campaign, the new government engaged in a bloody retribution against the remaining mulatto and urban supporters of the previous regime. Hastily ordered military tribunals quickly meted out death sentences to any perceived enemies.

Appalled by the rash bloodletting, Bassett took the bold act of confronting Saget's new ministers to express dismay at the continuing carnage. Although the American had no objection to imprisoning true enemies, he believed that murderous revenge was not a solution. "We know too, that this is a time of passion, and that therefore a fair and impartial trial could scarcely be given in the ordinary tribunals of the country. But for the sake of humanity—for the sake of the good name of the Haytian government abroad, I pray that these persons tried in this hasty and irregular manner may not be then hastily put to death," Bassett implored the new government.[3]

Fearing that he had overplayed his hand, the Haytian leader backed down in the face of strong U.S. protests, disbanding the tribunals and stopping the political massacre that they wrought. In their interactions, Saget appeared to Bassett as a mild, humane, and religious man—someone with whom he could do business. "If his counsels prevail, I am sure Hayti will be saved from much of the evidence and cruelty already upon us," he wrote Washington assessing the new government.[4]

But the risk that Ebenezer took facing down this unsteady new leadership met with a cold indifference from his bosses. Grant's administration was focused only on how the internal turmoil of Hayti could affect their greater goal of Dominican annexation.

Saget, meanwhile, feared for his long-term survival because of attempts on the part of the United States to grab control over his neighbor. Though he did not have forces strong enough to confront the power of the United States directly, the Haytian would do anything else to make Dominican annexation plans unpalatable to the American public and Congress.

International tension raged as Saget's troops began scurrying through Dominican territory, harassing Baez and backing insurgents Marcos Antonio Cabral and Gregorio Luperon (who were also ardent Dominican anti-annexationists). Just as the United States began secret negotiations with the Dominicans, alarmed intelligence sources clamored to Bassett that the Haytians were preparing for an all-out assault on Santo Domingo.

President Grant ordered Minister Resident Bassett to take a hard diplomatic line with the regime in Port-au-Prince. The president looked "with disfavor" upon Haytian involvement in Dominican affair, "and you will not fail to make that clear to any government that may exist in Hayti," Secretary Fish sternly instructed Bassett. "And you will at all times, and in every way in your power, discourage such [interference]," Fish admonished.[5]

From Washington's perspective Bassett had handled the transition from Salnave to Saget with relative aplomb. He had even earned a letter of commendation from the State Department, in which Fish described Bassett's actions as "discrete and well considered." But the task at hand would be a much bigger challenge. To make matters worse, Saget's partisans were extremely mistrustful of the U.S. envoy because Bassett recognized them as legitimate only after Salnave had been executed. Now, as they heard rumors of secret negotiations by his government, Bassett became their bête noire.

In fact, the American diplomat had been in contact with the Dominicans to let them know that in the event of any annexation, the United States would appoint an American citizen as governor of the new territory. Bassett may even have passed them intelligence information as well. He was certainly passing along intelligence from his local sources to the head of the American military in the region, Commander E. K. Owen, of the warship *Seminole*. Though Bassett was not the lead at negotiating the treaty with Dominican authorities, Haytians eyed the American Minister Resident suspiciously. As rumors of personal threats against him grew, informants warned Ebenezer that he should watch where he traveled, ate, and drank. Nonetheless, Bassett remained steadfast, keeping the legation open during normal business hours, six days a week.[6]

Reporting on the growing anti-Americanism within the ranks of the new regime, Ebenezer wrote numerous letters to Washington about a "great bitterness" against his countrymen.[7] He had even warned his superiors about British Consul General Spenser St. John, who had actively backed Saget's rebellion and continued to drive a wedge between the new government and the United States. Bassett further wrote, "I am sure that the influence he has with them will not be given to improve the existing popular feeling here against America and Americans."[8] But the warnings fell on disbelieving ears in the marble halls of the Executive Office Building.

"When it is considered what had been done by the United States for the African race within the past ten years," Fish incredulously replied, "and how noble and just a policy is now maintained towards that race in the internal laws of this country, it is difficult to understand how the prejudices growing out of the state of things before the war can survive."

Fish failed to understand how dangerous the situation was becoming on the ground, or how negative an effect relations with Santo Domingo could have in Port-au-Prince. But he remained steadfast to his envoy. "The Department places confidence in your judgment and discretion. It relies upon you to take every honorable way to prevent a collision . . . but it expects you to be firm in maintaining the rights of our citizens and the dignity of the government of the United States." Hundreds of miles from his wintry capital in America, Bassett was left dangling to negotiate for his own safety and help prevent any further deterioration.

Undaunted, Bassett pushed aggressively and repeatedly with the Haytian Foreign Minister and even with President Saget, not accepting vague denials of interference across the Dominican border. "The United States will look with decided disfavor upon any attempt," Bassett told his counterparts in Port-au-Prince, "to interfere with the domestic peace and internal affairs of the neighboring Republic of Dominica." When the initial response to this demand was not as clear as Bassett had preferred, he shot back: "In the absence of any declaration of a neutral policy on the part of your government as to the internal affairs of San Domingo, the United States . . . may have cause for much displeasure."[9]

Though the wording of such notes might seem benign to outside observers, in the diplomatic lingo of international conflict it was just short of calling the new Haytian government a pack of liars and threatening bombardment. Although there was no indication in any of the dispatches to Washington that Bassett may have disagreed with the annexation efforts, his repeated warnings to Fish about the growing bitterness served as more than just reportage on popular sentiment; they appear to reveal that Bassett disagreed with such efforts.[10] Nonetheless, his loyalty to the policy of President Grant rose above personal opinions. Bassett's sources, meanwhile, continued to tell him that President Saget had placed his forces at the disposal of the Dominican insurgents, and that the Haytian invasion was just days away.

Now fearing a wider conflict, Grant told Bassett to use a trump card. Bassett was to break diplomatic relations with Saget if negotiations to withdraw Haytian troops from the Dominican Republic were unsuccessful. Grant went further, saying that if Hayti refused, Bassett was to close down the U.S. Legation and join the regional naval commander. Seven American ships were dispatched to the region. War, it seemed, was now being seriously contemplated in Washington.[11]

Bassett sprang into action relying on the only means he had at his disposal to prevent conflict—himself. Using the negotiation skills he had acquired over the previous year on the island, he made an impassioned plea. He understood that an island-wide war would be disastrous.

Though the diplomat used all the tact that his good offices demanded, he did not refrain from ominously warning the Haytians. Bassett went so far as to assert to the Haytian foreign minister that if the Dominican rebels were receiving any support his country, "the responsibility of [the] acts [of the rebels] rest[ed] with [him]."[12] The saber rattling, combined with Bassett's diligent persuasion, seemed to have their desired effect. Haytian troops were withdrawn and hostilities temporarily ceased.

President Baez took advantage of the calm and hastily called a plebiscite so that the Dominican people could "voice" their support of American annexation. With four days' notice, the outcome of the plebiscite was not surprising: just fifteen people in the entire country "voted" against American protection.

"The news from the Antilles is exciting," *The New York Times* trumpeted of the fraudulent ballot. "The Dominican Republic has declared by popular vote for annexation to the United States, the majority being 'overwhelming,'"[13] It was hardly a surprising change of heart for the Dominican leader, who had once even opposed the leasing of Samana Bay to the United States. With angry troops stirring on his border, he felt he had no other hand to play in the game of great power politics.

The treaty was quickly negotiated between Baez and Babcock, and it was called to be ratified by March 29 of 1870. It outlined an American payment of debts at $1,500,000 and offered a process of U.S. citizenship for Dominicans, with the prospect of eventual admission to statehood. Most importantly from the U.S. military perspective, a fifty-year lease of the Samana Bay was to be made available to the United States.

But the treaty immediately fell into trouble with the U.S. Senate. Despite fierce and personal lobbying by President Grant, it failed on a tie vote of 28 to 28. Senator Charles Sumner, who had long been a vigorous supporter of Haytian and Dominican independence, saw Grant's efforts as nothing more than an attempt to extinguish the freedom of two Black Republics. Though both sides had crucial internal conflicts to overcome, Sumner hoped that the island would one day live united and in peace, as a symbol of the ability of former African slaves to govern themselves. His principled stance would come at a price: the senator had delivered Grant an early political defeat and made himself a pariah to the administration, which would eventually work to have him ousted as chairman of the Foreign Relations Committee.

President Grant's stubbornness may have made him a highly successful general, but it was beginning to cost him as president. He simply would not let go of the idea of annexation. At the end of 1870, he spent considerable time in his annual address to Congress on one matter: Santo Domingo. Grant recommended that a commission be appointed to further investigate the island. Vigorously defending the notion of Manifest Destiny, he concluded his speech with the almost laughable claim that lasting damage to the United States could ensue if Congress failed to act: "So convinced am I of the advantage to flow from the acquisition of San Domingo, and of the great disadvantage, I might almost say calamities, to flow from non-acquisition, that I believe the subject only has to be investigated to be approved."[14]

The Haytians were apoplectic. Saget sent Stephen Preston, his new ambassador to Washington, to make a formal complaint to Fish. Secretary Fish, in turn, instructed Bassett to lie low and not to stir up any further trouble by talking about the annexation of their neighbor, hoping that it might die under its own weight.[15]

Like a Haytian voodoo zombie, however, Grant's plan staggered ahead with the establishment of the Santo Domingo Commission. Three leading citizens were appointed to head the commission: Benjamin Wade, Samuel Howe, and Andrew White. Bassett's old friend Frederick Douglass was added as one of the secretaries of the mission, in an effort to show racial sensitivity. If Douglass accompanied the mission through the Dominican Republic and lent it an air of credibility, it would appear less as a takeover by white colonialists and might become more palatable to both the Haytians and those suspicious in the United States.

Interestingly, Douglass did not see himself as being used as a pawn in this process. He rationalized his presence and the whole annexation effort, even though it put him at odds with his close friend, Senator Sumner.

"To me it meant the alliance of a weak and defenseless people, having few or none of the attributes of a nation, torn and rent by internal feuds, unable to maintain order at home, or command respect abroad," Douglass later wrote of Grant's attempt to annex the Dominican Republic. "Since liberty and equality have become the law of our land, I am for extending our dominion whenever and wherever such extension can peaceably and honorably . . . be accomplished."[16]

The Haytians knew of the commission's travel, and they were determined to interfere with it. Insurgents were planning to harass the group as it set out on its expedition through the Dominican countryside. But Bassett's sources tipped him off to the attack, and he quickly dispatched his consular agent from Cap Haitien to warn Douglass and the others, preventing any harm to their fact-finding mission.

Weeks later the commission safely returned to the United States and dutifully filed a positive report, but no further action came from the Congress. Dominican annexation was now officially dead, but it did not dispel Haytian suspicions toward U.S. intentions. Through it all, Ebenezer Bassett worked diligently to repair the bilateral damage caused by these efforts.

Bassett sought to win over Haytian popular sympathies by trumpeting the recent passage of the Fifteenth Amendment, which guaranteed the right to vote for black men. Writing President Saget, Minister Resident Bassett noted that five million people of African descent, "brothers and kinsmen of ourselves and of the Haytian people," would now be able to exercise their ballot in the United States. The diplomat went on to praise President Grant, saying that "no one has done greater service for human freedom and the liberties of our race."

In fact, black voting was a matter about which Ebenezer Bassett cared deeply. As far back as his activist years in New Haven, his Convention of Colored Men sought to change Connecticut's state law forbidding blacks to vote. His activism in the Republican Party was an extension of that fight, and now it had finally born fruit. The election of 1870 was a landmark in American politics. Because of newly enfranchised black voters, Joseph Rainey, of South Carolina, became the first black member of the U.S. House of Representatives. That same year, the Mississippi legislature sent the first black man to serve in the U.S. Senate, Hiram Revels. Bassett glowed with pride at the changes taking place back in his home country.

Continuing his charm offensive, Bassett made a point of showing the American flag at public ceremonies to the Haytian people. He even served as the "godfather" at the ceremonial christening of a new bridge at the town of Bois de Chere. The diplomat—along with the Haytian president, Saget's wife, and several leading dignitaries—were all in attendance, and afterwards they returned to Bassett's residence for a grand reception. Wishing to ingratiate himself with Saget, the minister resident made a speech praising the Haytian head of state. He also played into the racial sympathies of his addressees, reminding them that, "as a man of color," he understood their desire keep Hayti a strong and independent nation. He went further by adding that his country had no designs whatsoever "against the sovereignty and independence of Hayti," only wishing to see their neighbor "independent, prosperous, and happy."

President Saget—whose mulatto skin seemed darker when offset by his long, graying sideburns and mustache—was gracious in his thanks. After a toast to the health of both presidents, the gathering broke into applause, and the Haytian band played "Hail Columbia," the piece written for George Washington's first inauguration in 1789 and America's first national anthem.[17]

Thinking that the ice was beginning to thaw between the two governments, Ebenezer and his family returned to the United States for a brief vacation back home. The year of violence, tropical illness, and heat had taken a heavy toll on the Bassett family. In addition, he received word that his mother, Susan, had become gravely ill. Now sixty-five years old and still mourning the loss of her husband a year earlier, Susan Bassett was not expected to live much longer. Ebenezer wanted to return to Connecticut for the family to be together one last time.[18]

When Ebenezer, his wife, and their four children arrived at the port of New York, they were treated as returning heroes. In a major "welcome home" reception at the Cooper Institute in New York City, Bassett was praised for having helped avert a conflict regarding the annexation of the Dominican Republic and for having supported black independence. Ebenezer rubbed shoulders with high-ranking African Americans as well as with international leaders. The president and vice president of Liberia were there to greet him, as were figures such as J. J. Wright, the black justice from the South Carolina Supreme Court. Letters of support from Frederick Douglass and leading black minister George T. Downing were read to the crowd.

Journalists asked Bassett about innuendos that the new Haytian government was displeased with him (and ironically unhappy with the fact that the American envoy was a black man). The diplomat refuted both rumors, saying that he had been welcomed "in a very cordial and fervent manner." Bassett went on to discuss his surprise at the fact that Haytians should be so prone to war, but that discontent had little means of expressing itself outside of "revolutionary plots." Nonetheless, he was optimistic, telling the gathering that a progressive spirit lived with this new government.[19]

After finishing up business and family affairs, that fall he returned to the Caribbean, and found that things had gone from a slow boil to a bubbling froth. His sources told him that once again Saget was supporting Dominican insurgents. The renewal of Haytian involvement in cross-border affairs brought out fury in Washington. Letters from Fish to Bassett demanded more intelligence concerning the supply of war materials. Bassett dutifully made his démarches to Haytian leaders in Port-au-Prince, who all denied anything but strict neutrality in the regrettably spiraling civil war of their neighbor.

Fish was beside himself. Not only had the poorly managed annexation of the Dominican Republic failed in the Congress, but now the situation was spinning out of control with increased fighting on the eastern part of the island. American involvement had only served to fan the flames. Now that the American Congress and public had so decisively rejected initiating the statehood process for Santo Domingo, Haytian authorities felt free to prey upon their vulnerable brethren. "The assurances offered to you by the Haytian government as to its disposition to keep wholly neutral in the contest between the Dominican parties . . . do not seem to be expressed in a way to inspire perfect confidence in their sincerity," Fish sarcastically wrote his envoy.

The secretary still failed to fully grasp the threat that Saget felt. "It may be easily understood that the Haytian, being mostly descended from those of African extraction, who once held in slavery won their freedom and independence by expelling their former masters, should be reluctant to allow any nation tolerating slavery to acquire dominion in St. Domingo," Fish continued in his letter to Bassett. "This feeling should not, however, include the United States, especially in view of the fact that the equality of races here before the law, is signally exemplified in the person of our diplomatic representative accredited to them."[20]

But the hands of both Secretary Fish and Minister Bassett were tied. Threats and prodding from the United States now rang hollow to the ears of Saget's forces. Haytian officials had even taken advantage of the illiteracy of their rural partisans by sending leaders into the mountains to read "proclamations" that the whites were approaching to reenslave everyone. Fomenting their opposition only became easier with time.

The old aphorism of diplomacy that it was better to ask for forgiveness than for permission was never truer given the limitations of communications in the nineteenth century. At times correspondence would take as long as ten weeks to pass between Washington and Hispaniola. Circumstances changed rapidly within the intrigue of Caribbean politics. This left Bassett with greater autonomy and required his utmost prudence in dealing with his hosts.

Desperate to put a lid on the growing conflict, Bassett repeatedly went to see the foreign minister. Making threats was not a common practice among diplomats, but Ebenezer had been forced to take a much stronger line with this new government. He accused the Haytian government of failing to act in good faith toward the United States. "You will pardon me for remarking," Bassett told the Haytian leaders, "it could behoove your government to bear in mind the hazard it might incur by provoking the resentment of the numbers in the United States who take a lively interest in the independence of San Domingo, and especially that it should be independent of Haiti."[21] Knowing when to show some of his cards was part of the finesse that Bassett had learned. Though he did not openly threaten Haytian leaders with violence, his choice of words made clear that he was willing to encourage his government to come down hard if Haytians continued meddling across the border.

Bassett was also quick to report back this stern warning to Washington. Not wanting to be accused of "clientitis," that is, of taking rather uncritically the word of the Haitian authorities who denied any machinations, he frequently reported their continual denial of aggression. But Ebenezer Bassett knew that at the very least Saget's forces would have to be much more cautious, as he had made clear that the unfavorable eye of America was looking down upon their every action. For all of his trouble, the Department paid Bassett back with another slight by continuing to refuse his request for an iron safe to protect files at the legation!

The winter of 1871 was unusually warm in Washington, with temperatures hovering in the 50s. The normally pleasant atmosphere of the Caribbean, however, became red hot, as another diplomatic imbroglio came to the front. The U.S.-flagged commercial ship *Hornet* had docked in Port-au-Prince, in what appeared to be an ordinary import/export mission. This event was noteworthy because trade between the United States and the tumultuous island had greatly decreased over the years of chaos. The cotton and coffee crops had been badly damaged that year due to heavy rains and insects, and newspapers reported that the produce deliveries "were lighter than ever before known."[22] The Department even denied Bassett his request for another consular officer there, saying that the "commerce of Port-au-Prince with the United States [did] not seem to be of sufficient importance to require the appointment."[23]

The *Hornet* was an 835-ton gunboat built for the Confederates as a blockade runner, and it remained an American naval vessel until it was decommissioned and sold to private merchants in 1869.[24] Upon seeing her arrival at Port-au-Prince and overhearing crew members bragging about neighboring Cuba's rebellion, Ramón Olivera, the Spanish envoy, flew into a rage and ordered the ship blockaded. Olivera had good reason for his suspicions. Twice before the ship had been seized by U.S. authorities for violating American neutrality laws by taking guns to Cuban insurgents, who had been fighting a long-standing battle against Iberian colonization. After checking the ship papers, however, Ebenezer Bassett found nothing out of place with the *Hornet*. Despite his suspicious, he could not substantiate the gossip and felt bound to support an American-flagged vessel.

As a series of earthquakes trembled along the Caribbean coast that winter, the government of Hayti became stuck in the resulting rubble, both figuratively and literally.

The Spanish, not wishing to create too many problems with the increasingly powerful United States Navy, turned its fury upon the island, arguing that Hayti was now aiding the Cuban insurgents. Besides moving their flotilla to establish the blockade, the Spanish even fired shots at another small ship that the Haytians had chartered, towing the boat back into the wharf and charging the Haytians with a violation of the blockade. Saget was powerless, knowing that Hayti could not stand against the stronger Spanish forces.

Bassett had developed good relationships with all of the ministers and consuls on the island, but he found that the insolence with which Olivera behaved made the situation intractable. The Spaniard had succeeded in frightening the Haytians, giving them a thirty-hour deadline to either turn over the American ship or face serious consequences. Haytian Foreign Minister Denis desperately asked for support from the United States. "We could only consent to accept safekeeping on condition that you give your entire approbation to the same," Denis wrote to Bassett.[25] No negotiations, Bassett replied; there was simply no evidence that the *Hornet* was helping Cuban insurgents. The deadline came and went, and Olivera packed his belongings and boarded one of the Spanish ships. Everyone in the city thought that the Spanish Armada would soon rain fire on the port.

Bassett refused to back down in the face of threats, however. The ship was a U.S.-flagged vessel, and it had not been intercepted doing anything illegal. He would not give his assent to anything other than a return to U.S. shores. While the ship sat in the wharf undergoing repairs, the blockade grew in size. Bassett wrote several times to Washington requesting a man of war to either convoy the *Hornet* away or quiet the increasingly vocal Spanish menaces.

Secretary Fish rebuffed the Spanish envoy in Washington and he left most of the negotiating up to Bassett. In Port-au-Prince, Ebenezer gathered the rest of the diplomatic corps to make a united defense on behalf of the U.S. ship. The other diplomats supported Bassett's action, and they pressed the Haytian authorities to neither turn over the *Hornet* to the Spanish nor pay any indemnity. Meanwhile, like sharks circling in the water, the Spanish continued to patrol the harbor for months, but they made no move against the stranded vessel for fear of an American backlash. A stalemate, it seemed, had been reached.

The impasse was finally resolved over a year later, when Bassett negotiated a way out suitable to all sides. Washington assented to his proposal that a U.S. military steamer escort the *Hornet* back to the port of Baltimore. The frigate *Congress* was dispatched by the Navy, and the *Hornet* was successfully brought back to the United States.

"The Conduct of the United States Minister, Mr. Bassett, in regard to the matter of the steamer *Hornet*, has given great satisfaction here," ran one glowing *New York Times* report after the incident. "It is generally conceded that the firm stand he took in the premises averted trouble between Hayti and Spain, which was at one time imminent, and saved the *Hornet* from capture."[26] While American media lauded its minister, Spain recalled its ambassador, replacing Olivera with someone more apt in the art of diplomacy and who, it was hoped, would not to be outmaneuvered again by Bassett.

Hayti had been tossed like a toy boat in the storm of big-power politics and chafed under Saget's leadership. In May of 1871 legislators took the extraordinary act of holding a no-confidence vote in Saget's cabinet, which resulted in their resignation *en masse.* Bassett had been following the backstabbing and violent willfulness of the country's leadership for two years now and he expected the worst from the embattled president. But, to his surprise, maturity and acceptance was the response. "It is said to be the first instance in the history of the country when the executive has, on a direct issue, yielded to the chamber," Bassett wrote Secretary Fish. Bassett also noted that jury trials against several conspirators were going forward, and that Saget had refused to sign death sentences for two of the convicted. It seemed that for all of Bassett's entreaties, democracy and respect for the rule of law were gaining a foothold after almost seventy years of independence.[27]

Haytian intrigue, subterfuge, and harassment were in large measure attributable to the United States' fixation on Santo Domingo, combined with Saget's desire to consolidate his own power. But despite the tense diplomatic tête-à-tête going on between the United States and Hayti, relations between the two countries never spun out of control, thanks to Bassett's ability to bridge the divide during difficult negotiations.

Ebenezer Bassett had endured the tropical heat, a civil war, overbearing Europeans, and even a foolish takeover attempt by his own government. By now, he was a ranking member of the diplomatic and consular corps on the island, both in longevity of service and bravery. Saget's government even seemed respectful of him and cooperated with Bassett against the Spanish. Perhaps that progressive spirit the American envisioned was coming to fruition. But as Ebenezer's experience on the island must have forewarned him, things in Hayti were never calm for long.

8

Diplomatic Immunity

The population of Port-au-Prince, suffering through years of warfare, famine, and natural disasters, stood at just over 30,000 people. The vast majority of Haytians eked out a subsistence living off the land or sea, residing in small wooden huts that offered little protection against the battering winds and rains of the hurricane season. Their surroundings were filthy; people regularly dumped waste and refuse out their doors into the unpaved streets. Government services in the city were negligible.

The debris of the city was home to packs of roaming dogs, growing swarms of ants, and the ubiquitous cockroach. These insects were particularly troublesome for Bassett. As an educator and lover of the classics, he had brought numerous volumes of literature so that he could read and educate his children just as he had taught countless students back in the United States. But the cockroaches, he soon found out, had "extraordinary omnivorous powers," ruining their books, paper, and even articles of clothing.[1]

Nonetheless, the hearty family thrived. In 1872 their oldest child, Charlotte, was sixteen; Ebenezer Junior was fourteen; Iphigenia was eight; and little Lizzie was just four years old. And Eliza Bassett had exciting news for everyone: she was pregnant. She would soon give birth to their fifth child, a boy they would name Ulysses S. Bassett, in honor of the president.

The Bassetts were religious and active in their Christian faith. Ebenezer's religious convictions as well as his position of authority made him all the more charitable when he came across unlucky American citizens far from home. Often these were sailors, but sometimes business people or even religious missionaries who made their way to his doorstep in dire straits. "I have been really obliged from motives of patriotism and humanity to afford from my very limited private means, assistance to our countrymen who have found themselves here comparatively destitute and for whom no public funds were provided," he matter-of-factly wrote Secretary Fish. "I have never refused to listen to and aid them as best I could."[2]

The official religion of Hayti was Catholicism, and the American diplomat soon learned to move with ease among the many priests of the community, especially because many had been educated in Europe and shared Bassett's love of literature. But the true national religion was Voodoo. Shrouded in ritual and mystery to the Western eye, the atavistic practices of Voodooism stem from African traditions brought by slaves to the New World. Related stories of undead zombies and cannibalism began appearing with more regularity. These stories commonly came from the provinces, where there was even less development and government was almost nonexistent.

From Jacmel—a city on the lower peninsula accessible only along mule paths through the mountains—came many of these growing stories of Voodoo cults. The capital became obsessed with one particularly hideous account of a woman who stood accused of killing and eating twenty-six children in a series of gruesome rituals.[3]

The reviling tale of cannibalism was sensational, but from Bassett's perspective it only served as a distraction on the cocktail circuit from the true problems that plagued Saget's administration. In 1872 his cabinet resigned again, and newspapers reported another brewing revolution. Papers in the United States labeled the Haytian leader "utterly incapable" and "far from being of a sound mind."[4]

In fact Saget, perhaps even because of Bassett's own influence, was behaving as few Haytian rulers had in the past. He pardoned political prisoners and sought to work constructively with the legislative branch. However, his internal foes viewed these acts as weakness and stopped at nothing— even plotting a "mysterious" fire at the new Presidential Palace to undermine his regime.

Holding on to power was never a simple task in Hayti, but it was presumed easier to do when there was an outside foe to unite disparate internal forces. The Dominican Republic had long played that foil, but with its annexation attempts by the United States Haytian anger turned from the east toward the north. In spite of this, Ebenezer Bassett was doing a masterful job of keeping bilateral relations on a relatively even keel. However, he found that as Saget came under increasing domestic pressure, the Haytian president resorted to the old tricks of a foreign bogeyman, turning Bassett's country into a tempting target.

The brief lull of good feelings came to an abrupt end on the afternoon of March 21, 1872, in the city of Saint Marc. The region, which had been populated by descendents of former Louisiana slaves, lay some fifty miles to the north of Port-au-Prince, along a horseshoe-shaped bay. It was a small community of less than ten thousand people, and unlike the capital it was built largely of stone structures. It was also home to an important deep-water harbor, making it a busy commercial center. As a result, the United States had appointed a commercial agent, Gustave Jastram, to handle the requests from ship captains and to promote American business interests there. What made that afternoon in March unusual was the fact that President Saget was touring the area. With his visit came a sight that was growing more common: protests.

Apparently, Saget was in no mood for the reception he received and ordered the arrest of a local Haytian general, Benoit Batraville, whom he accused of instigating the protests and plotting his overthrow. Jastram quickly became caught in the imbroglio when Haytian paramilitary forces snatched him from his offices and dragged him through the streets toward jail and a fate uncertain.

In reality, Jastram and the Batraville family were close. They conducted business together, and when several military officers came by the Batraville house on Saget's orders, Jastram was the first person the embattled general called to diffuse the situation. Treason was not an uncommon charge to be hurled against political foes. But the fact that Batraville had held a commanding position in the military made the charge all the more serious. Jastram rushed to his friend's house to find it surrounded. Breaking through the armed phalanx, he bounded upstairs, where he found the desperate general held by guards.

Batraville, seeing his old comrade, begged for assistance. Jastram could not offer diplomatic protection at a location outside of official U.S. government premises, however and returned to his office to seek more information about the case. Batraville was soon escorted from his house, passing by Jastram's store, which also served as the office of the commercial agent. Breaking free, the general ran toward Jastram, shouting, "In the name of humanity—protection of the American flag!" Now the case was clear-cut: a Haytian citizen was asking for asylum, and the commercial agent's office was considered a sanctuary, free from the interference of local laws and law enforcement.

Following the example of his predecessors under similar circumstances, Jastram granted Batraville refuge. The soldiers who had been following the general angrily demanded that the American turn over the fugitive, but the commercial officer refused: he had diplomatic immunity and his compound was exempt.

The escorts left in a huff but returned shortly thereafter with almost two dozen armed and furious men. They burst into the office, grabbing both the general and Jastram, who pleaded to be allowed contact with the American Minister Resident in Port-au-Prince. A mob had gathered outside Jastram's store, and the blazing Antilles heat caused tempers to flare even more as chaos ensued. Jastram feared for the life of General Batraville, and he was beginning to think that he himself might not escape Haytian justice.

Both the French and British consuls rushed to the scene as the crowd grew in size and agitation. Only after repeated efforts by the diplomats, with the French consul swearing to take Jastram into his custody, did they release the American. Jastram ran for the next ship setting sail for the capital, heading directly for the residence of Ebenezer Bassett.[5]

Listening to the story, Bassett became appalled by the barbarity of the action. Of equal importance, as the official representative of the United States, he understood that this attack on one of his consulates was more than just a matter of local intrigue. It represented a direct threat to the United States and a contravention of international law. Most importantly, Bassett felt this would have never happened to a representative of one of the major European powers.

Assured that Jastram was now at least safe, Bassett set out to see the highest authorities on the island to correct this diplomatic affront. "Such a proceeding has never before been ventured upon toward any duly recognized consular officer in the Haytian Republic," Bassett vociferously complained.[6] The foreign minister weakly promised an investigation, but Bassett knew that no one was taking the matter seriously. Not to be left stewing, he himself traveled by boat to Saint Marc and carried out an investigation, confirming Jastram's versions of events.

Weeks passed without action on the Haytian side, however. As the stonewalling continued, Bassett broke all diplomatic pretenses and confronted the foreign minister. Unless the Haytian government acted on his complaint, acknowledging the wrong and working to make amends, he would take it as a personal and national insult. "I shall feel constrained to take such a delay as evidence of an indisposition on the part of your government to make the reparation which I have asked," he said, threatening the Haytians with further action once word reached Washington.[7]

Such political hardball was becoming more common in Bassett's interactions with Saget's cabinet, but the case had now drawn international attention. "Outrage on the American Consulate at St. Marc," ran one front-page headline in an American newspaper, feeding the frenzy.[8] Still, the Haytian government felt no need to speed their "investigation" until vague threats became a little more concrete.

A few weeks later an American naval vessel suddenly appeared at Cap Hatien, in the north. The steamer *Nantasket* sent a small crew with one of their howitzers onto the beach, which caused "very considerable excitement," according to Bassett. The minister resident and the U.S. military commander innocently claimed such "deployment" was a misunderstanding; it was merely a military training exercise gone awry. But the timing and the implications were unmistakable.

The Haytian foreign minister, who earlier dismissed the American's warnings, was clearly shaken by the howitzer. Taking the unusual step of coming to Bassett's residence just outside of the city, the foreign minister sought assurances from his counterpart that the incident would not escalate further. Bassett used the opportunity as leverage to finally get an acknowledgment in the Jastram affair.

"In consequence," Foreign Minister Etheart wrote to Bassett, "my government makes it a duty to declare to your government that it regrets very much that Mr. Jastram has had cause to complain of the conduct of the authorities of Saint Marc, on the occasion of the arrest of General Batraville." He went on to promise the punishment of the individual involved and swore that nothing similar would happen again.[9] With that, Bassett finally sent his agent back to reopen the consulate in Saint Marc.

"The Department congratulates you," an overjoyed Secretary Fish wrote to his envoy after receiving the apology from the Haytians. "The energy and perseverance with which you have followed up that difficult case has at last been crowned with success," he continued.[10] Bassett beamed with this recognition from his superior, but despite promises to the contrary, the problems would not end so quickly.

It appeared that a full-fledged campaign had begun against the United States. Just days later, Bassett found himself coming to the rescue of another American citizen who, unluckily, happened to disembark in the capital.

Clement Eldredge, captain of the schooner *Lucy Holmes*, had gone ashore at Port-au-Prince on the night of July 11. After dining in the home of Oliver Cutts, a prominent American businessman, he walked toward the docks through the darkened streets. Suddenly, several men jumped from the shadows and charged him at gunpoint. Dressed in military uniforms, they proceeded to beat and force-march him through the town, shaking him down for money while raising their bayonets to his throat. Finally, they dumped him into the gutter after making the ship's owner promise to return with more money from his vessel. Instead, he returned to his friend Cutts's, who went directly to the residence of the American Minister.

Undoubtedly, the entire town knew of Bassett's success in getting Haytian authorities to admit defeat in the face of the Jastram case. But this only had emboldened locals against foreigners, who were seen as conspiring against Haytian independence. The diplomat quickly made his rounds once again. After taking Eldredge's official statement, Bassett turned to the Haytian Foreign Ministry. Though a domestic criminal case such as this would normally be within the purview of the Justice Ministry, Foreign Minister Etheart responded. He promised that the commanding guard of the station where the attack occurred would be "placed under severe punishment," and also apologized to Captain Eldredge.

Bassett had once again averted a dangerous situation for an American, but he was becoming more concerned with the growing level of violence in Hayti. "It can scarcely have escaped full and general knowledge that in a country like Hayti, where the government rests under constant apprehension of intrigue and insurrection against stability and authority and where offenses of a political character are numerous, and regarded as the gravest of transgressions in the state, arbitrary arrests and unwarranted infringements upon personal freedom and security should sometimes occur," he told the Secretary of State after quickly concluding this case. "Such arrests and infringements are, in fact, not altogether infrequent here. Nor is it perhaps quite unnatural that in Hayti, and in countries similarly constituted, there should be occasionally found to exist a sentiment somewhat unfavorable to foreigners domiciled there." But no matter the conditions, Bassett assured his boss, he continued to promptly intervene on behalf of any American claims.[11]

His words of warning about rising xenophobia were very prescient. Just two weeks later another case came before him, this one against Charles Teel, who had only months earlier been named American consular agent in Miragoane, along the southern peninsula. In this case, the U.S. official had been charged with "circulating false money." His home was ransacked, items from his store were confiscated, and he was finally arrested and taken from friends and family on horseback to a remote and dingy jail over twenty miles away.

Counterfeiting had in fact become so commonplace on the island that the Haytian government had taken the extreme step of making it an offense punishable by death. Now this accusation hung over an American diplomat, who sat in a cramped cell facing potential capital punishment.

Bassett was furious. He had become fed up with this series of attacks against his employees and his country. Perhaps the Haytians were simply testing his resolve, hoping that they could gradually wear him down; or perhaps they wanted to create so many problems that Washington would think their minister unable to handle difficult situations and look for a replacement. Though it would be a dangerous strategy—and one that might invoke an American military response—it was a gamble worth taking for a paranoid regime clinging to survival.

Undaunted, Ebenezer Bassett would not fold. Clearly, Americans were being singled out, and in spite of his earlier successes, something was deeply wrong in Port-au-Prince. "It is my impression that neither in England nor in France nor in Germany would a consular officer of the United States . . . even when charged with a crime, be subjected to the proceedings ordinarily taken against persons here," he told the Haytian government. While his consular agent sat in prison for another eighteen days, Bassett hounded every official he could find. To his surprise, he uncovered that the general who had arrested Teel also had a large personal debt with the American commercial agent. When he took this new evidence to the cabinet, the government was shamed into action.

The American had prevailed once again, gaining Teel's release without a trial and a tacit admission that the war of attrition against the minister resident was failing. But the provocation was far from over. Bassett continued in his quest for justice, arguing that the Haytian government ought to pay an indemnity to Teel. After the government offered a mere $1000 to end the case, an incensed Bassett demanded that it go before an arbitrator. To everyone's surprise, the arbitrator decided in favor of Teel and awarded him a sum of $10,000, which the Haytians reluctantly paid.[12] In spite of the pressure mounted by Saget to undermine the American diplomat, Fish held firm in his support, again writing to praise Bassett's "diligence and patriotic spirit."[13]

But it was not just attacks against consulates or American citizens that the Bassetts had to endure. The government directly increased the pressure against the envoy by striking at his very home. In the spring of that year, Eliza Bassett had sent her cook into town to purchase food at the local market. Once there, the poor Haytian woman was seized and arrested by the police. Panicked, Eliza ran to find her husband, begging him to find a way to free their trusted employee. Ebenezer marched directly to the man in charge of the police, and the woman was released (without charge or apparent explanation) to Bassett.

Months later, he would also suffer a similar indignity when armed men entered his official residence and grabbed two of his workmen without even so much as an explanation. Again, the diplomat was forced to make unofficial pleas to both the Interior and Foreign Ministry for their release.[14]

Unfortunately, Bassett also had a different set of attacks to overcome with his consular corps: three consuls died from tropical illness in those months' time. Besieged by both the natural forces of the Caribbean and the pressure from Saget's allies, life in the Republic was never an easy endeavor. But his perseverance against these challenges set even more firmly Ebenezer Bassett's steely determination and willingness to confront them on every level.

As a result of these continuing problems, Bassett asked permission to discuss changes in the consular convention between the United States and Hayti. Saget agreed to appoint someone, and negotiations began with a view to modifying the 37th clause of the existing treaty between the two countries. Bassett hoped to use this opportunity to more directly address the immunities and protections of diplomats and their homes and places of business.

Bassett laid out the argument for both the State Department and the Haytians that consular offices or dwellings should not generally be used as places of asylum, but given the history of the Republic, "where long usage had tolerated the right of asylum in foreign consulates in favor of persons charged with political offenses," the matter should be codified in treaty. Though he felt sure the proposal would meet with Secretary Fish's disapproval, Bassett pushed the issue anyway. While the matter had no basis in public law, it was invoked because of "laudable sentiments of humanity."[15]

Not just a theoretical sense of humanity spurred Bassett in this regard: the wanton killings during the previous civil war—and during the one he assumed might soon break out—led him to seek this clarification in the treaty. He could not imagine the repetition of a situation similar to the one involving Salnave's refugees without support from the United States government and full respect by Haytian commanders. But just as he feared, Secretary Fish slapped down this attempt to codify the asylum issue. "It is preferred that there should be no stipulation allowing the right of asylum to consular officers in Hayti," Fish responded.[16] The matter was left out, but Bassett knew it would not go away.

At some point in the summer of 1872, Bassett became aware that the Haytian ambassador in Washington, Stephen Preston, had gained access to sensitive communications between the U.S. Legation in Port-au-Prince and the Department of State. Panicked, Bassett fired off a series of confidential warnings to Secretary Fish, who gave the most unbelievable reply. Responding to the charge that Preston had "means for obtaining access to important dispatches which pass between the Department and your legation and that he has knowledge of all such dispatches," Fish told his envoy, " is not perceived with much credit." He went on, writing that "Mr. Preston's counsel since he has been in this country has not been such as to command much respect, or confidence in his character. My hesitation in giving credence to his asserted access to information does not rest upon my confidence that his nature is above reproach to improper means for the attainment of improper ends, but that there had recently been so very little in the correspondence relating to San Domingo that would tempt [him]."[17]

That the Secretary of State could make this claim even in the face of the ongoing harassment of consular agents and after the landing of a howitzer at Cap Hatien was unbelievable. Either he was naïve or he was truly disregarding what Bassett had been reporting for months. It was apparent to Bassett that letters were being intercepted, but there was no evidence that Fish did anything to change tactics or brought up the matter with Haytian authorities. In reality, this appeared to be one of the few times Fish simply ignored the good advice from his representative on the ground.

Bassett refused to be brushed aside, writing back that he was not "unmindful of the gravity of the allegations" against Preston. In fact, Bassett felt so strongly about the situation that he sent Abraham Crosswell, his new office clerk in Port-au-Prince, with a verbal message to the Secretary.[18]

The records do not indicate any final resolution of the Preston matter, but Hayti certainly felt threatened and clearly showed that they would do anything—even arrest accredited diplomats—to undermine American efforts on the island. For the Haytian government to have their ambassador in Washington act as a spy in order to collect information was completely understandable given the circumstances; not doing so would have been almost negligent. But Fish and Bassett let the matter drop. Perhaps they felt that given the low-level warfare going on between the two nations, the last thing they needed was another international incident to stir the press and public sentiment in both countries.

The importance of the island had clearly faded in the corridors of the American capitol. An election year was in full swing, with Grant running against *New York Tribune* editor Horace Greeley. Several parties other than the Democrats and Republicans ran that year, including the Equal Rights Party, with its presidential candidate Victoria Woodhull and vice presidential candidate Frederick Douglass. Though Douglass remained a supporter of Grant and never recognized his nomination under the Equal Rights banner, it was notable that this was the first election to feature a white woman (though women were not even allowed to vote) and a black man on the ticket. However, Grant remained popular, particularly with the newly enfranchised black voters, and he easily won a second term.

In Port-au-Prince, Ebenezer Bassett did not hide the Haytian disappointment over having to deal with another four years of a potentially hostile Grant administration. But the disconnect in Washington continued. Secretary Fish wrote at the end of that year saying that it was "not easily reconciled with the professed earnestness of their Minister to this country . . . related to the President in my presence that he was instructed to express the very cordial gratification of his government."

The "Minister" to whom Fish was referring was the same Stephen Preston who had been intercepting letters between Fish and Bassett; yet, somehow the Secretary of State could not fathom mendacity on the part of the Haytian envoy. Fish did acknowledge, albeit reluctantly, that some resentment might exist, and he told Bassett to engage in a public diplomacy campaign to alleviate this concern: "It may be such that you take some occasion to let this fact [Preston's positive comments about Grant] be made known to the authorities and to let it become known also to the public in some informed and unofficial way. You may speak of it without reserve."[19]

The resistance offered by Haytian authorities was a combination of self-preservation and vain efforts to influence the international balance of power. Saget's intransigence against American annexation of the Dominican Republic had not caused the failure of that enterprise, nor did he win the battle to undermine Bassett's authority. Yet, Saget proved himself a worthy adversary. He helped to sway American public opinion against a takeover of the Dominican portion of Hispaniola by creating chaos and thus kept the American Minister busy putting out other fires. But Saget's days were numbered. Grant had been guaranteed another four years in office, but pressure was mounting in the Haytian countryside for their president to step aside when his term ran out, just as he had agreed. Waiting in the wings was his fellow coup leader, now commander of the army, Michel Domingue. It only remained to be seen if a peaceful transfer of power would finally occur and if, for the first time, a Haytian president would leave office voluntarily—and alive.

9

"De'ye' mo'n gen mo'n"

The old Haytian Creole saying *"de'ye' mo'n gen mo'n,"* can be roughly translated as "behind the mountains, there are more mountains." It signifies not just the rugged landscape of the countryside, but more profoundly, the difficulties that Hayti continued to face—problems simply followed by more problems.

In Hayti, the dislike of Grant appeared more than just visceral. His second term saw another round of problems arise as Buenaventura Baez, the wily Dominican president, renewed his efforts to seek an American "protectorate." The continuing Cabral insurgency and Haytian animosity pushed Baez toward this alliance, but this time Grant had no stomach to take up another losing fight. The American president simply transmitted Baez's request for a protectorate to the Congress, asking that they look it over. Knowing that the approval of such a request was unlikely, Baez agreed instead to lease Samana Bay to a private American company, causing heartburn in Port-au-Prince but calming nerves by indicating that annexation was not imminent.

Seeing official American inaction and eager to finally defuse the long-standing problem, Dominican and Haytian officials met to begin negotiations for a treaty of friendship, calling for peace and a cessation of support for one another's insurgents. Meanwhile, Dominican rebel leaders secretly met with Bassett. Since he was accredited to both parts of the island, they hoped to gain support from the American government for their cause. Although they had previously been ardently opposed to annexation, their rebellion was in such disrepair that they sought to convince the American Minister Resident that they would make the best U.S. allies—if only he would intercede with Baez to help negotiate a cease-fire and a *de facto* partition of the country.

Bassett listened politely during these meetings but remained noncommittal. Though he could see the benefit of gaining an end to hostilities, he knew that Cabral was not offering to negotiate out of a position of strength. Bassett had to persuade the rebels that a great deal of what they were asking for would simply not work. It would only "concede to a dying insurrection . . . importance, recognition, and rights which three years of a certain kind of warfare had failed to win for the partisans," he told them. But he would work with them to negotiate a cease-fire and to establish safe zones within the country, in areas along the Haytian border and in Samana.[1]

Fish agreed with Bassett's suspicions but allowed him to continue the negotiations. Bassett instructed his consular agent in Santo Domingo, Fisher Ames, to meet with President Baez and discuss the terms of a settlement that he had outlined. Bassett's goal was to help put an end "to the shameful sham of arms" that had eaten up so many Dominican and Haytian resources and lives. "It is a work of peace," he instructed his consul.[2]

Ames succeeded in gaining the acquiescence of Baez, and the Dominican cease-fire was seemingly brokered. Baez's opponents within his own ruling party, however, were none too pleased with these maneuvers, and they began plotting his ouster, finally overthrowing him 1874. With Baez out of the picture, the new Dominican government of Ignacio Gonzalez signed the peace agreement with the Haytians almost immediately; it removed the issue of a protectorate and allowed bilateral conditions to stabilize while the Dominican government could confront its remaining rebels.

Though foreign turbulence gradually began to calm for the Saget regime, the Haytian head of state found no end of pressure mounting for a transfer of power to his rivals. Bassett continued to report on the ongoing political battles in Port-au-Prince, but now the majority of his work involved the traditional aspect of American diplomacy, that is, handling the numerous claims American business interests had against the state of Hayti. Dozens of Americans had lost property or investments during the Salnave years and the subsequent civil war. In total, over half a million dollars in claims by American citizens were pending, and little headway had been made toward their resolution.

"So far the just claims of American citizens are in sufferance," reported the *New York Times* in 1873. The newspaper was critical of Hayti's inaction and argued that the only person likely to receive payment was businessman Oliver Cutts, and simply because he had fathered seven children with his Haytian wife. "For out of the consideration of these children, the Government seems somewhat disposed to favor him within the limits of possibility," the paper editorialized. But they also took aim at Ebenezer Bassett, saying that unless the U.S. Minister was able to "show his teeth to the Government, like the representatives of Great Britain and France," the other American claimants would simply continue to wait.[3]

In fact, Bassett had been actively negotiating with the Foreign Ministry since the new regime came into power. Reporting on the situation to his boss in 1870, Bassett said: "Quite a number of claims by American citizens against the Haytian Government have been filed in this legation. These claims are generally presented as *ex parte* statements from persons and firms unknown to us, and their amounts seem to be somewhat arbitrarily fixed."[4] Nonetheless, he faithfully carried out his role as advocate for all Americans in their quest, no matter how implausible, for review and possible reimbursement.

For its part, the Haytian legislature was anxiously eager to repudiate any claims inherited from the despised Salnave regime, but Bassett refused to let the issue die. He tenaciously insisted on the establishment of a commission to examine the debts, and he told the Haytian government that he personally would choose two of its four members. Saget relented, but apparently the president also told his Haytian appointees to use the commission as a means of dragging out the process. In early 1871 Bassett wrote optimistically to Washington about the resolution of several claims, particularly the $300,000 owed to Oliver Cutts, but adverse public opinion and indifference on the part of commissioners eventually made that impossible. Promised a resolution by the first of March, 1871, a frustrated Bassett wrote back to Washington: "Indeed, the first days of February, of March and of April are now gone, and our claims are yet in no way adjusted."[5]

Although Fish had forbidden the American Minister to exert "official" pressure, he was encouraged to use his "good offices" to seek a resolution. Other countries had flexed their muscle, taking a more militant and hardening line to resolve their citizens' claims. Germany simply sent two warships to Port-au-Prince in 1872 and threatened to destroy the Haytian Navy if a payment was not made that day.

Though the United States could be accused of many high-handed grabs at power, these raw demonstrations of force were certainly not the norm for this American Legation. Ebenezer Bassett was loath to call for the use force in these situations. Diplomatic settlement was a point that Bassett strongly advocated with his superiors, who may have shared with him this inclination regarding private claims. "The other great powers have sought redress for grievances here by a display of force . . . But we have dealt with them more generously. We have never brought force to bear upon them, as others whom they now affect to love have done, and I judge they think we never will and never can do.[6]

Bassett was also reluctant to encourage actions such as Germany's because of the historical and racial ties between Hayti and the United States. Europeans interacting with black leaders often resorted to brute force as their first course of action rather than their last. For the Americans, most especially for Bassett, the importance of the Black Republic meant more because of its symbolism. It was important for many Americans to see Hayti succeed, and Bassett's sensitivities on this point made his diplomacy more nuanced and active than the coarse threats of European gunboat diplomacy. However, as Bassett feared, the diplomatic solution lent credibility to the "weakness factor"—the idea that the U.S. would never resort to force on such a matter. The Haytians seemed to think that if they dragged out the negotiations long enough, perhaps they could evade any payments.

Furthermore, the economy of Hayti was in a shambles, and part of the delay in Haytian negotiation was caused by the dire financial straits of the country. Bassett reported that the last time the Haytian currency, the gorde, traded at a 1 to 1 rate with the U.S. dollar was in 1827. The years of warfare and inflation caused this rate to change to 2000 to 1 during the Guerre de Cacos. Though the Saget administration had returned stability to the currency, the exchange rate was still 200 to 1, making all claims that much more expensive for the broken treasury.[7]

As inflation hit the island once again in 1873, President Saget decided to simply withdraw the use of paper currency. To the shock of most Haytians, only transactions in hard currency were considered proper. When the editor of Le Peuple, a newspaper in the capital, wrote a scathing commentary against this decision, he was simply arrested and left in one of the wretched Haytian prisons.[8]

The difficulty in settling the claims was also compounded because of the political turmoil within the legislature. The Corps Legislatif, the Haytian legislative body, had been scheduled to attend their annual meeting in the spring of 1873; it was this legislature that was to eventually vote on the next president.

The backers of the Liberal opposition attempted to boost their candidates in the legislative elections that year. The campaign had been an ugly one; some candidates even claimed that their opponents were secretly spies for Ebenezer Bassett. But dirty tactics were not enough for the ruling regime. When the balance appeared to be tipping against it, the opposition was squelched as Saget's troops marched to the polls and arbitrarily arrested several partisans, leaving numerous legislative seats vacant in Port-au-Prince.

When the deputies did eventually meet, a political battle broke out between supporters of the President and those of his opponents. In the stalemate, a group of legislators simply walked out, leaving the body without a quorum and no way to function. The fight continued for weeks, and Bassett warned his capital, "in a word, it would now seem that nothing short of an armed revolution can avert a practical dictatorship of Hayti."[9]

Soon thereafter, several cabinet ministers, including the foreign minister, resigned. This minister, with whom Bassett had actually developed a close friendship, confided to the American that he simply could not take the political heat and that he feared retribution against Saget supporters would begin the day they left office. With his friend no longer in the cabinet, Bassett now had few people with whom he could actually negotiate regarding business claims—or any other matter.

Despite the turmoil, Bassett remained determined and addressed his concerns with Saget's new cabinet. Always one to value personal diplomacy, Bassett was quick to offer dinner parties at his home outside the city, doing his best to court the newest officials. His wife Eliza had become one of the most renowned hostesses in Port-au-Prince, and invitations to their *soirées* were in high demand.

Bassett's persistence appeared to be paying off by late 1873. He explained to the State Department that it now looked like Saget was ready to make payment in some of the Salnave claims. Only the obvious and noncontroversial cases would be resolved, but it was at least some progress. By the following February, Bassett won for J. R. Lavender a payment of $12,000.[10] Months later, he also succeeded in gaining the payments on seven additional claims (one for as little as 80 dollars, but in total over $17,000).[11]

The timing was unmistakably politically motivated, given the internal upheavals. Perhaps Saget thought that by negotiating, he could keep the United States on his side in the coming power struggle. Bassett was optimistic about further success in the claims negotiation, and he counseled Secretary Fish to remain patient. "History, it has been thought by respectable authority," Bassett wrote to Fish, "points to the facts that when a government once takes a step, even though feeble, toward the right direction, it is generally carried further in that direction than it originally intended."[12] But as further negotiations proceeded, all hell broke loose.

It started in the port city of Gonaïves, known as the Independence City, because it was the location where Jean-Jacques Dessalines had first declared to the world that Hayti was an independent country. That rebellious spirit continued as many of the Liberals opposed to Saget's rule began organizing themselves from this northern region.

The Gonaïves uprising campaign was led by local supporters of one of the major opposition leaders, Louis Lysius Félicité Salomon, who was exiled in Jamaica.

Bassett described the dynamic political exile as "a black man of remark-able moderation, ability, and culture."[13] Supporters of Salomon had been dispersed and silenced prior to the legislative election, but they were slowly reorganizing their opposition. After the military took over several of the polling stations and proclaimed martial law, the Salomon support-ers attempted their feeble revenge in Gonaïves. It was a minor uprising in the scheme of Hayti's bloody history, but it was one that portended greater problems.

Reporting on the outbreak, Bassett wrote that the insurrection consisted of only thirty men who managed to sneak into the local fort but never gained full control of it. By daybreak, they had been routed, killed, or chased into the woods by the military. It was the aftermath of this small uprising, however, that caused the greatest concern to the American Minister.[14]

The government's response to the revolt was a series of "frightful executions" that were "visited almost indiscriminately upon everyone to whom the slightest suspicion of complicity or sympathy with the insur-gents could be traced," Bassett wrote of the events. "Men were taken from their homes and led off to execution without ceremony and without warning. No form of trial was had in any case, as far as I have learned or believe." Bassett said he heard of a list of 34 rebels that were "officially" to be executed, but in reality, sources told him, that number was double. "In some cases, I am assured, the bodies of those who had fallen were allowed to lie unburied in the scorching sun, and to be devoured by ravenous animals," he continued. "It is even said that in at least one well-marked case these animals began their sickening work before the life of the human victim was extinct."[15]

The scene was one of total carnage, and Ebenezer Bassett dutifully recorded the facts of the day and filed his report to Washington. But he was not just attempting to bear history's witness to these events. In the days before widespread concerns about human rights, Bassett was an early voice crying out against these abuses, and he constantly pressed his outrage with the government in Port-au-Prince.

In addition, the fighting led a small number of insurgents to flee toward his consular office in Gonaïves. The issue of asylum had grown so pre-carious that Great Britain decided to cease the practice on the Dominican side of the boarder. In spite of the bloodthirsty vengeance that govern-ment authorities were exacting upon their enemies, Saget did not order any of his troops to forcibly remove the refugees from the American Con-sulate or to threaten the consular officer there. He did, however, place a guard at the consulate to prevent any escape. Forced to return to Saget's cabinet to resolve the situation, Minister Bassett strenuously objected to this treatment. Bassett's constant battles a year earlier were now paying dividends, as the unofficial "right" to asylum and the sanctity of diplomatic grounds were once again, at least temporarily, respected. The guard was removed, and the refugees were allowed to go free.

Though the right for asylum was not officially recognized by U.S. policy, Bassett advised his consuls to use their judgment and "moral influence" of their official position "in behalf of humanity." And when these gentle suasions were not sufficient, Bassett was willing to let his officers provide some protection from the wanton killings. For him, it was simply the right thing to do.[16]

News of the political murders made their way north, with one report referring to the events as another in Hayti's "usual topsy-turvy condition." Calling Saget's government a "rapacious clique" serving its own purposes, "like vultures preying upon a carcass," the *New York Times* said that even "better class of the people who have been so unsparingly victimized, are struggling hard to extricate themselves" from this latest wrong.[17]

Despite the previous and continued warnings from Washington to avoid direct confrontations, Bassett was willing to push the issue to the brink again with the Haytians because he viewed it as morally right. Hamilton Fish was forced to admit, even though somewhat reluctantly, the horrors of the government backlash. And as long as his consulates were not being violated, the secretary wrote back to his minister resident, "your proceeding . . . in regard to the refugees who obtained shelter in the United States consular office at Gonaïves is approved."[18]

Amid all the chaos, Bassett took a moment to write to Washington requesting additional assistance for his office. He noted his own personal declining health, as he said, "from the constantly enervating climate." He also stated that because the pressure of work and the tropical conditions made him unable to always carry out his duties, he had been forced to hire a clerk, whom he had paid out of his own pocket the annual salary of $1000 during the previous four years. The consular fees he collected were enough to cover this cost, and he asked Washington if it were possible to use that money to relieve him of this burden.[19] No, Fish responded "with regret."[20]

If the show of force in Gonaïves was meant to have a chilling effect on the stalled political process, it succeeded. The Corps Legislatif failed to meet, additional supporters of Salomon were arrested, and the legislature, without an exit from the standoff, was paralyzed. Ebenezer became increasingly worried that the escalation would cause the country to slide into full-scale civil war. And in the absence of a legislature, he thought, General Domingue would wind up dropping into the throne of power "as unceremoniously and naturally as an apple falls to earth." Intrigue and menace, Bassett warned Washington, "were the order of the day."[21]

Because there were several months left before the end of Saget's term, the minister resident's sources told him that no one would act before the spring of 1874. Then, all bets were off. Bassett thought that even if there were no bloodshed, the unstable situation would an open invitation to widespread corruption, and those backed by the most powerful, both politically and financially, would be able to buy their way into power. In order to describe this scenario to Secretary Fish, the former classics teacher quoted the wisdom of Jugurtha, the north African leader, in the rebellion against the Roman Empire: "*Omis Romae venalia,*" or "All of Rome is for sale."

"And here it may not be altogether astounding," Bassett continued, "if we see a fuming member of the [Salomon] opposition of today turn up tomorrow a flaming Dominguist." (Domingue was presumed to succeed Saget.) Either way Hayti seemed to be on the verge of another catastrophe, brought about by greed and the exercise of raw power.[22]

With all sides fearing the worst, a compromise was reached whereby members of the legislature briefly convened. The clouds of war lifted temporarily, but everyone knew that this simply postponed the inevitable.

The tempest of political turmoil was not all that swirled around the island during the late summer. The rainy season in the Caribbean unleashed its fury with biblical destruction as hurricane winds and floods lashed the Antilles. Like some omen of retribution, the terrible storm inflicted incredible damage, especially in Jacmel and the southern peninsula of Hayti. The wooden huts of the rural area were yanked from their flimsy foundations. Whole trees, torn at their very roots, were tossed like mere twigs. When the rains stopped and survivors went out to survey the damage, they found that all the foreign ships that had taken refuge in the harbor were destroyed and washed ashore.

Keeping track of those killed in the natural disaster was hard in remote areas, and reports could only state that "considerable loss of life" had occurred.[23] Ebenezer Bassett and his family remained boarded in their home while the full force of the storm spared Port-au-Prince, preventing a total calamity. But they were cut off from most of the countryside: the roads were impassable for weeks.

After both violent storms and intrigue, Bassett wearily made his way to bid farewell to 1873. The year-end celebration at Saget's palace featured all the powerful players in Haytian life. As dean of the diplomatic corps, Bassett spoke to the gathering, wishing the leadership well with usual pleasantries. He congratulated the president for his ability to maintain peace and tranquility in spite of strong pressure to violently battle opponents. The fact that incidents such as those in Gonaïves were not more common, Bassett thought, was due to Saget's desire to complete his term as nobly as possible.[24]

Bassett made his way through the formalities of this ceremony, but he was growing increasingly preoccupied and ill by this time. Worries over the troubling signals he saw before him, the pressure from work, and unsanitary conditions in the wake of the hurricane led Bassett to grow physically ever weaker as he started the new year.

In fact, the year 1874 was not an easy one for the United States either. A major financial crisis hit the country the previous autumn; now currency speculation and bankruptcies continued to rise as the nation careened through a recession. President Grant became so apprehensive about the matter that he advocated returning the nation to the gold standard to alleviate the series of runs that had led to business and investment crashes.

It was not simply economic turmoil that the federal government faced, however. The course of Reconstruction was wearing thin with many of the states of the former Confederacy. The Civil War had ended almost a decade earlier and the eleven rebellious states had been forced to free all slaves, instituting new laws guaranteeing equality and protection for all citizens that led to rising black political power. The results of the 1874 midterm elections reflected not just the discontent with the economic collapse of the country but also the souring political sentiments toward Reconstruction. That year brought Grant one of his worst defeats as Democrats took control of the House of Representatives and were set to challenge his leadership.

The thin cloak of federal protection might have caused a backlash from the white former slaveowners, but Grant was quick to ominously warn the new Congress of the growing menace posed by groups of armed and masked gangs appearing throughout the countryside. These so-called White Leagues conducted drills and military demonstrations in states across the South, but the actions of their members included more than mere intimidating shows of force, as they also began a targeted killing spree, aimed "to spread terror" against blacks, Grant told the legislators.

The president had even ordered over four thousand federal troops to monitor the elections of 1874 in Louisiana, Alabama, Georgia, Florida, the Carolinas, Kentucky, Tennessee, Arkansas, Mississippi, Virginia, and Maryland. "This embraces the garrisons of all the forts from Delaware to the Gulf of Mexico," Grant told the Congress. Despite federal protection (or in part because of it), the Republican Party took heavy losses at the polls, and many began to question how much longer the entire Reconstruction experiment—and particularly the ability of African Americans to actively participate in national decisions—could survive.

President Grant, however, made no apologies for his defense of civil rights. Even in the face of electoral defeat, he remained steadfast in his commitment: "Treat the negro as a citizen and a voter—as he is and must remain—and soon parties will be divided, not on the color line, but on principle. There we shall have no complaint of sectional interference."

He also remained steadfast with his African American appointees. Grant had not only kept Ebenezer Bassett as his envoy in Port au Prince, but he had also appointed James Milton Turner as minister to Liberia. Though pressure may have been building to replace these African American diplomats with white ones, Grant strenuously resisted.

The political climate was no better for Bassett in the Caribbean than for his party back home. Pressure continued to mount on Saget to relinquish power in favor of his ally, General Michel Domingue. The American Minister constantly gauged the opinion of the changing political winds and told Washington that he was certain Domingue would be the next president. In spite of appearances otherwise, he said Domingue was not a popular figure. Having earlier described Domingue as "a pure black of unintellectual mould,"[25] and in whose "expressionless face" he saw "the forebodings of further trouble to Haiti,"[26] Bassett did not look with favor at this changing of the guard. Even worse, he felt that President Saget would probably not go quietly into the sunset: "It must be remembered that no Haytian chief of state has ever, of his own accord, given up power, except President Pierrot, who is said to have retired in disgust in 1846. It does not appear to run in Haytian blood voluntarily to renounce authority once obtained."[27]

It was not that Domingue was just a stupid man or that Bassett saw him as intellectually inferior. Rather, he exercised his command with such brutality that it had made him notorious. "I was obliged myself to form a very unfavorable opinion of him," the diplomat wrote of the heir apparent. "I have found that the cruelties which Domingue is said to have committed somewhat openly in a time of civil inquietude and actual hostilities have really been sanctioned and substantially repeated." With the blood of Gonaïves still staining the island, Bassett reported: "I feel a shudder of horror when I think now of the truly dreadful sacrifices of human life and the fierce persecutions which have in one way or another received the direct approval, the sanction, or the connivance of all branches of this government."[28]

The one thing that Domingue had in his favor was his loyalty to Saget's regime. In Haytian politics, disagreements within political parties were just as destructive as attacks from the opposition. But Domingue remained loyal, waiting in the wings for his turn at the helm. Somehow, Bassett hoped, this fidelity might make him a better interlocutor for the United States.

That spring, as the end of Saget's term drew near with no resolution in sight, the ambassadors of Great Britain, France, and Germany took the extraordinary step of requesting naval vessels from their respective capitals. Worried by the rising tension, Bassett, by April of 1874, felt compelled to do the same: "I have the honor to state that all attempts at reconciliation between the opposing political parties up to this moment seem so critical that I feel warranted in taking the responsibility to request that a war vessel of our government be directed to touch here as soon as possible, under such orders as may allow it to rest in these waters a few days, according to need, and to afford, under the laws, the protection to our interests which circumstances may appear to demand."[29]

Meanwhile, Domingue grew impatient as the political process stuttered in the capital, and he began gathering his army from the southern part of the island. Newspaper reports said that foreigners were hurriedly transporting any valuables to their respective legations and consulates for safekeeping as they began an exodus from the country. "Every appearance indicated probable bloodshed," ran one article. "The American Minister, Hon. E. D. Bassett, was actively engaged in looking after the interests of resident Americans . . . [but] business was entirely prostrated and the rainy season had thus far proved very unhealthy, the mortality rate among the natives from fever being very large."[30]

Knowing that a civil war could destroy the already ravished country, the White House quickly agreed to Bassett's plea and sent a gunboat, the *Kansas*, from Key West, to protect U.S. interests and promote calm. It appeared not a minute too soon. The Liberal Party, which had been so fractured that it could not field a candidate to replace Saget, saw Domingue marching toward Port-au-Prince with his troops. Though the Liberals hated Saget and had caused him no end of grief during the previous four years, they found him to be a better option than Domingue. Race, it seemed was also a factor for the opposition. Domingue's base was formed not just by the Nationalist Party that his military wing supported but also by the masses of dark-skinned people who were fearful of a return of mixed-race elites to Haytian leadership.

For Bassett, race had always been viewed through the American perspective. One drop of "black" blood in the polarized American context made him black. But in the Haytian context, his light skin made for an entirely different classification. Haytians had developed complex categories for noting race. Besides the category "black," there were also multiple subcategories of what would be considered "mulatto" in the United States. Any children born from one mulatto and one black parent were called "griffes" (for boys) or "griffonnas" (for girls). The child born to a griffe and a black was categorized as a "marabou."[31] The list continued in specificity and was confusing to outsiders. But for the Haytians, specificity in race was important, and the Nationalists would use it politically as much as they could against the lighter-skinned Liberals.

These issues were a distant distraction to Bassett's capital, however. When the minister resident offhandedly wrote in a note that he had put the legation flags at half-staff in memory of the passing of Senator Charles Sumner, he was chastised at length by his boss for the action.

A year earlier, the Haytian government had decided to hang portraits of Sumner in the Legislature in honor of the American's decades of friendship and struggle in support of their independence and cause. So great was their admiration of Sumner that when news of his death reached the island in April 1874, the government put its flags at half-mast and marked the day with official mourning. Bassett and his next-door neighbor, the British Consul General, also lowered their flags to half-staff.

When Secretary Fish read about this action, he rebuked his minister. The old enmity between Grant officials and Charles Sumner, Grant's great nemesis in the Republican Party, would not end even in death. Fish responded that it was "not usual, nor [was] it proper unless in the case of the decease of the President for a Minister in a foreign country to exhibit official signs of mourning without special orders from the Department."[32]

Though apparently Fish had time to deal with such trivia, Bassett now had precious little free time for any but the most pressing of matters. His diplomatic despatches, normally written in elegant calligraphy, became sloppier and hastened, as the tension and his illness—likely yellow fever, dengue, or malaria—progressed. Most tragic for the family, however, was the death of their young daughter, Iphigenia.[33] News of the loss of the little girl crushed the already weakened heart of Ebenezer. Nonetheless, he bravely continued to work, trying his best to carry out his duties, while preparing for civil war.

Taking the initiative of writing a confidential despatch to all his consular and commercial agents on the island, he warned them that there might be "irregularities" that would result in numerous people seeking political asylum in their offices. He fully acknowledged that there was no legal basis to accept these potential refugees and that neither he nor the Department might be presumed to assist with possible resulting legal problems. However, given the fact that they were consular officers "of a great Christian state," he told them, "you may be expected judiciously to use, on all proper occasions, the moral influence of your official position and your general good offices in behalf of moderation . . ."[34] By not telling them outright to turn away possible victims of political violence, Bassett left open enough wiggle room, he hoped, for them to operate. However, he undoubtedly wondered how much patience

Secretary Fish would have if all the U.S. Consulates became overrun by terrified, fleeing Haytians.

May 15th was the deadline for Saget, and even though Domingue had brought his troops to the outskirts of town, the president sought some way to hold on to the throne. But with less than 72 hours remaining in his term, a committee formed by community leaders came to the national palace to seek an audience with the president. These community leaders pleaded with him to resign. They had all lived through the bloodshed of the Guerre de Cacos, and they asked him not to allow it to happen again. Reluctantly, Saget agreed, turning over power to his cabinet, which could then arrange a transfer to the next executive.

As night closed around Port-au-Prince, Domingue's troops quietly crept into the capital and set up on the Champ de Mars. Leaving home on horseback early that morning to open the legation, Bassett was shocked to see thousands of troops now inside the city. He knew vague details of the meeting Saget held the day before, and he could not understand why troops had moved in this show of force. "I think I never saw a more determined looking set of men," he told Secretary Fish. As the day progressed, the army moved from the parade grounds into the very heart of the city. Leaving nothing to chance, Domingue would ensure that Saget was true to his word. This would be the first time in Haytian history that a president had ever voluntarily stepped down from office, Bassett thought, if having to do so under the watchful eyes of thousands of armed and angry soldiers could be considered "voluntary."

As he was preparing to leave, President Saget took his closest advisors and paid a call on Ebenezer Bassett and his family at their house. He told the Americans that he was returning to Saint Marc, where his family was waiting.

It was a tremendous gesture for the head of state to pay one of his last official calls on Bassett. Their relationship had started off very poorly, with the United States refusing to recognize his insurgency and maintaining close ties to the hated Salnave. The conflicts over consular protections, American property claims, and annexation of the Dominican Republic had led to a war of attrition against the minister resident over the years.

Bassett understood that many of these acts by the authorities were done out of their perceived self-interest. To overcome this, he had gone to great lengths to cultivate strong personal ties with Saget and his family in spite of lingering problems. The relationship had paid dividends when Bassett was able to freely approach the president on almost any matter, and in fact he had probably been able to save many lives through this personal diplomacy. And he found the Haytian president to be a sophisticated man, attempting to do the best for his country in the face of extreme odds. He also admired Saget's respect for the rule of law. And choosing to step down at the end of his term was the ultimate sign that Saget respected the law and political institutions above all else. It was a bittersweet moment for both men.

The next morning Saget formally announced his resignation to the Haytian people. He added that even though the legislature had asked him to remain, he could not allow himself to do so. "At the moment of returning to my fireside I shall not dishonor my gray hairs by any act for which my political conscience would fundamentally reproach me," Saget said. "In consequence, I hand over the power to the council of minister; the people will be called later, and in the manner which shall be judged the wisest, to proclaim the election of the chief of the executive power . . . I have also taken all the proper measures to secure peace and guarantee life and property during all the time of the vacancy of the presidency, in investing with the commandment in chief of the Haytian army, General Domingue . . ."

Looking like a beaten and haggard man, Saget left the palace escorted by Domingue and his throng of supporters and past the military procession that lined the roads. The cabinet had given him a $4000 annual retirement salary as well as a personal honor guard of fifteen men as part of his agreement to leave. Watching him, Bassett wrote of this historic occasion: "I hope that the precedent established in this instance may prove a salutary one for the future of this, in some sense, sorely afflicted country."[35]

In the meantime, the various warships from Europe and the United States remained in the harbor, reminding Domingue that even though he held all of the power, he needed to tread lightly. Elections were quickly called, and four weeks later the Assembly unanimously elected Michel Domingue President of the Republic of Hayti "for a period which shall be determined by the new constitution."

To everyone's surprise, not only had the Haytian Assembly members lifted Domingue to power, but they now decreed that a new constitution would be written, their eighth since independence. Bassett wondered what unlimited powers Domingue would try to secure for himself. But taking the oath of office on that hot June afternoon, the new president spoke of reconciliation and of respecting the views of opponents. He then met with members of the diplomatic corps. As the dean, Bassett spoke on behalf of the group, thanking the new leader.

Domingue remained ambitious, but he was of such an advanced age (he was 74 years old when he became president) that Bassett wondered how well he could pull the levers of power. A short, stout man, he nevertheless impressed the American as someone dignified and in excellent health, neither appearing happy nor burdened by this new position. In spite of his brutal reputation in the quest for power, now that he possessed it, Bassett guessed that Domingue would "be naturally a lover of justice and the good opinion of others."[36]

As Bassett now saw him, Domingue was a "complete master of the situation."[37] Peace, it seemed, was finally at hand.

Wedding of Tobiah and Rachael. Warren, Israel P. Chauncey Judd. Naugatuck, CT: The Perry Press, 1874 (Chapter 20).

Headstone of Bassett Family, Grove St. Cemetery, New Haven, CT. Courtesy of Marian O'Keefe.

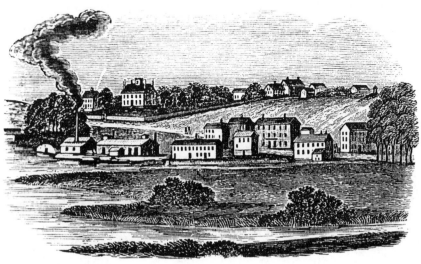

Southeastern view of Birmingham, Derby (1836). Courtesy of the Derby Historical Society, Derby, CT.

Frederick Douglass (ca. between 1865 and 1880, forming a part of the Brady-Handy Photograph Collection). Courtesy of the Library of Congress Prints and Photographs Division, Washington, D.C., 20540.

Public square, Birmingham, Derby (date unknown). Courtesy of the Derby Historical Society, Derby, CT.

First home of the Normal School (date unknown). Courtesy of the Special Collections Department, Elihu Burritt Library, Central Connecticut State University.

Normal school (date unknown). Courtesy of the Special Collections Department, Elihu Burritt Library, Central Connecticut State University.

Bassett student photograph (1855). Courtesy of the Special Collections Department, Elihu Burritt Library, Central Connecticut State University.

Southeast view of Derby Landing (date unknown). Courtesy of the Derby Historical Society, Derby, CT.

PROF. C. L. REASON   HON. E. D. BASSETT

PROF. ROBT. CAMPBELL   MARTHA F. MINTON   PROF. OCTAVIUS V. CATTO

PROF. JACOB C. WHITE, JR.   R. E. DeR. VENNING

Fanny Jackson Coppin. *Reminiscences of School Life, and Hints on Teaching.*
Philadelphia: L.J. Coppin, 1913 (page 140).

Distinguished Colored Men: Head-and-shoulders portraits of Frederick Douglass, Robert Brown Elliott, Blanche K. Bruce, William Wells Brown, MD, Prof. R. T. Greener, Rt. Rev. Richard Allen, J. H. Rainey, E. D. Bassett, John Mercer Langston, P. B. S. Pinchback, and Henry Highland, garnet published by A. Muller & Co., ca. 1883. Chicago, IL: Geo. F. Cram. Courtesy of the Library of Congress Prints and Photographs Division, Washington, D.C., 20540.

Ebenezer D. Bassett, Colored Minister to Hayti.
Harper's Weekly, May 1, 1869 (page 285).

Ulysses S. Grant, 1885
Aug. 6. Courtesy of the
Library of Congress
Prints and Photographs
Division, Washington,
D.C., 20540.

Fish, Hon. Hamilton of NY (ca. between 1865 and 1880, forming a part of the Brady-Handy Photograph Collection). Courtesy of the Library of Congress Prints and Photographs Division, Washington, D.C., 20540.

John Langston (date unknown). Courtesy of the Library of Congress Prints and Photographs Division, Washington, D.C., 20540.

10

Lover of Justice

Right away it became clear that Ebenezer Bassett's perception of Michel Domingue as a "lover of justice" had been wildly optimistic. Due to his personal relationships with so many members of the new administration, Bassett had written to Washington, "I am now almost convinced that our position with the incoming, will be much better than it has ever been."[1]

But the troubling signs started even before the new leader took the reigns of power. Upon the sight of Domingue's troops entering the city, several political opponents hastily sought refuge in the British Legation, including Saget's former finance minister, Charles Haentjens. No one had come to Bassett for similar protection, but Domingue sought out the American Minister to intercede and resolve this first crisis of his presidency. Pulling Bassett aside, Domingue confidentially told the diplomat: "I have no idea of persecuting anyone. Such is not my policy."[2] He asked Bassett to speak with his friend and neighbor, British Consul General Spenser St. John. Ebenezer stuck to his guns, politely declining to encourage the turning over of anyone seeking the political protection of a foreign flag. He did assist in negotiating an eventual resolution, however, and all refugees were sent to a neighboring island. The American must have had a gnawing feeling that he was soon to see history repeat itself.

Just as disturbing as the continuing political instability were some of the legal changes that the new government was bringing to the fore. Because of the protracted Salnave claims, for which Bassett was still trying to gain a final resolution of several hundred thousand dollars, popular sentiment was turning strongly against foreigners. With the Dominguists swept into power, their new constitution built upon this resentment by forbidding non-Haytians to own immovable property and "in case of losses by civil or political disturbances no indemnity can be claimed from the State."[3] This meant that protections and the rule of law would become even more fickle. In addition, Domingue was granted expanding powers in the new constitution, including an eight-year term of office.

Nonetheless, everyone remained on their best behavior as the honeymoon continued. By that summer, the new president held a grand *soirée*, which several foreigners attended, and the attitude was decidedly pro-American. So confident was Bassett that he soon asked for a leave of absence to return to the United States: "[T]he public tranquility, and the restoration of good faith toward our countrymen, appear in some measure to have been guaranteed in this country under the administration of President Domingue," he wrote to Hamilton Fish that summer.[4] It would be the first time in four years that he would return home.

After so many years in the tropics, his lingering health problems had finally worn him down to the point of collapse. He had scheduled his trip for that August, but he had grown so ill that he was unable to even leave the house. He had been diagnosed with "rheumatic neuralgia in the neck and head, aggravated by a serious and obstinate bilious attack." In short, he suffered acute and almost constant pain caused by damage to his nerves or spine. Coupled with that, he seemed to have either developed gall bladder problems or perhaps some other gastric disorder. The combination of those problems and the difficulties he continued to have with the heat caused him to teeter on the edge of health. For a full month he writhed in agony, unable to conduct any of his usual business, much less leave for a lengthy sea voyage home.[5]

Finally, by October he was well enough to travel, and he made his way back to New Haven, Connecticut, where he immediately went into the care of a doctor. Additional bed rest prescribed for the normally energetic diplomat was the only remedy available. By the end of that month, his energies had returned sufficiently for him to send a telegram to the State Department, indicating that he could finally travel to Washington, D.C. and meet with the Secretary of State to apprise him of the new government.[6]

In many ways, it was lucky for Ebenezer and his family to have gotten out of the Caribbean that fall. Once again, fierce hurricanes struck in Barbados, Jamaica, and Hayti, causing a great deal of damage and destroying an already bad infrastructure outside the capital.

Bassett and his family were gone for a total of ninety-five days, enough time to get him on his feet again and to give his family an opportunity to reacquaint themselves with their relatives and friends back in Connecticut. Two of Eliza and Ebenezer's children had limited recollection of the

United States, whereas the oldest was now beginning to prepare for an eventual return to attend college. But everyone remained concerned about Ebenezer's strain and weakness as he gradually recovered.

Upon their return on January 17, 1875, the Bassetts were greeted with a warm welcome home reception by the Haytians, where all classes of people cheered their return with "almost an ovation."[7] Most surprisingly, Minister Septimus Rameau, Domingue's nephew—and whom Bassett described as "the chiefest of advisors, if not the controlling one"—was extremely gracious with the returning diplomat. Rameau now exercised almost complete control over all aspects of the government. While his uncle continued as president, Rameau used his guile and knowledge of political maneuvering to isolate enemies, looking for ways to amass a fortune for himself in the process.[8]

The feelings of friendship and his reinvigorated health made Bassett even more focused on strengthening American relationships with Hayti. He had requested an autographed picture of President Grant as well as a signed letter congratulating Domingue on his new leadership role. Bassett went over to the palace to personally present these mementos to Domingue, which pleased the elder general. As a fellow military man, Domingue held Grant's accomplishments in high regard, and he undeniably viewed the American president like himself: as a savior of his people.

Bassett also used flattery and played upon Domingue's vanity to make headway with him, especially because British Consul, Spenser St. John, had moved on to his next assignment. St. John had interfered very insidiously with Hayti's political affairs to further Britain's hegemonic efforts in the Caribbean, and his influence had been great with Saget. But St. John found himself on the outs with this new regime, disdainfully referring to Domingue as "an ignorant and ferocious negro."[9] Bassett moved to fill that vacuum, becoming the undisputed leading foreign dignitary in Port-au-Prince. Telling Domingue that "there had never been a chief of state in Hayti more favorably known or more widely esteemed in the United States than his Excellency," Bassett ingratiated himself well and hoped to cement a relationship that he knew would require a great deal of maintenance.[10]

The new president was a complex man, and Bassett must have known that he should be handled with care. In spite of earlier declarations of dislike for the Haytian leader, Ebenezer Bassett went out of his way to cultivate the best personal bond. But it was a true challenge for Bassett, as not only was Domingue a feared and ruthless leader, but he was also rumored to be a practitioner of a strange sect of Voodoo.[11]

The Voodoo stories that earlier had been occasional cocktail gossip became even more frequent and gruesome. News of a "society of cannibals" in the interior of the country broke when one man carrying a decapitated woman's head in a basket was found by authorities. Later, a woman's body was recovered, "with portions missing," and presumably, according to press reports, the missing portions had been eaten. Over eighty people were allegedly involved in the particular cult. "It has been proved that they were addicted to eating human flesh, and all will be executed."[12]

The crackdown on a supposed cannibal cult, which in reality was not related to the practice of Voodoo, was most likely a strike at Domingue's political enemies. As the year 1875 progressed, the Haytian leader began orchestrating political persecutions to strengthen his power. Well aware of his advanced age, many of Domingue's advisors, principally Septimus Rameau, were also jockeying for position. Rameau wanted to be as well-placed as possible for what he assumed would be a short tenure for the septuagenarian. By encouraging Domingue to dislodge any foe, Rameau hoped to turn up the real heat against any future challengers.

That heat went from figurative to literal by February, when nearby Croix de Boussales almost completely burned to the ground. Over eight hundred houses were destroyed, including the commercial warehouse of Oliver Cutts, an American businessman.

Fire was a common method of waging political terror. During the Saget years, the National Palace had been set ablaze, and Port-au-Prince regularly saw fires as a means of expression. Naturally, the loss incurred by Cutts, the largest American plaintiff from the "Salnave Claims," left an indelible mark in everyone's mind. Although the destruction had the appearance of an accident, it was difficult for many to believe that sinister motives were not really behind the inferno.[13]

Just a few weeks later, General Joseph Lamothe was charged by the National Assembly with "unfaithfulness" during his tenure as Saget's minister of the interior and foreign affairs. It was clear that Domingue's allies were orchestrating a political payback, and Lamothe quickly ran for cover to the British Legation. Ebenezer Bassett was again called in to help negotiate between the English *chargé d'affaires* and the government of Hayti. Rameau maintained his denial that any political persecution was underway, stating that it was a judicial matter involving Lamothe's oversight (and presumed corruption) while in the previous cabinet. The new British Consul, Major Robert Stuart, did not want to simply turn over the high-ranking Haytian, but Rameau wanted the body immediately. Bassett offered a compromise, one that created angst in Washington.

The American joined his British colleague in a meeting at the Presidential Palace, during which they both voiced their support for the right of asylum. Rameau demurred, again insisting that Lamothe was not deserving of political refugee status. Bassett insisted that diplomatic property be respected. They finally agreed that Lamothe could return home and that a proper judicial hearing could begin against him only if Lamothe first agreed to pay a "security sufficient for the sums alleged" in his misappropriation of state resources. Rameau's greed apparently overtook his sense of vengeance, and he consented.[14] The harassment of the British did not end with Lamothe's release, however, as police officers continued to intimidate English vice-consuls and citizens in locations around the country.

Bassett had laid down a marker to Washington, letting them know about his actions in support of the British asylum case. Not surprisingly, Fish responded coolly weeks later: "The Department regrets to notice that you have assented to doctrines on the subject which are believed to be in themselves untenable and which may be regarded as at variance with the instructions to you of the 16th of December, 1869 . . ."[15] The disagreement between the Secretary of State, who wished to simply avoid future conflicts by denying that the right to asylum even existed, and his minister— who continued to insist that some form of protection be offered—was about to come into full flower, and with the most dangerous consequences of all for Ebenezer Bassett and his entire family.

The first news of trouble hit U.S. shores in a report from the *New York Times* stating that Port-au-Prince was under a state of siege. Forty foreigners, including the servant of Major Stuart, had been killed. In reality, it was much worse than the ten-line story indicated. [16]

May 1st was a national holiday in the country, known as *Fête de l'Agriculture.* May Day, a traditional celebration tied to the spring planting and to fertility, was a time of parties and family gatherings. In a country so heavily dependent on the successful production of crops, May Day took on special significance for many Haytians because it was also a time when people would be expected to let down their guard. Knowing this, Domingue readied his forces to wipe out the last remnants of any opposition.

Bassett awoke that morning planning to attend an early reception at the palace. But the tropical weather and his continuing struggle with illness had once again caught up with him. After straining to get out of bed, he slowly dressed. Despite his pain, he decided nonetheless to open the legation in case any Americans had come into the capital during the holiday. About 10 o'clock that morning, he finally arrived downtown and almost immediately heard the crack of muskets near his office.

It turned out that former general Monplaisir Pierre had come under fire in what would prove to be a three-pronged attack by Domingue's forces. Pierre had been the war minister under Saget, and in 1874 he ran a nominal campaign for president among the disunited Liberals in opposition to Domingue. The Haytian President clearly feared Monplaisir Pierre's ability not just to wage war on the battlefield but also to potentially rally supporters and undermine his grip on power.

Pierre knew that the charges of conspiracy were a mockery and that, if arrested, he would never see the inside of a jail cell—much less make it into court. As soldiers approached, the general made use of the only remedy available and barricaded himself inside his home.

Surrounding the house, the troops began firing indiscriminately. When that failed to bring him out, cannons from nearby streets were brought to bear against the house. The rage of the attack was so mindless and wanton that the soldiers paid little attention to where they aimed. One shell landed in the yard of the U.S. Legation. Though Bassett was uninjured, the rampage continued for hours. Terrified, Ebenezer Bassett watched out his window as soldiers gunned down people in the streets, including a small servant boy of the nearby British Legation. During a lull in the firing, Bassett and Major Stuart of the British Consulate made their way over to the palace to plead for a cease-fire.

Domingue personally met with the two diplomats, politely explaining that although it was regrettable, the military had been forced to capture Pierre. The president claimed to have uncovered a plot against the government, and Pierre was among the coup leaders. Almost oblivious to the shelling going on around them, Domingue calmly told them he had no choice, informing them that the city was now under martial law.

At this news, Bassett blanched. Surely a peaceful resolution might be found, Bassett replied, who could only imagine the continued killings and persecution to take place under the guise of martial law. All the while, he watched in amazement as orders where given, aids rushed about, and a general state of war drew upon them.

Taking the president aside privately, the American diplomat urged a slower course of action. Though not denying the gravity of the situation, Bassett cajoled him into not declaring a state of emergency, which he advised would only make things worse. The plea worked. Domingue told his staff that they must continue to pursue the coup plotters, but that martial law was not necessary. Bassett wearily trudged back to the legation, and soon afterward, the attack on Pierre's house was over. Peering out, the American found it impossible to tell which was more riddled with holes: the wooden structure or the general's body. In addition, sixteen Haytian soldiers died in the day-long siege.

It was then that Bassett learned of another attack taking place, this time against General Brice. The young general had been one of the military leaders to bring down former President Salnave during the siege of Port-au-Prince in 1870. Since then, he too had become a political figure, serving for a period of time as leader of the lower house in the Corps Législatif.

Thirty armed men surrounded Brice's home, and the commander approached him saying, "General, I have come to arrest you." With none of his family members or supporters nearby, Brice defied the troops, yelling "I will resist alone!" In the volley of fire exchanged between the two sides, Brice was shot in the leg but somehow managed to cross the street into the British Consulate. He would have been given asylum, but the bullet wound was too severe and he died later that evening. Before they discovered that Brice had died, Haytians troops fired several shots into the consulate, wounding one of the employees.

As the sun began to set, an exhausted Bassett cautiously made his way home to check on his family. Unknown to him at the time, Domingue had also unleashed the third prong of attacks, this time in the hills near Bassett's home and against his most feared enemy: Boisrond Canal.

General Pierre Boisrond Canal was another of the young leaders who had successfully ousted Salnave from power. Canal was a less political figure than the other two, but he was charismatic and popular nonetheless. Now living on his large farm just outside the city, the light-skinned Haytian and his family and friends were celebrating the agricultural festivities when they saw half a regiment marching toward them. Knowing something dastardly was in the works, Canal armed his able-bodied relatives and lay in wait. Though vastly outnumbered, he had more time to prepare than either Brice or Pierre had been afforded. A skirmish ensued during which Canal and his relatives attacked and retreated, then attacked again, successfully holding the troops at bay throughout that day and into the next.

From their house in Petionville, Bassett and his family could hear occasional shots throughout that Sunday. The American Minister was also hearing rumors from his neighbors that Canal might head into the poor neighborhoods of the capital to recruit soldiers and launch a full-scale movement against Domingue. But as Sunday night fell, silence retuned to the suburban enclave. The Bassetts retired, hoping that peace would find them for a good night's sleep.

The knock that came to his door at 3 o'clock that Monday morning shattered the illusion of any settlement to this latest uprising. As the proud Canal and his two young relatives staggered into Bassett's home and humbled themselves by asking for protection, Bassett's best instincts took over. Looking at the weary, terrified men, and knowing that Domingue's army was probably just steps behind them, he shut the door and provided the three with the delicate veil of protection that diplomatic immunity offered.

After seeing that his new "guests" were given food, water, medical care, and clothing, Bassett must have sat with his head in his hands thinking of how he would explain this to a displeased Washington. "It may be that the instinct for humanity got the better of me," he wrote. "The men before me were not my personal friends. They had never visited my house before, nor I theirs. I had no merely personal interest in them," he noted in his letter days later to Hamilton Fish.

The next morning, Bassett dressed to open the legation as though nothing unusual had happened. He warned everyone in the house to remain quiet until he could assess the situation in the palace.

News of the refugees leaked throughout the city almost immediately, however, and Bassett's office was inundated with people asking whether the rumors that Canal had escaped and was hiding in his house were true.

As the minister resident began making discrete inquiries, he learned that massive arrests were taking place throughout the city. Martial law was now in effect, and people were fleeing in every direction trying to just stay alive. Calling on the palace, Bassett found that both President Domingue and Minister Rameau were cordial, but their emotions were raw. He could tell that it was no time to raise this sensitive issue. Finally, during the afternoon, the Port-au-Prince district attorney, a close friend, came by and warned Bassett that he should return home at once.

Panicked, he fled and found hundreds of men outside his gates. More troops were on the way, and it was clear that the worst-kept secret in Hayti was at an end. Assured that everyone inside was safe, he returned to file a formal protest with the foreign minister, who simply demanded to know the name of every refugee. Bassett politely refused to name any and left. But he soon began to receive threats of violence against himself and his family. Despite further efforts by the diplomatic corps to calm emotions, glares—bloodshot with anger—were the only responses they received.

One thing became clear to Bassett as the situation began to deteriorate: Canal, despite claims that he was leading a coup against the government, was popularly regarded as one of the best citizens in Hayti. His bravery, integrity, and ability were almost universally acknowledged and this heightened fear of him by the increasingly paranoid Domingue and his tight circle of allies, especially Septimus Rameau.

The crisis had dragged on for several days before the American was able to pen his first diplomatic note back to Washington. Reflecting on all that was still unfolding, Bassett handwrote a twenty-one page despatch to Secretary Fish. All of Hayti had become "stirred up" in an incident that "burst forth like a tornado upon the country." Vividly describing the state of affairs, he said that "violent language and violent acts have been evoked; persons have been shot down in the streets and in their homes, arbitrarily arrested, exiled, and outlawed; cannon have been fired upon a private dwelling in the city."

Nevertheless, the envoy continued to remain optimistic for an eventual cooling of passions. He had dealt with numerous cases of refugees in the past, some taking weeks to resolve, but the consummate diplomat had always been successful. Still, things seemed different this time around. "I must confess," he continued to Fish, "that the presence of a thousand armed men around my country residence . . . with discontent stamped on their faces and Henry rifles in their hands does not quite give the best possible ground to my hope."[17]

An unsympathetic Secretary Fish was angry at what he read. Finally able to respond, the secretary replied a month after initial hostilities began: "It is regretted that you deemed yourself justified by an impulse of humanity to grant such an asylum. You have repeatedly been instructed that such a practice has no basis in public law and so far as this government is concerned is believed to be contrary to all sound policy."

Not once asking about Bassett's well-being or offering any words of support, Fish continued to berate his minister. He noted that the Haytian Ambassador to Washington, Stephen Preston, had been in complaining about the refugees, demanding that they be turned over immediately. "I answered him, however, that though it might have been preferable that you should not have received those persons, it was not deemed expedient to comply with his request." Fish replied to Preston that if Domingue were to ask for a trial, Bassett would be authorized to give up Canal, but only if Domingue guaranteed no punishment greater than banishment from the country.[18]

Fish simply wanted to be rid of this problem as quickly as possible. However, he did not force his envoy to merely hand over the refugees; to do so would be a capitulation to the Haytian demand, and American prestige required more. Fish appeared more concerned with international respect than with the lives of the Haytians or the unfolding events. With a simple assurance that the refugees could be exiled safely, the secretary thought the entire incident would be instantly resolved.

Bassett knew that promises not to harm Canal would be lies, as the Haytians continued to up the ante. "What is said by this government about 'law' and 'justice' is a sham, a delusion, a snare," Bassett shot back to his boss.[19]

The Haytian Foreign Minister kept pestering Bassett to hand over a list of everyone in his house. Then, through Stephen Preston in Washington, he made the scurrilous charge that the refugees had come with arms and ammunition, as though the three men were ready to strike at the entire army decamped outside Bassett's doorstep. In reality, Canal and his young relatives were carrying a few small arms when they arrived, exhausted, at Bassett's house in the middle of the night. But Bassett had taken the weapons away and locked them up. Preston's démarche to Secretary Fish, however, raised a wild specter of rebels armed to the teeth and only increased the fury of the secretary of state.

In addition, several other individuals—personal friends of Bassett's—were trapped inside the American Minister's house. Bassett convinced Domingue to let these friends embark unharmed and even to allow one of Canal's relatives, Floriot, to leave as well. He continued negotiating with Rameau, and soon he was successful also at arranging for former foreign minister Etheart and former senator Duval to be set free, both of whom were hiding in the neighboring British Consul's residence. By May 19, General Canal and his younger brother were the only refugees remaining at Bassett's house.

Though the minister resident had made some progress, the target of Domingue's ire remained untouched. As long as Canal was safe, the Haytian government would continue its brinkmanship. Nonetheless, the American held firm to his conviction that the general would be shot down if it were not for his protection. Despite incurring the wrath of his superiors in Washington and putting all of his credibility on the line, Bassett wrote:

> I am not unaware that the ground taken in my several despatches . . . may not be in accord with the requirements of public law . . . nor am I unmindful of the views entertained by the Department as they are expressed to me in your No. 24, of December 16, 1869, but circumstances seemed to crowd in upon me without warning, and in such a way as to leave me almost no choice. Men maddened by passion, inflamed, as I am credibly informed, by rum, and elated by consciousness of armed power, were pursuing their fellow countrymen with red-handed violence. To have closed my door upon the men pursued would have been for me to deny them their last chance of escape from being brutally put to death before my eyes.[20]

It was not simply a matter of humanity that led Bassett to throw the protective cloak over his refugees. He was also keenly aware that he could not give one inch in this staring match. To surrender would invite a rampaging mob to overrun not only his home but all consulates protected by the American flag.

As a result of the standoff, Bassett's home remained surrounded by over one thousand soldiers. The nightly rhythm of loud taunts, screams, and the beating of metal objects kept the family huddled inside, trying to gain a few hours of restless sleep. In his May 8th despatch, in which he reported the incident, Bassett first suggested that a U.S. warship be sent to Hayti. He argued at the time that such a show of force would exert "a wholesome influence" and strengthen "our own moral force" in resolving the matter, just as Spain and Britain had done.[21] As the conflict dragged on for weeks, with both Bassett and Domingue digging in their heels, government officials in Washington only sat paralyzed. The diplomat continued to plea for a warship through the summer, but Fish, piqued at his minister and in dithering discussions with Ambassador Preston, left the situation in a quagmire.

Bassett was clearly frustrated with his boss's timidity as well. "One word from you will, in short, give relief from all this sore and trying difficulty," he said in again asking for a ship weeks later. "I am equally well convinced that any other proceeding . . . will only increase the difficulty, increase also the presumption and insolence of these peculiar people toward our country and our countrymen."[22]

As weeks became months, Haytian authorities continued to turn up the pressure. Domingue issued a decree ordering any citizen to shoot Canal down on sight. Then he arranged for hasty military tribunals to try Canal for treason. Bassett took note of these efforts as a means to sway Hamilton Fish into ordering Canal's release. Calling the trials a "farce," Bassett begged his superior "to concede to this government nothing whatever further than what is already conceded."[23]

In spite of the displeasure of both Fish and Rameau, Bassett's heroic stance had won him supporters among the Haytians. The whole affair had turned popular opinion in favor of the United States and made Canal into a cult hero. "The prevailing sentiment is unmistakably in favor of [Canal], and in our favor, because we have firmly protected him against violence," Bassett wrote. No doubt part of the support for both Canal and Bassett was because of the brutality with which the regime continued to act against any and all presumed opponents. Political arrests and killings continued, and Bassett concluded, "the awful fact stares me in the face that we are all under a reign of terror."[24]

The wilting heat of the Caribbean summer came full blast upon Bassett, with no resolution in sight. As he tried to find a solution for the crisis, he doubled over once again with the illness that had plagued him almost continually over the previous several years. His despatches back to Washington became less frequent as he was on many occasions forced to remain in bed under the care of a doctor. Nevertheless, his personal secretary managed to keep the legation open and brought correspondence to his bedside so that Ebenezer could remain engaged in his duties. His work ethic, combined with the torments of Haytian soldiers outside his gates, undoubtedly only served to worsen his condition. But he persevered in spite of the pain and pressure to turn over Canal to the authorities. Canal, Bassett demanded, must be escorted to a ship and allowed to leave Hayti unharmed.

While this siege carried on, Ebenezer Bassett was under another kind of attack, this time from an erstwhile friend. Abraham Crosswell was the former U.S. Consul in Cap Hatien, and he had served as a private secretary to Bassett. He and Bassett had a falling out, however, and Bassett fired him in May of 1873. Crosswell had then gone to work with another foreign resident in Port-au-Prince to set up Farmer, Crosswell and Company, a firm involved in the import and export of goods. Crosswell complained that his former boss had become derelict in his duty, failing to keep the legation offices open and not providing consular services to ship captains that were in need of official certifications.

Ironically, Bassett had fired Crosswell for just these reasons: not keeping the office open during some of Bassett's absences. Now the diplomat had to explain his actions to the State Department, whose officials closely examined Bassett's every move. Vehemently denying the charges, he assured Assistant Secretary John Cadwalader of always maintaining the strictest compliance with business hours, despite the siege at his residence and his own ill health. On the rare occasions when he was not personally present, his new secretary, C. A. Kearney, was always at the office.

"I feel constrained to observe most respectfully that I scarcely know how the allegations set forth in the said enclosures could be more suitably answered than by a serious and solemn denial," Bassett told the Assistant Secretary. He called Crosswell's charges "most extraordinary and without foundation in truth" and went on to add that his former employee was a "smart, scheming, boasting, utterly unprincipled young man. Truth and honor are, as I was at last obliged to recognize, nothing, absolutely nothing, to him."[25]

Bassett was continuing to pay not only for the office rental out of his own pocket (at $150 per year) but also for Kearney's salary (as he had previously done with Crosswell). Nevertheless, the State Department felt compelled to open an investigation into the claims.

Kearney also wrote to the State Department, defending his boss and explaining that even when Bassett went home early because of illness, he continued to work in his sickbed. The young assistant lived with the Bassett family and added that "the business of his office seems to occupy almost all his attention."[26] For several months, the State Department kept the "investigation" open and Ebenezer in suspense as to possible disciplinary action against him. But with the Canal situation still unresolved, Bassett had little time to worry about matters of less significance.

By summer's end, it looked like Secretary Fish had finally had enough. Perhaps a more visible threat, he concluded, would cause the Domingue regime to crack. "It has been determined to apply to the Navy Department to order a man of war to Port-au-Prince with a view to your protection from insult," Fish wrote to Bassett. "That the embarrassing question adverted to may be satisfactorily adjusted before she arrives, is much to be desired."[27]

Meanwhile, Fish publicly denied that anything was amiss. He told the *New York Times* that there was "no trouble" with the Domingue government despite the circumstances at the official residence. "The action of Minister Bassett was dictated by feelings of humanity rather than policy, it being certain that the refugees would have been summarily executed had he surrendered them," the paper reported after speaking with Fish. The secretary also moved to position himself to take credit for what he hoped would be a resolution to the standoff, claiming he had "succeeded in persuading the Haytian government to grant amnesty to Cannale [*sic*] and his followers, provided they leave the country, and the United States steamer *Powhatan* has been ordered to Hayti to take them off."[28]

In fact, just as the *Powhatan* was preparing to leave, Ambassador Preston rushed in to tell Fish that Domingue was ready to capitulate. Bassett could escort Canal safely out only if the *Powhatan* would turn back and not enter Haytian waters. Fish agreed and instructed Bassett that a deal had been set. Though Ebenezer had been crying out with that same request for months, it was a welcomed relief when he finally received the news.

Now with an official deal in hand, Bassett set out to speak with President Domingue. In a cordial meeting on October 2nd, the Haytian president said he would gather his cabinet and make immediate arrangements. By 8:00 p.m. of the next day, Bassett was greeted by the ministers of war and foreign affairs, who informed him that everything had been arranged: "We have come to announce to you formally that the government has decided to embark Boisrond Canal and his brother. Their embarkation now depends on you." Domingue had commuted Canal's death sentence to banishment for life. And Bassett was told to have the refugees ready the next evening.

The following night General Thelemaque called upon the Bassett home at 10 o'clock, saying that he was ready to escort the two toward the port. Bassett, his secretary Kearney, the French *chargé d'affaires*, and the two Haytians refugees all mounted horses and made the three-mile ride under cover of darkness.

Just after midnight, on October 5, 1875, Canal embraced Bassett and boarded the American-flagged ship *Varnum H. Hill*, which set sail for Jamaica.[29]

Canal had been held captive as a refugee inside the Bassett home for over five months. The next day the American diplomat telegrammed the State Department to inform them that the crisis had finally passed: "Refugees amicably embarked and soldiers withdrawn from around my premises yesterday."[30]

Still irritated by the entire affair, Secretary Fish offered no words of congratulations or well wishes. He had earlier accused Bassett of allowing his partiality toward Canal to cloud his judgment. Now that the refugees were safely gone, Fish continued to take a strained tone with his envoy, "bearing in mind the personal inconveniences to which your according of asylum to the Refugees appears to have subjected you, the Department accepts your assurances that you did not intentionally violate the law," the Secretary coldly wrote him.[31]

And even though the once stellar relationship between Washington and Bassett had become tarnished, he was at least out of danger of losing his job over the Canal matter. A few weeks later, Assistant Secretary Cadwalader even wrote Bassett to inform him that the investigation on Crosswell's allegations had also been resolved, with the State Department finding no cause for complaint.[32]

As his principled and heroic actions demonstrated, the true "lover of justice" had been Ebenezer Bassett. Though he undoubtedly paid a high price by having irritated the powerful figures who ran the State Department, he nonetheless stood up to Secretary of State Fish and to the brutal Domingue dictatorship. By demanding humane treatment for an honorable patriot to the Haytian homeland, Ebenezer Bassett had served not only the best interests of the United States but also of the people of Hayti. Unfortunately, it was only a matter of time before total chaos returned to the island.

Leaving Hayti

Even after the exile of Boisrond Canal, repression did not cease. It was not long before Ebenezer Bassett became convinced that yet another violent revolution was in the works. In spite of the plea that the diplomat offered to the president at the New Year's celebration for "public peace" and "domestic tranquility," the year 1876 offered little hope of either in the tumultuous republic.[1]

Bassett knew that Domingue and Rameau would do anything to hold on to power. Rameau was particularly ruthless in his efforts to crush all signs of dissent. American newspapers referred to him as Hayti's "most unpopular man" and to President Domingue as a mere "figure-head."[2]

Soon enough the American yet again felt the political pressure when Haytian General Bonhomme, one of the leading figures on the island, ran into the U.S. Legation in great agitation, crying to Bassett that the government had ordered his arrest. He knew that if he did not get help, his arrest meant his death sentence. Bassett, accompanied by the ministers of Spain and France, looked at him with tedium as they recalled the previous year's siege. Surely there must be another way aside from simply granting asylum, the ministers cried in unison. Indeed there was. With Bassett's help, Bonhomme was able to make his way to a ship and quietly leave the island. With this crisis averted, they hoped that emotions would calm as well.

However, things continued to collapse under the weight of repression, which finally reached a breaking point in the city of Jacmel. Rebels attempted a landing on the seaport, and several days of fighting broke out between the government and revolutionary forces. In response, martial law was declared again, even in Port-au-Prince. Bassett had just recently been elected president of the Foreign Club, a leading social organization for diplomats and expatriate merchants, and he refused to comply with Rameau's demands to close down. Bassett's stance may once again have endeared him to the press and common Haytians, but he caused heartburn with the ruling elites.[3]

Even after the fighting cooled in Jacmel and the government regained control, Bassett was certain that this was just the opening salvo. "I may reaffirm my conviction that some sort of an armed movement against the existing government of Hayti cannot be far distant," he wrote to Secretary Fish. He mentioned that the British, Spanish, French, and Germans had all brought warships around the island to protect their citizens and investments. "I feel warranted in suggesting," he wrote to the secretary, "that if there be a national vessel of our Government within easy proximity to this port, her commander be requested to touch here at an early date."[4]

All the while, Haytian Ambassador Stephen Preston paid several visits to Secretary Fish, officially presenting a démarche about Bassett's perceived partiality toward Canal, even now that he was in exile. At this same time Bassett became aware once again that Preston was intercepting the diplomatic mail and was privy to many of the sensitive communications between Port-au-Prince and Washington. This suspicion was first leaked by one of the closest advisors to Rameau and was confirmed by one of Bassett's closest friends, the former Haytian Consul in New York, C. A. Van Bokkelen. Rameau had become almost hysterical during the Canal crisis and would now resort to anything to ensure he gained the upper hand.[5]

Uninterested in repeated charges of espionage, Fish brushed him aside once again and demanded a reply to Preston's claim of favoritism on Bassett's part. When Bassett responded simply with a denial, his boss was unsatisfied. The secretary wrote back: "You do not fully meet the charge. The Diplomatic Representative of a friendly power should not allow himself to be made an agent of parties attempting to overthrow the government to which he is accredited. That government may be bad, but it is the duty of an accredited Minister to that government to act in good faith toward it, so long as its people are pleased to endure it."[6]

Initially, Bassett's relationship with Canal may have been one only of general acquaintance, but it clearly had changed after Bassett had lodged the dissident for half a year. The two became closer because of the ordeal, and Bassett's dislike toward the governing circle was only heightened by the unfair treatment he received. Nonetheless, he strived to remain a true professional, maintaining good relations with the leadership and always working to further bilateral relations despite the worsening conditions. It was all the more ironic that Preston complained to Fish about Minister Bassett, for Ebenezer's sources told him that Preston was actually sympathetic toward Canal. The crafty, politically-minded minister in Washington was clearly playing all sides off one another to ensure his own position of power. But none of that mattered to the Secretary of State, who still appeared to bear a grudge against Bassett's earlier actions.[7]

This state of affairs was all the more paradoxical because Ebenezer Bassett was not only fastidious in his diplomatic dealings but was thoroughly honest in other matters of his job. He himself brought to the attention of the State Department his having to credit the U.S. government for an inadvertent overdraw of consular fees: "It is due myself to express my sincere regret that a miscalculation made when I was recently in the United States, should have led to the regrettable mistaken of overdrawing my account by even a single dollar . . . No similar error has ever before occurred in my account with the government, no similar one shall ever hereafter occur."[8] The total accounting error was just $130.41, but Bassett berated himself for the error.

As the ruling structure began to completely collapse around Rameau, his suspicion of foreigners only worsened. The government penalized merchants based on nationality by passing a so-called License Decree. Non-Haytians were required to pay taxes far above the normal rate, which would drive most foreigners out of business. When Bassett and other diplomats challenged this change, Rameau rudely dismissed them from the palace.

The darkened mood of the country grew more desperate with Rameau acting "as if the whole public treasury, the whole country and everyone in it belonged to him personally." Rameau's heinous brutality targeted even the members of Domingue's cabinet, who dared not to cross him in fear for their very lives. "No similar state of affairs has ever before existed in this country," Bassett reported to Washington. This was a striking statement given Haytian history, which was marked by wars, coups, and killings. But Bassett also knew that no matter how much power Rameau wielded, the Haytian people were bound to rise against him.[9]

It did not even take one month for his prediction to come true. As renewed battles broke throughout the countryside, the minister sent a cable back to Fish: "Civil war just inaugurated. Atrocities feared. Immediate presence of American war vessel desirable."[10]

The fighting spread to cities just outside the capital, and Bassett heard rumors that Rameau was soon to make use of the "ignorant blacks of the mountains," whom he would call to come down and indiscriminately kill people.[11] As the tensions mounted, Bassett was unfortunately stuck once again with another attack of his tropical illness. Because Rameau had taken such a personal dislike toward him and because his health was frail, Bassett feared not to be able to defend himself and his family. Despite several days of illness and fever, he continued to work furiously through the crisis. "He will never forgive my conduct in protecting General Canal," the envoy wrote back to Washington about Rameau's vendetta, "and will never cease to try to do me directly or indirectly any injury that may be within his power and that his unhappily inspired heart and brain may conceive."[12]

The enmity between the two grew so great that when Bassett came to again discuss the License Decree penalizing foreign merchants, Rameau exploded rather than acknowledge that the law would violate the 1864 treaty between the two countries. He told the minister that Hayti was officially withdrawing from the treaty. In addition, he informed the entire diplomatic corps that from that moment on, anyone involved in opposition to the government would be considered an outlaw and could be pursued and arrested "wherever he may be found in Haytian territory." This implied that no foreign legation or consulate was a safe haven and that soldiers could enter any premises at any time. Bassett overheard his nemesis scoff that this would finally "put foreigners in their places."[13]

But the situation on the battlefield deteriorated even more rapidly than Rameau could master, and just days later the final axe fell quickly. It was gruesome even in the annals of Haytian coups. As his ministers and military leaders abandoned him, Rameau had given an order to kill all political prisoners. But instead, the prison guards left the prison gates wide open for hundreds to escape and join the rebellion.[14]

Cities fell quickly in line with the revolutionaries, despite having no charismatic leader to follow as they had in previous civil wars. The revolutionaries were simply trying to rid themselves of the odious Rameau. Bassett held daily meetings at his legation with the other diplomatic representatives, and despite the concern of widespread bloodshed, in reality the revolutionary forces aligned themselves so quickly that protracted battles were few and far between.

When it became clear that Port-au-Prince itself would fall and that Domingue and Rameau had but a few hours left, Bassett called at the palace to play a role in the peaceful final turnover. At first Domingue was resistant to the American's plea, but as it became apparent that the end truly was near and the Haytian leader asked Bassett to negotiate a cease-fire. Domingue said he would resign if he could sail safely from the harbor.

Bassett and his British counterpart mounted their horses and rode toward the approaching rebel forces that General Lorquet commanded just north of the city to pass him the message of surrender. As they got closer to a line of several hundred troops, the two became terror-stricken, fearing that they might have run into a trap. The soldiers were wild with excitement, and Bassett could not tell which side they were on—or even if they simply wished to kill everyone in their path.

Suddenly, one of the officers recognized the American Minister and galloped over to the surrounded foreigners. When he explained to the enraged guards who these men were and what their mission was, loud cries rang out: "Vive les ministres d'Amérique et de l'Angleterre!"

"They are going to save our society; they are here to help rid us of Domingue," the officer cried out. Deafening cheers continued as Bassett explained the cease-fire. But the commander told Bassett that the main forces still lay several miles to the north. Hearing this news, Bassett thought it best to return to the capital to see what had transpired during his brief absence.

Back in town, it was clear that the end was already at hand. Rameau had attempted to remove all of the money that the government borrowed from the French to start up their national bank. The money was kept in the grand government vault, and Rameau had ordered boxes full of gold to be moved to a waiting ship in the harbor; but when the residents of the city realized what was happening, they savagely attacked the men who were transporting the gold. Breaking open the iron safes, the mob began removing more gold; what they could not personally cart off, they simply flung into the harbor to prevent Rameau from stealing it.

Meanwhile, Rameau and his uncle were cornered in a palace that had quickly become surrounded by that same angry mob. Only the Spanish and French consuls were present, and the two Haytians begged for diplomatic asylum and the protection of the diplomats' foreign flags. The irony of such a request from these two defeated dictators was not lost on the diplomats, but they courageously agreed to escort them toward the French Legation, just a few steps from the front door of the palace. Forcing their way through the angry crowd, they locked arms around Rameau, practically carrying him as the mass of ferocious faces around them grew more violent.

The Haytian people, despite their fury at their former rulers, were calm enough to recognize that none of the diplomats were to blame for their situation, and they took great care not to harm the Spanish or French consuls. However, as the convoy came within steps of the door to the French legation, someone from the crowd reached out to trip Rameau. As he stumbled toward the ground and out of the grasp of the hands of the two envoys, shots rang out, riddling his body with bullets. At the same time, Domingue was struck with the butt of a gun, and a bayonet was thrust into his side. However, he collapsed into the doorway of the legation and out of vigilante hands.

The sister of General Brice—the man who had so mercilessly been hunted down a year earlier and whose death started the chain of events—approached the corpse of Rameau and dipped a handkerchief into his blood, lifting it up for the crowd to see: their vengeance was complete.[15]

Safely in the diplomats' protection, Domingue was soon put onboard a ship bound for nearby St. Thomas, but Rameau's body lay in the street for hours as gawkers passed by to see if it were true. Someone castrated him, stuffed his penis in his mouth, and threw his body onto a dung heap, where it remained unburied in the Caribbean sun for another thirty-six hours.[16]

"I venture to predict that the memory of Septimus Rameau will, for an indefinite period, be held in execration by the Haytian people," Bassett harshly wrote, summing up the events for Washington. The only condolences that came from the American capital were Hamilton Fish's words: "It is to be hoped that the new government of Hayti may be wise, and secure to the people what they are entitled to expect from that government."[17]

Two days later, General Boisrond Canal and over one hundred of his exiled Haytian followers made their triumphant return from Jamaica. Crowds swarmed at the port, cheering their arrival. It was a jubilant time, as dancing and rhythmic drum-led songs filled the air. It was also an opportunity for the American Minister Resident to shine.

Days later, after being inaugurated as provisional president, Canal was going to the National Cathedral with his entourage when he recognized his old protector across the street. Shouting and pointing over to Bassett, the rest of the crowd turned. With a delirious, deafening roar, the thousands that had gathered to celebrate Canal were suddenly celebrating Ebenezer Bassett. Hats and handkerchiefs filled the air as the waving crowd poured their emotion and affection onto the normally stoic diplomat. Though it could not have erased the pain through which he and his family had suffered, Bassett must have felt that justice and right had indeed prevailed.[18]

As the new government began to stretch its wings, Ebenezer felt it was time to take his family back again to the United States. The previous year had been hard on him physically and emotionally. He continued to suffer and needed the time to recuperate as the heat of the summer set in. Returning to Connecticut, he found himself hailed as a hero by his hometown as well. He was even invited to Yale University, where he delivered a speech at the Law School on the "The Right of Asylum."[19]

The summer of 1876 not only saw the celebration of a new Haytian government but also marked the centennial anniversary of the United States. President Grant took his last few months in office to mark the full honor of a resurgent nation. As tradition dictated, the American president would not run for a third term. But he clearly kept his political eye on those members of the so-called radical wing of his party, seeking to promote the causes of his supporters on racial issues even while marking this historic occasion.

In his address to Congress commemorating one hundred years of U.S. independence, Grant noted that over that time, the nation had grown from three million to over forty million people, and the thirteen colonies were now thirty-eight states. In a nod to the work done over the previous century— which included recovering from a civil war and trying to establish an egalitarian society—Grant said, "Our liberties remain unimpaired; the bondmen have been freed from slavery; we have become possessed of the respect, if not the friendship, of all civilized nations . . . We are a republic whereof one man is as good as another before the law. Under such a form of government it is of the greatest importance that all should be possessed of education and intelligence enough to cast a vote with a right understanding of its meaning. A large association of ignorant men cannot, of any considerable period, oppose a successful resistance to tyranny."[20]

Grant's imminent retirement threw the Republican Party nomination wide open, with several party stalwarts vying for a slot. James Blaine, a politician from Maine who had served as Speaker of the House, was the early front-runner that year. Considered a strong candidate, he had many friends among the black community who had been supporters of Grant, but Blaine was not on the radical wing of the party when it came to racial issues. However, Blaine's eventual loss of the Republican nomination to Ohio governor Rutherford Hayes was less because of his support for racial equality than because of charges tying Blaine to corruption.

The Republican Hayes went on to defeat the Democratic standard-bearer, Samuel Tilden, in a hotly contested and controversial general election that fall. Though Tilden won the majority of the popular vote, disputed votes in Florida, Louisiana, Oregon, and South Carolina led to a crisis resulting in a congressionally established electoral commission to certify the electors. The standoff was only resolved when both parties reached the so-called Compromise of 1877, whereby Tilden would concede on condition that federal troops be recalled from the southern states and the Reconstruction period be brought to an end.[21]

This was especially ironic considering that the 1876 election had the highest voter turnout as a percentage of the voting-age population in U.S. history.[22] Such voter turnout was an indication of the impact of Reconstruction and the newfound independence of black voters that accompanied it. Though Tilden may have captured more popular votes across the nation, clearly the voice of black voters was not to be ignored. And although Hayes would keep his word and begin dismantling those very protections of Reconstruction that enabled black voters to remain engaged in the political process, he was far more sensitive to racial issues than the Democratic Party would have been had it occupied the White House.

As Hayes took his place in Washington, he began looking to fill the numerous patronage placements available for a victorious candidate. The diplomatic positions at the State Department were among the thousands across the government to be doled out, and Hayes naturally looked at his earliest supporters in the race. Bassett certainly was a stalwart Republican, but would he have the connections to the new administration to allow him to continue in diplomatic service? He did not even know Williams Evarts, who would be Hayes's Secretary of State. After spending the rest of the autumn making consultations in the United States, Bassett finally had to return to his post of duty and await an uncertain fate.

Back in Hayti, Canal's first few months in power had not been easy ones. It began with such hope, but it quickly turned unsteady with the arrival of an unexpected visitor who made quite a stir. General Louis Lysius Félicité Salomon, who had lived in exile in Jamaica for the previous seventeen years, came back to Port-au-Prince when he heard that Canal's government wanted to reach out to many of the politically persecuted under previous regimes. Bassett described the general as the "Haytian Frederick Douglass" and as a man of "rare intelligence, commanding presence and manners." He was also dark-skinned, in contrast to the mulatto Canal, and he had the support of the many Haytians, who were suspicious of the elitist, mixed-race leaders who now ruled the country.

"The esteem in which he is held by the blacks of this country as a rule amounts almost to an adoration of him," Bassett wrote of Salomon. The exile also had the advantage of not having played a role in the bitter fratricidal wars over the previous decade; unlike so many other leaders, he was not tainted by corruption or murderous vengeance. His return to Port-au-Prince caused the lighter-skinned military leaders to accuse him of attempting to take the presidency. Their threat in turn created resentment among the legions of black Haytians who adored the charismatic leader.

Bassett found himself having to intervene personally in the boiling tensions that mounted. After unsuccessful talks between the two sides, Bassett feared that the fragile peace would soon collapse into chaos. Reluctantly, he went to Salomon's house and suggested that—given the personal danger the general faced and the potential of conflict in the countryside—it might be best if Salomon left Hayti temporarily. General Salomon saw the wisdom of the American's advice, and he even asked Bassett to escort him to the wharf to see his party embark safely.

Though Ebenezer was himself a great admirer of Boisrond Canal, he was struck by the awe and respect displayed by ordinary citizens for

Salomon as he accompanied the exile to the boat. "It is indeed remarkable how sometimes among thousands, one single man by his mere presence inspire[s] and command[s] the rest," Bassett wrote of the encounter.[23]

With the crisis quickly averted, things seemed to be finally on the right track. Commerce between the United States and the Republic steadily grew. The New York Consulate reported large increases of both imports and exports and noted in particular that exports from the port of New York had gone from $2.3 million in 1872 to the current level of $3.9 million.[24]

For the first time in Haytian history, the executive also made efforts to truly rule democratically, paying more than lip service to the notion that the Corps Législatif should be an equal and strong branch of the government. Canal also made special efforts to tighten relations with the United States and Bassett personally. When the American Minister went to pay his respects to the president for the New Year of 1877, he was greeted at the palace as never before. An honor guard stood waiting for Bassett's arrival, and Canal met the American in full formal dress. The meeting was marked by the full pomp and circumstance of the visit of a head of state. The military regalia must have reminded Ebenezer of the Black Governor ceremonies that gave such pride to his father. Canal was jovial, and he expressed great friendship and gratitude toward him, even ordering a thirteen-gun salute outside the palace when Bassett made his exit.[25]

Canal's compromising attitude toward governance, however, made him look weak in the eyes of his political enemies, and the backstabbing among the elite members began almost immediately. Newspapers soon reported that even though "peace prevailed throughout the country," trouble simmered below the surface. Opponents of Canal sought to take advantage of the leader's "humane disposition" and support of the rule of law.[26] But these conflicts became more than rhetorical when the president became gravely ill that spring. Trouble rolled out into the open as several candidates jockeyed to position themselves as his successor. Bedridden, Canal went under the care of an American doctor as an insurgency movement broke out just outside of the capital. Though the rebellion was quickly put down, fear settled upon the countryside, and Bassett noted that Canal's absence or death would only "create great public insecurity and would probably plunge the country again into civil strife."[27]

Though Canal and the nation slowly recovered, Ebenezer Bassett's days were now numbered. That July the White House reserved the post in Hayti for one of its fervent black political supporters: former Ohio resident John M. Langston. Langston was born a slave in Virginia, but his family members eventually earned their freedom and moved to Ohio. There Langston graduated from Oberlin College, eventually becoming the first black admitted to the state bar. Langston was also the first black man to win an elected office in the country, serving as a clerk in Brownhelm Township during the 1850s.

Like Bassett, the Ohioan also recruited black soldiers for the Civil War, and he was later rewarded by President Andrew Johnson for this service by an appointment as Inspector General of the Bureau of Refugees, Freedman and Abandoned Lands, a position that brought him to the nation's capital. It was through their mutual work during the war that Bassett and Langston came to know one another. Though not close friends, Langston wrote a letter recommending Bassett's appointment as minister to Hayti, calling him "one of the ablest and most influential colored citizens."[28]

Langston remained active in the party but moved over to become a professor and, eventually, dean of Howard Law School in Washington, D.C. His connections and work on behalf of the victorious Rutherford Hayes, however, were what enabled him to become one of the leading candidates for a diplomatic posting. Langston opted for Hayti because of his interest in working with the first Black Republic, feeling that the assignment would be one of symbolic importance for the African American community as much as for the Haytians.[29]

The note to Bassett from Secretary of State Evarts breaking the news was short and to the point. President Hayes planned to make "certain changes in the Diplomatic service," and he "would be pleased to have your resignation."[30] There was no discussion, explanation, or offer of support. It must have been stunning for him to receive. Nonetheless, he responded with the dignity and grace that had marked his entire tenure as the first black diplomat:

> After having fulfilled to the best of my ability and discretion for more than eight years consecutively the office of United States Minister Resident and Consul General to Haiti, I have the honor to request you to be pleased to inform the President that I hereby place my resignation of that office at his disposition, with many and truly sincere thanks for the consideration which I have uniformly received from the President and from the Department.
>
> I am, Sir, your obedient servant,
>
> Ebenezer D. Bassett.[31]

The family began making preparations for a return to the United States, packing their house and saying their tearful goodbyes to the many friends they had made over the years. It was an especially difficult time; Eliza had just given birth to their sixth child, a baby girl named Olive, and had lost a boy that same year, an infant they had named after Frederick Douglass.[32] Moving was always difficult, but with the newborn in tow and mourning the death of another, the family was stretched to its limits.

Though Bassett was preparing to leave, he did not cease working as tirelessly as ever in his duties. He was able to successfully negotiate several more payments for American citizens that were worth over $168,000 and that dated back to the Salnave claims. Still, it must have stung when he read the newspaper reports of Langston's nomination officially being sent to the Senate for confirmation.

Interestingly, in contrast with his own nomination, no mention was made of Langston's race either in the media reports or in Secretary Evarts's letters to the new minister. Race, though clearly an issue, was no longer the most pressing factor in the nomination. Bassett had broken new ground with his appointment. He had performed his duties with such courage and skill that he was the victim of his own success, encouraging the president to nominate other black leaders to diplomatic positions, including his own.

Langston was quickly confirmed by the Senate and prepared for his own mission heading the U.S. Legation. As Langston was leaving New York, Bassett finally received a long-overdue letter from the State Department. Williams Evarts had not been Bassett's supervisor through the civil wars, coups, illnesses, or intrigues, but he knew of his impressive record of successes as minister resident, and the Department was effusive in acknowledging Bassett's ability.

"I cannot allow this opportunity to pass," wrote acting Secretary F. W. Seward, "without expressing to you the appreciation of the Department for the very satisfactory manner in which you have discharged your duties of the mission at Port-au-Prince during your term of office. This commendation of your services is the more especially merited because at various times your duties have been of such a delicate nature as to have required the exercise of much tact and discretion."[33]

On the morning of the 22nd of November, *The Andes* arrived at the harbor carrying Ebenezer's replacement. Bassett and Major Stuart, the British Consul General, along with the leading American citizens on the island, were there to greet the newcomer, who spoke no French or Creole. Bassett had arranged for a carriage to bring Langston back to his home. If Bassett had any resentment at having to turn over his post of duty to the new minister, he showed no signs of it. "The consideration and hospitality with which Mr. and Mrs. Bassett received and treated [me] . . . are profoundly appreciated," Langston later wrote in his autobiography.[34]

Ebenezer then made arrangements with the Haytian Foreign Minister for Langston to have an audience with President Canal to present his credentials. The ceremony was set for November 27th. While busying Langston with the details of the day-to-day work of running a legation, Ebenezer made the final rounds of good-byes. He was clearly emotional at having to bid farewell to so many friends, not the least of whom was the president himself.

The entire cabinet, every leading Haytian, and many American figures were present late that morning at the palace. Gathering before the heat of the day broke with its normal fury upon the city, the Haytian National Band greeted them with an entrance march as the National Guard moved solemnly into the ornate reception room. Bassett stood by Langston's side as the president approached the two men.

Having formally written out his letter of recall to Canal, Bassett spoke first and with great emotion while handing him the diplomatic correspondence. He told the president that he was leaving Hispaniola, a place where he had "passed many happy days," but that his "official residence has ended." At a moment that must have brought a tear to everyone's eyes, Bassett presented Langston to the president and added: "In all probability I shall no more see either your Excellency, whom I have learned to esteem, or your Excellency's fellow countrymen, all of whom have shown me only the kindest personal regards and the most exalted attention."

He alluded to the rapid and, at times, furious series of events that carried both men to this place. He concluded by calling Canal "my personal friend," and wishing him "happiness, success, and prosperity."

After Langston introduced himself, Canal gazed into Bassett's face, seeing the man who had saved his life and had helped his country avert so many crises. Deeply touched, everyone in the audience was indulgent under the circumstances. "At the moment of taking leave of you, Mr. Bassett, I cannot defend myself against a legitimate and profound emotion," Canal told the gathering. The president continued:

> You have not only been the intelligent diplomat to whom the President of the United States himself and all of us here render under homage, but moreover the friend of Hayti as well as my personal one. Your departure renders me more keen in my heart the thankful sentiment of sympathy which you have always shown to my country, and the recollection still so recent of those critical moments when a happy circumstance permitted you to mingle your devotion for the persecuted friend with the care of the dignity of your country and the honor of your flag. Neither threats, nor promises, nothing was able to shake you in the defense of justice, humanity and friendship. Mr. Langston will therefore easily understand and excuse the emotion which such a separation causes me.

> The necessities of politics may well separate us, My dear Bassett, the natural instability of all human things may tomorrow change my situation as it did yours, but there remains between you and myself a bond which neither the whims of fortune, nor the inconstancy of events can reach, that it's the thought of the perils which we have braved for the defense of our mutual

rights, and your conduct in private as well as in public has till this day only served to render more firm the ties of friendship.[35]

Soon thereafter, Ebenezer, Eliza, and their children made the way from their home—on the hillside of Petionville, overlooking the port—on the morning of December 1st, 1877. As they boarded the steamship *The Atlas,* they feared that it would be their last sight of the Haytian shoreline. Emotions ran high as they set sail on a two-week trip that finally brought them back to New York by midmonth, in time for winter and the holidays.

Mr. Consul General

It was an unusual transition. Since leaving Hayti, Bassett had been searching for another overseas assignment with the State Department. The hardships of life in a developing country had taken their toll on him physically, but he had been bitten by a more potent bug—that of foreign service. The diplomatic corps of the late nineteenth century was not the regularized, professional organization of later years. It was not until the passage of the Rogers Act in 1924, establishing a unified consular and diplomatic corps based on examination and merit, that the stage was set for greater involvement by true international professionals, regardless of race or political connections. Prior to that, diplomatic appointments were solely doled out using the patronage system of the day. Who you knew was what mattered most.

Though Bassett knew a great deal about running a U.S. Legation and the intricacies of international diplomacy, he was also familiar with the whims and fickle desires of the bureaucracy back in Washington. His eight years in Hayti meant that he had been away from the parlor game for too long. All of his excellent connections in the Grant administration had now been replaced by a new group wishing to make its mark upon the Hayes Administration foreign policy. Soon after his return to America, Ebenezer made his way down to Washington to meet with Secretary Evarts. Though they discussed other potential foreign postings, Bassett had no political chits to call in with the powers that be in the American capital.

Ebenezer was still a young man. At just forty-four years old, he had developed a wealth of experience and was eager to continue pursuing his professional interests. But, like all fathers of several small children, he worried about feeding, clothing, and educating his family. And returning to live in United States, a land that some of his family had never called home, was not an easy transition. Used to the ways and customs of Hayti, they would have no doubt struggled with the initial period of culture shock—not to mention the cold climate of New England winters.

Surrounded by relatives, the Bassetts returned to the comfort of New Haven. The oldest daughter, Charlotte, decided to pursue her interests in education and soon moved to Philadelphia, where she boarded with another family and several of her fellow teachers.[1] In a proud moment for her father, she would eventually join the staff at Ebenezer's old school, the Institute for Colored Youth. Her years in Port-au-Prince served her well when she became the teacher of French to a school that continued to grow in size and prestige.

As for the rest of the Bassetts, they moved into the house at 142 Grove Street. Their oldest son, Ebenezer Junior, would soon join his sister, heading off to complete his high school education at the Institute of Colored Youth and then begin his studies in 1881 at Yale University.[2] Their other daughters Lizzie and Olive attended grade school in New Haven. Their son Ulysses was at the prestigious Hopkins Grammar School, which had been founded in 1660 as one of the first institutions of education in America.[3]

The Bassett family continued to grow as Eliza gave birth to their family's newest member, Wendell P. Bassett, in 1879. They were clearly a member of the black elite within the city, relatively prosperous and prominent within the community. They even had the comfort of additional helpers in the house, which consisted of two servants, (a young man named Edward and an older nanny Ellen) who kept the family organized.[4]

Little further is known about Bassett's first year back in the United States. What is certain was that he reengaged with the academic and political community in Connecticut and nearby New York City. He also became active in humanitarian causes, such as supporting the "Arkansas Refugees," a group of over one hundred blacks who fled from southern white persecution to New York in early 1880. Like many poor, rural blacks, they found their limited defense under the law stripped away with the end of Reconstruction and federal protection. Harassed, unfairly taxed, and their property outright stolen by whites, they decided not to take the abuse any longer and made the trek to New York. Led by Reverend Simon Davis, the Arkansas Refugees were trying to gather enough financial support to set sail for Liberia and begin a new life on this former American colony. Bassett donated to their cause and helped the group.[5]

Bassett also maintained his connections with friends in Hayti, and he must have been troubled by some of the signs he saw since leaving the island. The Corps Législatif became the setting for a major political power struggle in Port-au-Prince as conditions once again began to worsen.

Boisrond Canal, though light-skinned and having displaced the Nationalist Domingue, was soon on the outs with his fellow Liberals in the legislature. His party was overcome with cannibalistic maneuvering as they devoured one another for the opportunity to take over the country. This forced Canal to rely more heavily on the Nationalists, who drew most of their support from the dark-skinned majority that made up nine-tenths of the country. It was an uneasy alliance, and one that reached the breaking point by the summer of 1879.

Canal had now ruled Hayti for three years. The Corps that was to gather that year would also select another leader at the end of Canal's term. But squabbles over who actually had the right to be members of the Chamber reminded everyone of the final months of the Saget administration, where petty struggles led to an eventual take-over by Domingue. No one wanted a repeat of that calamity, but neither did anyone see any exit.

Finally it came to blows when two Liberal members of the Corps, Edmond Paul and Boyer Bazelais, broke away and launched a military strike against the government. The fighting that ensued resulted in over one hundred and fifty deaths, including those of several legislators and cabinet officials. The new U.S. Minister Resident John Langston could not broker an accord and fretted from the sidelines: "[I]f such movements are continued but a little longer, the ruin of this country, its utter desolation, cannot be prevented," he wrote to Secretary Evarts.[6]

Though the violence was increasing, it was nothing like the destruction that Bassett had witnessed in earlier civil wars. The restrained fighting was probably due to the fact that President Canal, unlike previous dictators, was not a bloodthirsty man. In fact, during a temporary lull in the fighting, Canal issued a statement offering amnesty to all except for Paul and Bazelais. This was an incredible gesture but only showed further weakness to those jealous for power. As rebellious troops in the northern part of the country consolidated their ranks, they began a movement toward Port-au-Prince. Langston became convinced that "the wisest course for [Canal] to pursue is to resign." Only his removal from the scene would allow emotions to calm and hopefully order to be restored.

That idea was provident; on July 8, 1879, Canal and his senior advisors abdicated and left for St. Thomas aboard a French vessel. As the president headed toward the docks, a large crowd of his followers joined him, applauding and cheering their leader. Canal had left in disgust, but even at his lowest point, many Haytians recognized what Langston wrote to the State Department of the events: "It is safe to state that it will be a long time before this unfortunate country will see his equal in patriotism and intelligent devotion in its Presidential chair."[7]

What was interesting about this crisis was the limited involvement of the American Minister throughout the whole affair. Unlike Bassett, who not only chronicled the most minuet details of the events and was an active participant in shaping history, Langston seemed more out of the loop. To distinguish himself from his predecessor, Langston had also made it his policy to not receive any asylees. Though Secretary of State Evarts took a softer line than his predecessor on the issue of political refugees, Langston was an absolutist. And as a result, he was not called by Canal or other political leaders for his advice and negotiations as Bassett had constantly been. Perhaps a stronger hand by the American Minister might have prevented Hayti's loss of its great leader.

It was not long until the Haytian people turned to yet another figure, perhaps even more mythologically powerful, to unite their country. General Louis Lysius Félicité Salomon retuned yet again from his exile in Jamaica, making a glorious homecoming to the land of his birth.

Though Bassett was close to Canal and personally disappointed that he had not been able to complete his term of office, he also greatly admired the new president. And Salomon could only think back to those days of 1876, when he stepped foot on his homeland after so many years only to be met with anger and suspicion by many of the light-skinned, elite Haytians. Bassett's efforts to diffuse that crisis and personally assist Salomon board a ship for temporary safe passage from the chaos left a lasting impression on the leader. Salomon was in power only a few months when he looked to repay a debt that he had long held with the American who had saved his life.

Through his envoy in Washington, Stephen Preston, the new Haytian president made an offer to the former American Minister. He proposed to make Ebenezer the new Haytian Consul in New York City. Bassett, who had been anxiously looking to return to diplomacy after two years away, eagerly accepted in November of 1879. He and his family could remain in nearby New Haven while he commuted into the city at number 7 Bowling Green to serve in the prestigious appointment.[8]

It was not necessarily unusual for an American to take the position of a foreign consul in the nineteenth century. Bassett had befriended the former Haytian Consul in New York, another American citizen C.A. Van Bokkelen, who would even stay with the Bassetts during their years in Port-au-Prince. Bassett's former American clerk in Port-au-Prince, Henry A. Kearney, had resigned in 1876 to take that posting in New York when Boisond Canal offered the same position to him. Kearney lived with the

Bassetts through the siege of Canal's asylum. Those two men had also found a tight bond and the Haytian president rewarded Kearney for his steadfast friendship with the appointment.

But Kearney made way for his former boss when the new Haytian president wanted to make changes. Salomon needed fresh blood and prized personal loyalty. Though the move made little press in the major American newspapers, the African American press, such as *The People's Advocate*, took note right away.

> E.D. Bassett, late Minister to Hayti, today received an appointment as Haytian Consul in New York City, a position affording a yearly compensation of something over $6000 in commissions. The position was not sought by Mr. Bassett. He received a very friendly letter from President Salomon of Hayti, saying that upon Mr. Bassett's departure from Hayti, Mr. Salomon, who was then a private citizen, was grieved, and mentally determined that if he ever became President of Hayti, he would appoint Mr. Bassett to the New York Consulate.[9]

The fact that Bassett had asked for, but did not receive another diplomatic appointment from his own Secretary of State was not overlooked by the black community. Here was a man who stood firm in the face of extreme pressure to surrender Haytian dissidents but never backed down even with threats to his own life. But he was also a man whose scholarship and bookish manner may have put off certain people, making further appointments with the Hayes administration unlikely.

Ironically, Bassett quickly became a confidante to the man who had been his old nemesis, Haytian Minister Preston. The fact that Preston had been able to survive as the head of the Legation in Washington through the administrations of Saget, Domingue, Canal, and now Salomon, was nothing short of remarkable. In his decade of service, Preston had been an active ambassador, not below snooping into official correspondence for intelligence on what Americans were planning with respect to Hispaniola. He also nurtured multiple political patrons through the years, always able to shift his loyalties or have allies convince each new administration of his unbending devotion to their government. He also had the advantage of being the veteran in Washington who was known to make things happen. Secretary Fish had commented about Preston's unsavory reputation, but that unsavoriness had made him invaluable to Port-au-Prince in their battles against the goliath to the north.

While Preston dealt with the political issues of the Hayes administration, which included keeping Dominican annexation as far from favor as possible, Bassett was free to deal with the commercial and trade issues that the Port of New York required. As the busiest port in the United

States, and the most important one for bilateral trade between the two countries, the New York Consulate offered the kind of high profile that Bassett felt he deserved. He relished the opportunity.

Almost immediately he became involved in a controversy that had bubbled since his time in Hayti. The initial wrangling grew out of a new law passed by the Haytian legislature in 1876 that called for a one percent charge for all merchandise that left the United States for Hayti. Though the so-called "consular tax" was presumably collected to offset Haytian consular expenses, it was simply a lucrative export tax on American goods, something illegal under American law.

Though Bassett had dealt with the matter only slightly during his waning months, it became a fixation for John Langston. The Haytians were unwilling to budge, in part because they continued to rely on the revenue. And Langston held Bassett's earlier failure to wipe away the tax as a black mark that he would not repeat. Calling it a contravention of the "spirit and the letter of the Treaty of November 1864," which established commercial relations between the two countries, Langston hammered away month after month with Foreign Minister Felix Carrie. However, Carrie rebuffed him at every turn. Langston even enlisted the help of the British and French consuls in their plea of the inequality, but their hosts continued to turn a deaf ear. With nothing being offered as compensation and no punitive action in sight to withdraw the tax, the Haytian government had no incentive to actually negotiate.[10]

Clearly growing exasperated, Langston finally threw up his hands when Carrie was replaced as foreign minister by L. Etheart, the man who had actually written the law in the Corps Législatif.[11] A lesson that Bassett had learned early in his dealings with the Salnave claims was that it required a great deal of tact, patience, and good feelings to win the day in this diplomatic war of attrition. Langston lacked patience, and his limited understanding of the culture only served to make matters worse. Pouring salt on the wound, the foreign minister would frequently remind Langston that his predecessor had made no complaints about the law.

The diplomatic parrying continued on the consular charges through 1879. Because Langston had been unable to successfully negotiate the situation, the matter was transferred to Secretary of State Evarts, who took up the matter with Haytian Minister Preston. But nothing happened over many months in Washington either, until Ebenezer Bassett became consul in New York.

While the official records offered no indication of the role he may have played, it seemed quite reasonable that Bassett may have been able to bridge the gap between the two sides. The bickering correspondence over several years that had found no resolution was settled only months later.

Bassett's knowledge of both the Haytian political and legal system may have forged the compromise that allowed John Langston to write his boss, "in view of the importance which our government attaches to the subject, [the Haytian] government has decided . . . to abolish the charge of one percent for consular visas."[12] Bassett's slow and steady course, even under his new employers, had finally paid dividends.

Now that Ebenezer Bassett was again a member of the diplomatic corps, he resurfaced in the American media as someone to watch. His attendance at a reception at the Academy of Music in New York was noted in January 1882,[13] as was his speech at the Lincoln birthday banquet a month later.[14]

He had even become the man for foreign "dignitaries" to visit during their sojourn in the United States. Princess Olive, the daughter of former Haytian "Emperor" Soulouque came to New York and stayed with the Bassetts. Her visit created a minor stir among the African American media in the northeast. Reporters "flocked" to Bassett's home to get a glimpse of a reclusive, but striking woman. Actually they were old family friends— when her father lost power in 1856, she went off to study in Belgium but occasionally visited the Bassetts while they were stationed in Port-au-Prince. Still Ebenezer found himself trying to ward off the 1880s version of the paparazzi, and the princess managed her stay in the United States without incident.[15]

The initial years of Salomon had been ones of great optimism. Admired as the new "Father of the Country," Salomon brought stability to the normally troubled waters of state. The economy seemed to perk along and there was a sense of hope for the future. The leader established plans for repayment of foreign debt, reconstructed the moribund educational system, and instituted agricultural advances. But just as Bassett had seen in his days as minister, the pendulum of chaos inevitably swung once again out of control on the island.

Those hungry for power soon began plotting ways to grab control. As usual, several of the port cities in the north and south of the country were the scenes of intrigue by 1882 and 1883. Unlike Canal's lenient attitude toward those who opposed his rule, Salomon took a hard line with the expatriate rebels and their recruits in the military. In an effort to swiftly crush their spirit, Salomon ordered the capture and execution of dozens of people. Salomon even traveled to Cap Haitien to confront several of the presumed coup plotters personally.

Although these actions were cheered by many Haytians, a deep mistrust was simultaneously borne of these acts. American Minister John Langston sent back to Washington hinting of future concerns. "At this writing the tranquility of the country is nowhere disturbed," he wrote the

Secretary of State. "The quiet is, in fact, profound, but of such character as to compel the feeling whether it may not be ominous of early and dreadful outbreaks as has been the case so many times heretofore in the experience of past administrations of this country." He also concluded that Salomon, having been "pressed to extreme measures," would be forced to continue them.[16]

The Haytian government suspected that several Americans were involved with plots to overthrow Salomon. The exile Bazelais received support from an American ship, the *Tropic*, which sailed from Philadelphia and later deposited insurgents at the port of Miragoane. Other Americans were also suspected of illegal involvement, and leaders in both capitals feared that the issue could reach a breaking point, both bilaterally and for the government of Hayti.

Bassett stepped into the mêlée, trying to stop private Americans from breaking U.S. neutrality laws and profiteering from the fighting. Writing a letter to the collector of the Port of New York, Bassett requested that they stop additional ships from setting sail toward the Haytian cities of Miragoane, Jeremie, and Jacmel, all of which were now under siege by Bazelais's rebels. The towns had been emptied as insurgents took hold of the arsenals and Salomon's troops responded with an incessant bombardment.[17]

The Haytian Consul General accused several American-flagged ships, the *Azelda*, the *Laura*, and the *Mary E. Hogan*, of illegally running guns from New York to support Bazelais. "I have reason to believe that [the ships have] a lot of arms and ammunition on board designed to give aid to the rebels in Hayti," Bassett was quoted in the press. He then quickly signed an affidavit before the U.S. District Attorney declaring that the schooners carried 43 cases of weapons. Most disturbing was the fact that one of the vessels was owned by his former friend and secretary (and the man that had proceeded him as Haytian consul), Henry Kearney.[18]

However, Bassett had been unable to present hard evidence of a crime. Most probably the ships had clandestinely unloaded once questions were asked in New York. Certain of malfeasance, and pressed by President Salomon to do something, Bassett kept the matter tied up administratively, remaining at a stalemate before the district attorney. Finally Treasury Secretary Charles Folger was forced to step in and authorized the vessel's release.[19] But the delay had been enough for Salomon's forces as the rebels withered without their supplies, and Bazelais was killed in the last of the fighting. Bassett's timely insertion into the matter helped save Hayti from another all-out civil war.

Worsening the strained relations between himself and Bassett's replacement in Port-au-Prince, President Salomon even wrote a letter to

Langston that offered as its first words of thanks to Bassett.[20] Langston, who had also tried to insert himself into the negotiations during the summer sieges, only received a letter of rebuke from the State Department, saying that his actions taken to negotiate a peace "cannot be regarded as one having the official sanction of support of this government."[21]

Ebenezer Bassett was soon put again in an uncomfortable position as an American in the uniform of the Haytian Consul. When Stephen Preston was requested to make a special trip to Europe and needed to leave someone as *chargé d'affairs* of the Haytian Legation, he naturally turned to his senior and most experienced diplomat. It created an awkward moment for an American to represent a foreign power before the very government that he had once served. His temporary "promotion" was prominently reported in the media as the new "Haytian Minister."[22] But this moved was frowned upon by the State Department in Washington, who turned down the request, feeling that it would become a conflict of interest.

Nevertheless, Preston got around the formal designation of *charge d'affairs* for Bassett while effectively leaving him in charge: "I admit that Mr. Bassett, as the principal consular officer of Hayti in this country," Preston wrote to the new Secretary of State Frederick Frelinghuysen, "and as having charge of the business of this Legation, may, in that capacity, correspond with Your Excellency on all questions that may arise during my absence. I am very glad, and I take note of the fact that your declination to receive Mr. Bassett as a diplomatic officer is due to no personal feeling, but that, on the contrary, 'the archives of the Department of State afford ample proof that, if a contrary decision were deemed warrantable, there could be no reason to distrust his prudence or intelligence.'"[23]

While serving as de facto Haytian *chargé*, Bassett tried his best to stay out of the limelight, but with the unfortunate passing of President U. S. Grant in July of 1885, he found himself in the news once again. Just as the veterans that made up his army joined to commemorate the war hero, so too did members of his administration, including the diplomatic and consular corps. They gathered at the Windsor Hotel in New York City to plan their role in honoring the leader. Bassett, along with colleagues that had served in Belgium, Germany, Japan, Siam, and Brazil, all planned their participation in remembrance as the nation mourned.[24]

News accounts of the day of burial were as poetic and somber as the occasion merited. "The day broke heavy and sullen, as though the smoke of his hundred battles yet hung in the sky," read the first line from the *New York Times*. Grant's funeral procession through the streets of New York caused the already crowded city to burst with a gathering of unprecedented size. A record 1.5 million visitors poured into the streets from around the country.

Major General Winfield Scott Hancock led the funeral procession. President Grover Cleveland, the first Democrat to win the White House after the Civil War and only in office a few months, followed the casket surrounded by Grant's cabinet officers and staff. Veterans of the Grand Army of the Republic made a long column following the political elite in an impressive sight to behold as they filled Fifth Avenue. Following soon behind this mass of soldiers came the carriages of the former Presidents Rutherford Hayes and Chester Arthur and immediately behind them were the diplomatic corps, with Bassett featured prominently leading the way. The entire procession wound its way up the island of Manhattan through the day, placing the revered patriot in his final resting spot overlooking the Hudson River.[25]

Bassett also became involved in a public debate surrounding the very name of General Grant. Though he was known universally as U. S. Grant, it was not his actual name. Bassett had earlier inquired with Grant's personal secretary General Babcock, about the General's "Christian" name. Babcock confirmed for Bassett that Grant's birth name had actually been Hiram Ulysses Grant but that while at West Point, he had been listed by a typographical error as Ulysses S. Grant, perhaps confused with his brother, Simpson Grant. Ebenezer had even named his fifth child Ulysses in his honor, so it was of some surprise to the diplomat that the President had actually been named Hiram. Bassett took the occasion to tell the media what he had learned and to set the historical record straight.[26]

Bassett remained as the head of the Haytian Embassy with Preston's continued absence. As such he was required to conduct the official business of the Haytian government before the Secretary of State. One issue that he suggested to Secretary Frelinghuysen was an exchange of military officers from the U.S. to the Haytian navy. Bassett knew of the lack of professionalism in the Haytian military and thought an exchange of officers and engineers would prove beneficial. He took the matter up with William Chandler, the Secretary of the Navy and apparently worked out a deal for voluntary "leaves of absence" for the Americans to participate in the Haytian training.[27]

Bassett also confronted one of the more painful and uncomfortable assignments of his career when his long-time friend Charles Van Bokkelen was arrested in Port-au-Prince for bankruptcy. Though an American citizen, Van Bokkelen had been the Haytian Consul in New York from 1870 until 1876 and then returned to Port-au-Prince to open his business. They had developed quiet a friendship over the years and it was difficult to see his friend thrown into debtor's prison in 1884.

The matter, however, became one of official interest to the Department of State, because Van Bokkelen had been treated differently under Haytian law than a Haytian citizen. In the mind of both Minister Langston and Secretary of State Frelinghuysen, this was a violation of the treaty between the two countries. Langston argued and pestered the Haytian government, frequently bringing up the matter with President Salomon himself. But the courts had spoken, and they ordered him held in prison.

Bassett was asked to defend the Haytian government before Washington and had to lay aside his personal feelings in an official note to the State Department, arguing that the judiciary had acted properly: "I do not think that there is any spirit of unfairness towards Mr. Van Bokkelen or discrimination against him in these proceedings. He is, as I understand it, in detention under the customary administration of the law of Hayti, which certainly differs from that of the United States."[28]

Van Bokkelen lingered in jail as his health deteriorated. Meanwhile, President Cleveland wanted to make a change in his diplomatic representation and asked for Langston's resignation. In his place, he sent another African American, John E. W. Thompson, who took up residence in June of 1885.[29]

Just as Langston was preparing to leave the post, the government of Hayti turned Van Bokkelen over to the departing minister by decision of President Salomon himself. Much to everyone's surprise, Van Bokkelen was simply released after fifteen months in jail without any written explanation or official communication. It seemed to Langston that he had finally worn down the Haytian president, but the timing with the arrival of the new minister resident was more than suspicious.[30]

Thompson was from New York and had studied at Yale Medical School. He had set up a private practice in the city in 1884, and it was likely that he had known the Bassetts as well.[31] Though no record exists of any correspondence, Bassett must have initially felt relieved that Langston was to be replaced. It could have been that Bassett pressed upon the Haytian leader to release his friend as another gesture to the United States, and one that would allow the new minister resident to begin his tour without this thorn in the bilateral relationship. Unfortunately, Van Bokkelen died just a few months after his release.[32]

Bassett's worked settled down to normal as he resumed oversight of only the consulate in New York with the return of Preston to Washington. When a trade dispute surfaced involving Hayti's desire to limit the type of kerosene that could be imported to the island, Bassett stepped in to resolve the conflict. American merchants claimed that they were unfairly treated when the Haytian government wanted to ban any oil that burned below 150 degrees Fahrenheit. Given the scars that the country suffered over the years with its many fires, such limitations seemed reasonable to the Haytians; cheaper and poorer quality kerosene was simply a danger to public safety. Bassett began consulting chemical experts to gain their views on the level of explosiveness that could be properly handled by common people. The experts agreed that the type of cheap kerosene used in Hayti was dangerous "beyond all doubt."

Armed with this information and making a plea toward humanitarian concerns for the well-being of uneducated people who understood little about how to use the combustible, Bassett convinced Minister Thompson and the State Department to allow only higher-grade kerosene for export from the United States.[33]

At home in New Haven, the family had suffered yet another blow, with the loss of young Olive Bassett in 1884. The death of their youngest girl must have been a particularly lonely event for Eliza and Ebenezer. Their oldest, Charlotte, was living a few hours south and teaching full time at the Institute for Colored Youth, leaving only Lizzie, Ulysses, and Wendell at home with their mother.

The difficulties spread to Ebenezer's work as the political situation in Hayti slid once again toward anarchy. President Salomon had initially won a seven-year term of office, but he had changed the constitution, enabling him to seek reelection in 1886. The move smacked of dictatorship, and Liberal and Nationalist forces began to arm themselves in response.

Along the margins lurked Boisrond Canal, who made his way back to Port-au-Prince and was rebuilding his base of support. Crucial among Canal's allies was Francois Legitime, a member of the Haytian Senate, and a man who had also been exiled by Salomon. By the late 1880s, the Haytian president had grown ill and was quite elderly at this point. With challenges from Canal and Legitime, he saw himself losing more control over the situation. Soon, flames raged again through the city, and despite Bassett's efforts to reduce the impact of accidental fires with a higher quality kerosene, these burnings were no accident. The resulting instability caused Salomon's army commander from the north, General Thelemaque, to declare a rebellion and march toward Port-au-Prince. Surrounded by enemies and rather than suffer a fate similar to that of Domingue, the noble Salomon left in August 1888 and died a few weeks later after an operation in Paris.[34]

With Salomon out of the picture, Canal assumed control once again as the head of the provisional government. Bassett must have felt relieved that his old friend was back in power, but that relief was short lived. General Thelemaque continued his march from the north, finally arriving at the capital. The rivalry between the Liberal Party and the Nationals boiled over into full-scale war. During one skirmish, Thelemaque was killed—assassinated, his followers claimed—and Hayti teetered on the brink of a bloodbath.

Canal stepped (or was perhaps shoved) aside to make room for Legitime to rally the remnants of the Liberals. Meanwhile the popular general, Florvil Hyppolite, took up the mantle of the slain hero Thelemaque and the Nationals as the fires of war now raged throughout the country. In fact, Hyppolite's forces had control or laid siege to large portions of territory in Hayti. Legitime's stronghold remained Port-au-Prince, and because that was the seat of government, it seemed easy for him to claim the right of recognition as the true Haytian government.

However, Stephen Preston and Ebenezer Bassett were caught in a bind. Their sympathies were with the Liberal faction, but they had been unable to convince the Secretary of State that the U.S. government should formally recognize Legitime's authority. With too many variables at play, new Secretary of State Thomas Bayard simply chose to wait and let matters work themselves out, writing his envoy in Hayti to "carefully avoid taking sides."[35]

In the meantime, a panicked Minister Resident, John Thompson, continually wrote to Washington for war ships to help calm the situation. Anarchy prevailed, and in response Legitime declared blockades of several ports actually under the control of Hyppolite's forces. American merchant vessels had been drawn into the fray when a U.S.-flagged ship (ironically named *Haytian Republic*) ran into one of these blockades outside the city of St. Marc and was captured as a prize of war by Legitime's navy.

Seeking to make sense of the chaos, U.S. media went to Ebenezer Bassett for his take on what was happening. He told reporters that Legitime's forces had blockaded ports from Jacmel in the south up through Gonaives, Cap Haïtien, and even Port de Paix in the far north. Optimistically he told reporters that "the insurgent force is in the neighborhood of 10,000 men and is now confined exclusively to the North. It is not expected that the insurgents can hold out much longer against government forces."[36]

Bassett continued this Pollyannaish approach in late November 1888, asserting that things were improving after Salomon's fall. "There is every prospect that peace will soon reign in Hayti," he told the *Chicago Tribune*. "I am informed that high dignitaries of the Roman Catholic Church have succeeded in setting a movement on foot, the object of which is to settle the misunderstanding between the Haytian Government and the insurgents . . . The insurgents have nearly reached the bottom of their pile of money and that fact no doubt makes them all the more willing to talk of peace. We shall all be thankful when peace once more reigns in Hayti."[37]

But peace was nowhere near at hand and Legitime's actions in seizing the steamer *Haytian Republic* had absolutely enraged Washington. Secretary of State Bayard told Thompson to "protest instantly" against the illegal act, finally ordering a war ship to sail for Haytian waters.[38]

Rather than cave into Washington's demands, Legitime set up a tribunal to investigate the capture of the American ship, and not surprisingly the tribunal found that no wrong had been committed. Adding insult to injury, the crew members had been held captive by authorities during an investigative process and were only released when Minister Thompson personally appealed to Legitime. After being held almost one month, they were finally put aboard a Dutch ship and sent back to New York. Ebenezer Bassett went out to greet them upon their arrival, but rather than finding comfort in the meeting, he found himself questioned unsympathetically about his brutal new "government" in Port-au-Prince.[39]

During all the confusion, newspaper stories appeared saying Bassett had been recalled as the consul general, and many were wondering if Bassett could have done more to prevent this situation. "Mr. Bassett declined to say anything about the matter, and Minister Preston said that he knew nothing about it. It was admitted that Mr. Singleton is now Acting Consul-General," reported the *New York Times* toward the end of that year of turmoil.[40]

The rebel Hippolyte now boldly claimed control of the government, "appointing" a new minister in Washington and consul general in New York. "Hyppolite's faction had a representative in New York last month in the person of Gen. Papillon," reported one daily. "His presence greatly annoyed Consul General Bassett and that official—who is a reticent official, by the way—insisted upon believing and announcing that all sorts of plots to fit out and send supply ships to Hippolyte's forces from this country were being put into execution in New York and Brooklyn. He made a great fuss about the steamer *Samana* which was fitting out in Brooklyn along the middle of November."[41]

In fact, American privateers were openly taking advantage of the situation in the Caribbean to trade arms and ammunition to whichever side was willing to pay. Though Stephen Preston begged the State Department to put a stop to these mercenaries (at least those supplying Hyppolite), those calls fell on deaf ears in Washington. Clearly the treatment after the capture of the *Haytian Republic* had won no friends in the North American capital. In fact, Secretary Bayard told Preston that "the right of the Haytian Government to call on this Government to stop sales of munitions of war to persons who may be concerned in a Haytian insurrection is in no sense conceded." Incredibly, the Secretary of State was telling another friendly power that nothing would be done to stop gasoline from being poured on the fire of civil war—that arms could flow freely.[42]

It looked suspiciously like the U.S. government was not simply turning a blind eye to mercenary activities. At the very least, they were giving tacit support to those around Hyppolite and even clandestinely supporting them. Secretary of State Bayard received letters from Hyppolite's faction protesting any interactions with Preston and Bassett as illegitimate: "On behalf of the Central Provisional Revolutionary Committee of the North Republic of Haiti, the undersigned most respectfully protests against the recognition of Mr. Preston as Minister Resident of the Republic of Haiti and of Mr. Bassett as Consul General of said Republic at the City of New York," came the first official word from U.S.-based supporters of Hyppolite. "Mr. Bassett assumes by virtue of powers which have ceased to exist, as I have stated, to prohibit the shipment of this or that merchandise to the north of Haiti, claiming that without his express permission, no goods may enter there."[43] Hyppolite's supporters further claimed that not only was Bassett trying to stop arms from their cause, he was actually helping ship arms to Legitime's forces.

In spite of the criticisms, Bassett continued his furious protests as the arming of boats in New York harbor continued, going so far as to post a watch when suspicious vessels were being loaded. At the slightest provocation, Bassett would complain to the Collector of the Port and asked the ship to be searched. The *Samana* had been one vessel of particular concern because it was to set sail not for Haytian waters, but rather for the Dominican port of Monte Christi, along the northern frontier near Hayti's border.

Bassett now found himself accusing the Dominican government of playing a role in the conflict by allowing its ports to be used as the supply line for Hyppolite's campaign. It would be a surprise to no one that Dominican leaders saw an opportunity to help support a regime on their western border more favorably inclined toward them. Bassett made it an international issue after speaking and writing numerous times to the Dominican Consul in New York. Officially the Dominicans denied any knowledge or involvement in the conflict, but the arms race continued unabated.

A second ship was also accused of gun-running and the normally dispassionate Bassett made something of a name for himself in the press with his vociferous claims. "[The *Saginaw*] which sailed from New York

Nov. 6 also caused Mr. Bassett a great deal of worry," reported a Chicago paper. "He moaned so long and loudly that she was carrying arms, powder, and supplies to Hyppolite's forces that Collector Magone finally sent the revenue cutter *Chandler* down the bay . . . Those who know anything about revenue cutters will of course understand that this revenue cutter didn't come within telescopic range of the *Saginaw's* stern."[44]

It was apparent to all that this was a futile exercise. American ships were being used to ferry weapons and soldiers in the Haytian conflict, and Legitime's hold on power was becoming more tenuous by the month. By 1889, the ships sailing to Dominican ports for off-loading to Hyppolite's partisans became more common as several additional steamers set sail from New York.

In the end, it all became too much for Ebenezer Bassett to handle. Seeing that Legitime's days were numbered (Boisrond Canal and other supporters would eventually abandon the island once again), the Consul General of Hayti for the City of New York resigned his position. Not in a loud show of protest, but in the quiet dignity that had always been his way, Ebenezer Bassett returned to New Haven.

13

A Hero's Return?

An obscure Naval captain and lecturer, Alfred Thayer Mahan, published *The Influence of Sea Power upon History* in the year 1890, spurring renewed thinking in Washington. Mahan argued that a great world power, such as the British Empire, had achieved its position through naval strength. The lesson for the United States was clear—to counteract European superiority, it was imperative to control the seas. In real terms this meant focusing energies on building a canal through Central America in order to connect the Atlantic and Pacific Oceans. It also meant that the United States must solidify its position in the Caribbean as the guardian of that canal.

For the new American President, Benjamin Harrison, this fit in nicely with the expansionist foreign policy of "manifest destiny." Harrison brought back James Blaine as Secretary of State, who had earlier served in that role under the brief administration of President James Garfield. Blaine also maintained the view that Latin America was crucial in the geostrategic game for control. And one of Blaine's first pieces of that strategy was to gain a foothold for a naval coaling station in Mole St. Nicholas, a bay along the northwestern coast of Hayti.

Also with the change of administrations would come the traditional resignations of the appointees from the outgoing Cleveland government. This meant that John Thompson would soon be leaving Port-au-Prince as minister resident and it provided an opportunity for a new appointment, most likely another leading black candidate for the Black Republic.

Because Bassett had quietly resigned his consulate, he began pressing everyone he knew for that coveted foreign service appointment. Speculation even reached the newspapers, as one *New York Times* article featured a front page headline "Wants to Be Minister."

"The Hon. E.D. Bassett, a resident of this city and until recently Haytian Consul at New York, is a candidate for the position of the United States Minister at Hayti, and his friends in New England are confident of his appointment," asserted the *Times* piece.[1]

However, Bassett required the support of political patrons for the position. In addition to calling in his chits with the senators from his home states of Connecticut and New York, he also needed the support of the most important black American of his day.

Bassett and Frederick Douglass had known one another for over thirty years, having first met in the 1850s. Douglass was now in his twilight, but at seventy years old he was still the preeminent black voice in the nation. He had served as president of the Freedman's Bank, as Marshal for the District of Columbia, and as Recorder of Deeds in Washington. But he also longed to add a diplomatic posting to his stellar resume, and short of elected office, it was the only thing that he had not accomplished by this point in his life.

Douglass remained in occasional contact with Bassett through the decades. However, their friendship had trailed off as the two moved in their different directions. The last record of correspondence between the two had been in 1871. However, as Legitime was falling from power in Hayti, Bassett began looking again for support from the State Department and he naturally turned to his old ally.

Perhaps what rekindled their relationship was a chance meeting in New Haven during the 1888 presidential campaign. Douglass had come to town to stump for Republican candidate Benjamin Harrison, and while he was there he visited the Bassett family. They discussed Hayti, politics, and—most touching for the elder statesman—the death of Frederick Douglass Bassett, the child that had died in Port-au-Prince. Ebenezer and Eliza told Douglass that their son was always on their mind, and it was not possible to think of the infant without also thinking of the man they so admired.[2]

So when it became clear by early 1889 that General Legitime was not likely to hold on to power much longer, Bassett took the opportunity to write again to his friend and ask for assistance. He told Douglass that he was seeking a position in the foreign service because he was, "in view of so many years of experience, better fitted [for it] than for any thing else."

It was true, at this point, given eight years as minister resident and now almost ten years as consul general, Bassett had amassed a unique wealth of experience. However, Bassett knew that the issue of his working for a foreign government, even serving as *chargé d'affaires* for a time, would rub some people the wrong way. Most damaging, he feared, was that he was seen to represent a government now extremely unpopular in Hayti, and one not officially recognized by the United States government. Nonetheless, he told Douglass that he had "no enemies" in Hayti, having always conducted himself with great caution and professionalism.[3]

Although Bassett's name may have been put forward, there was little support by the new Secretary of State. Blaine held expansionist views, and Mahan's book on the importance of sea power only stoked those fires. Thus the United States' backing of Hyppolite, in the face of British and French backing of Legitime, moved from quiet to blatant support. The U.S. Navy opened the blockaded ports of the northern coast and American vessels freely moved in and supplied the rebels with materiel. Hayti's civil war had now officially become a focal point in the great game, whereby European powers sought to regain a foothold in the hemisphere and the American government attempted to checkmate those moves. This left Bassett stuck as a pawn in the middle of the chessboard, without a knight for protection.

Making matters worse, Bassett had simply chosen to be loyal to the "wrong" side in the Haytian conflict. By remaining in his job and working officially for Legitime, Ebenezer Bassett found himself on the outs with Blaine and his supporters, who wanted the regime to change to one more beholden to the United States. Although Bassett claimed to Douglass and anyone who would listen that he neither backed Legitime nor opposed Hyppolite, he failed to gain any traction.

The response from the White House came soon enough. President Harrison would not nominate Bassett for the position in Port-au-Prince. Rather, he chose with the man who had campaigned on his behalf and offered further political support for the Republican Party in upcoming elections, the most famous black man in the world—Frederick Douglass.

On June 25, 1889, Douglass wrote to Blaine accepting the offer of the position. As newspapers heralded the appointment, Bassett must have been crushed when he saw the headlines. But instead of sulking, he wrote a five page congratulatory letter to his idol; one he marked: "Confidential."

"The offer of the mission to you is a tribute to your high character and to the unsurpassed eminence which the rare unanimity the American people assign to you," Bassett extolled to Douglass just days after the news broke. "You will see that I have never wavered in my esteem, my veneration for you. Believe one then that I indulge in no mere flattery now."

Bassett went on to offer his services, saying that he would be more than happy to brief him about all aspects of Haytian life. "I know them, their language, and their inspirations just as you know the people of the District of Columbia," he continued.

Getting to the more difficult part of the letter, Bassett then pleaded with his long-time friend for additional assistance. If Douglass would only put in a good word with President Harrison, perhaps something else might be available, even a posting in Jamaica or St. Thomas. It seemed that the Bassett family had in fact fallen onto hard times.

Perhaps in part because of the instability in Port-au-Prince, full funds to which he was accustomed may not have been available during the last months of his consul generalship. In addition, a series of bad investment decisions had led his family to the brink of financial disaster. "All my accumulations have been swept away by the bad faith or mismanagement of men who were in the highest esteem of their respective communities and whom I thought above reproach," he confided to Douglass. Although he did not go on to further describe these individuals, they were certainly associates from his time in Port-au-Prince. Just as he had seen his old friend Charles Van Bokkelen die at an early age, a broken and imprisoned man for his financial gambles with Hayti, Bassett feared for the worst himself. He still had school-aged children; and with no savings or an immediate hope of future employment, he felt desperate and feared he had nowhere else to turn.

"But I have never yet looked into the face of any man before [of] whom I was afraid or ashamed. And in view of my past record, I think that the interests of us all would be served by my keeping well afloat," Bassett wrote, pouring his heart out to Douglass. Humbling himself even more he offered to join him as his secretary, noting that the U.S. government made "a small allowance for this." It would be small indeed, just a fraction of what he had been earning both as consul general and previously as minister resident, but Bassett had no other choice.[4]

Bassett not only provided Douglass with his knowledge of Hayti's history, he also supplied him with up-to-date intelligence from his intimate sources, particularly Stephen Preston. In the months between the announcement of Douglass' assignment and his leaving for Hayti, Bassett wrote a series of letters to the future minister resident, marking them all "Confidential." In them he quoted from conversations and letters he received from Preston, who still remained as Haytian Minister in Washington. Preston noted that his highly placed sources told him it was President Harrison personally, rather than Blaine, who wanted Douglass for the position. "He does not regard lightly the colored vote as Mr. Blaine does," Preston said. He also reported that President Harrison was against intervention in Hayti, something that he felt Blaine and several military leaders had been more active in promoting.

Preston also reiterated what several shipping merchants were saying; they were furious with the appointment of Douglass, fearing he would not support their commercial schemes and interests in Hayti. "They know that Mr. Douglass is not to be bought and that *he* will *not* be their instrument," Bassett quoted Preston as saying.

In a telling statement, Preston mentioned that in spite of the pressure, no Haytian government would yield the Mole St. Nicholas, neither to European nor American military. "Viva Hayti!" Preston had exclaimed to Bassett.[5]

Bassett also warned Douglass not to go to Hayti until after September of that year, fearing that presenting his letter of credence to the dying Legitime government would start him off on the wrong foot. It was apparently an opinion shared by both Douglass and the State Department, as he remained in his Anacostia home over the summer months, receiving a recess appointment while Congress was out of session.

In the meantime stories began appearing about a gradual takeover of Hayti by the United States. They surfaced in part because of the rumors that efforts would soon be underway to secure the Mole, but they exploded in Haytian circles when it was recalled that Douglass had taken part in the Santo Domingo Commission over a decade earlier in Grant's attempt to annex the Dominican Republic. Now people were fearful that Douglass was being sent down there to lay the groundwork for another annexation. Bassett urged Douglass to knock these stories down. "Haytians generally are very sensitive to this matter of losing their autonomy," he wrote Douglass. "It is the one subject in which they all intensely agree."[6]

Given all the fierce lobbying that Bassett had made toward Douglass, and given the fact that he had been unable to secure another appointment, the two returned to conversations about Bassett joining him as his secretary. Bassett proposed that Douglass recommend to the Secretary of State a new position of deputy consul general, but even that was turned down by the bureaucracy. However, with the wealth of information that Bassett supplied the abolitionist leader, and because he himself spoke no French, Douglass saw the wisdom of having the experienced diplomat at his side. Especially because he understood how tricky any negotiations would be for the Mole, Douglass felt he could not have chosen a stronger or more trusted person to lean upon before embarking.

Although the salary would only pay $850 annually, Bassett stressed that there were other "legitimate perquisites" that the consulate general had at its fingertips. Assistance with housing and the cheap cost of living on the island were enough for Ebenezer Bassett to take the plunge and return again to the Pearl of the Antilles.

Back on the island, the lame duck Minister Resident John Thompson tried to handle the delicate negotiation between Hyppolite and the remnants of the Legitime regime. Finally overcome by loses, Legitime succumbed to the pressure and resigned the presidency in August of 1889, just as Douglass was preparing to assume his new duties.[7]

Bassett warned Douglass of the still unfolding events with respect to the Mole and the new Hyppolite regime. It was being reported in American newspapers that since finally gaining power, Hyppolite was rethinking his promise to lease the harbor to the U.S. Navy. In an ominous statement of the dangers that lie ahead Bassett warned Douglass: "Great governments do not readily relinquish schemes like that of ours to acquire a foothold in the great pathway of the world's commerce to the isthmus canal."

What was more, they were not only about to enter complicated maneuvers with the Haytian government, but they were also coming into a chaotic situation as regarded lines of authority by the U.S. government. Bassett charged that Minister Thompson had become simply a "figurehead." U.S. Naval Admiral Bancroft Gherardi, who commanded the Caribbean fleet and had been instrumental in supplying Hyppolite's forces during the conflict, was the "real Minister."

"Thompson is a man without ability or even experience outside of Hayti," Bassett vented. Though he had hoped Thompson would be an improvement over John Langston, Bassett had been sorely disappointed in the weakness Thompson had shown by letting Admiral Gherardi run the show.[8]

Making matters worse, Thompson turned out not only to be inexperienced, but apparently also corrupt. He was reported to have been involved in an effort to pocket $25,000 of the money awarded from the arbitrator of the case surrounding the detention of the ship *Haytian Republic.* Bassett told Douglass that it had resulted in a complaint lodged against Thompson during the end of the Cleveland administration—but that nothing had been done about it. These were charges similar to ones that General Legitime himself made against Thompson, though none of them were ever proven.

In spite of the various challenges that awaited them, Bassett was supremely confident that they would master the situation. "I have no fears on the score of your and myself being able to face the music and to hold our own in the diplomatic dance around the Haytian plum when once we are on the scene."[9]

As Frederick Douglass and his second wife, Helen, prepared to finally leave, a media frenzy developed around their mission, particularly because Helen was a white woman heading to the Black Republic. Douglass had apparently been slated to sail with a different captain aboard the U.S. naval vessel, *Kearsarge,* but that captain had refused to serve as host to a black man, even one so distinguished as Frederick Douglass. The Secretary of the Navy was forced to relieve him of his command. They departed with a new captain, seen off by tremendous crowds from the Brooklyn port on October 1, 1889.[10]

On board with them was Ebenezer Bassett, officially described as Douglass's secretary. It must have been a bittersweet reminder of his sendoff almost two decades earlier. But none of those crowds were there to see him that day.

Even as the newspapers were filled with stories of the Great Douglass, it was obvious that Bassett would be no ordinary assistant.

"Mr. Douglass is well advanced in years and although in good health, cannot be expected to attend to the routine duties of the office," ran one piece. "The diplomatic language of Hayti is French, and Mr. Bassett is an accomplished French scholar. He spent several years on the island and is familiar with the people and their institutions. For this reason he has been chosen by Mr. Douglass to go with him and act as a sort of sub-Minister. . . . Mr. Bassett's position will be more important than that of private secretary. He will be Minister Douglass's right-hand man while in Hayti, and be responsible to the Minister for the conduct of the office."

The press also raised another reason Bassett chose to accompany Douglass, in spite of no official title. "If [Douglass] resigns, it may be in the order of things for Bassett to succeed the Ministry. He knows the country from top to bottom and it would not be surprising to me to see him Minister to Hayti again before another year has passed."[11]

This may have been Bassett's strategy all along as well, but in spite of his bravado about being able to face the music, he would soon realize that things were going to become much more difficult than he had imagined.

The first year in Hayti was one during which the new regime struggled to quickly get on its feet. Among the choices of Hyppolite's cabinet, Bassett must have noted with great interest, was Septimus Rameau's nephew, Dantes. Stephen Preston, who had managed to maneuver, snake-like, through so many changes of Haytian administrations, had finally reached the end of his run of luck. Hannibal Price would replace him as minister in Washington.

As the new legislature was chosen in early 1890, Bassett helped Douglass untangle the confusing system and personalities that would become valuable contacts for the Americans. Reporting back to Washington, Douglass' notes read more like drafts that Bassett himself had put together; the sense of history and nuanced analysis was something that the freshly arrived Douglass would not have managed on his own.

"No matter what party is in power here, the administration is usually charged with the exercise of improper and undue influence to defeat the popular will. The present administration has not escaped this common reproach," Douglass told the State Department once the new Corps Legislatif had been seated. These were words for which Bassett knew the reality only all too well.[12]

Nevertheless, all ran fairly smooth, if not routine during those first months in place. Progress seemed on the way as construction of a cable was completed connecting Port-au-Prince to Mole St. Nicolas, which in turn connected the country to other islands and the United States. This increased the importance of the Mole as a strategic communication center as well.

Bassett, who was clearly in the background, helped Douglass interpret and come to know all the influencers on the island. President Hyppolite himself said that Douglass was a symbol of "the greatest proof of respect which the Government of the United States has given to us."[13] If Bassett chaffed under the role of second fiddle, he showed no signs of strain or jealousy.

Douglass and Bassett both returned to the United States the summer of 1890 as the new Haytian legislature got off the ground and a sense of normalcy returned to the island. While Douglass went back to his home in Anacostia, Bassett traveled to New Haven, where he was greeted by his group of friends as a returning hero.

"The 'boys' up at the club received me with cheers, and gave me a right royal reception. Indeed if I were only just a few years younger, I might, from the greeting that I received on every hand here, flatter myself that I belong to the class known up this way as 'little great men of a country village,'" Bassett lightly bragged to Douglass.[14]

It was not only a simple matter of basking in the glory of friends back home, but it was also time for Bassett to do some serious consultation during this vacation. Continuing newspaper reports of shipping companies being unhappy with Douglass' work concerned Ebenezer. He knew from his many years of experience that the New York shippers could be a fickle lot, and not above bending the law when it was to their advantage, as the munitions runners found during the Haytian civil war. This was particularly true of the Clyde Steamer line, which wanted a special concession as a reward for their work in supplying Hyppolite during the war. Bassett went to meet with the shippers in New York and what he found was a cordial reception, but an unwillingness to engage in real discussions about the so-called complaints.

Bassett wrote over twenty letters that summer to Douglass, keeping him up-to-date on the political happenings of the country, offering advice on actions to take while in Washington, and constantly asking the Douglass family to visit them in Connecticut. But the tropics had not been kind to the aged leader, and Douglass spent a great part of the summer recuperating at his home. Another common subject in all of that correspondence was Bassett's desire to gain another posting of his own as minister resident. He busily lobbied the senators in his home state and asked Douglass to meet with Secretary Blaine at the State Department as well. Although Bassett may have burned his bridges earlier by working for the Legitime regime, he hoped that his dedication to Douglass and the U.S. mission in Port-au-Prince would now sway opinions in his favor.

Ironically, Bassett seemed to be concerned that his race would be an issue for receiving a future appointment. Whether he could take Douglass' job once he eventually resigned, or obtain another posting, the fact was that black men had only been appointed to Hayti and Liberia in the diplomatic corps. And the mood of the 1890s political landscape had changed a great deal since the era of Reconstruction.

Writing Douglass again on the matter of an appointment, Bassett wondered: "I presume that there is no question of my capacity to fill the place out there or any other like it. But there will remain the question as to my *representative* character," he wrote, in a reference to his color. It was clear that Bassett felt limited by race as a symbol or even as a barrier to overcome.

It was also apparent that personal loyalty was the most important aspect for Bassett in his relationship with Douglass. Concluding the letter he said: "Also my plans are more for returning with you. I'll stick it out down there with you just as long as you wish to stay." He closed by noting optimistically that his first year had gone fairly well, and said "it is not at all likely that your next year there will be any less victorious than the first."[15]

Though there was incredible respect for the legendary figure that Frederick Douglass projected, it was one thing to worship that image from afar and another to have to negotiate with the actual man. He had not even been in Port-au-Prince for half a year when stories began leaking out about how suspicious Haytians were of him and how unpopular a minister resident he was turning out to be.

John Langston, who, since returning to the United States, had served in the U.S. House of Representatives, speculated that from the very start, the government was against Douglass. "He now goes back to the country on a war vessel, and his secretary, Mr. Bassett, was as Consul in New York in the pay of the party which is now out of power in Hayti. It may be that the Haytians fear Douglass, I do not know."[16]

Fear was not an emotion that either Douglass or Bassett wished to strike with their new interlocutors. But fear was something that seemed to suit Admiral Gherardi just fine. It would become Gherardi's favored method as he pressed Washington to do away with all restrictions, allowing him to gain the Mole.

Just as Douglass and Bassett were preparing to return to Port-au-Prince in October of 1890, Douglass received a letter from the State Department requesting that he remain in Washington for important meetings. Bassett, who had sent his luggage to New York for departure, was left literally holding the bag. Rumors abounded that Douglass was about to be forced out of office. Even worse, he was hearing the rumors that Blaine had involved them in some nefarious schemes, to which Bassett wrote Douglass, "You are not the kind of man to carry out down there!" Bassett warned his friend that it appeared some trap was being laid, though the details he apparently did not know.[17]

Indeed, Douglass sent Bassett ahead to return to Port-au-Prince alone, while he remained in Washington for the mysterious meetings. It turned out that these were the initial discussions about plans to obtain the Mole St. Nicholas. Bassett was skeptical that this could successfully be negotiated, knowing the existential fears that Haytian people felt about their hard-won territorial integrity. He remembered one of his first issues was to negotiate with President Salnave, who offered him the Mole as he was about to fall from power. Then, as now, such moves were made from desperation and resulted in a backlash. But little did they realize the surprise in store for them all.

Douglass returned that November and soon made quiet inquiries with the Haytian Foreign Minister about a lease of the Mole. He found Minister Antenor Firmin almost frightened by the possibility. Douglass later wrote to Blaine of the meeting that Hayti "began life with all the world against them," and it would be a difficult process under which to conduct all the negotiation. Nevertheless, with time and patience he thought it could be successful.[18]

Time, however, was not on Douglass' side. Just a few weeks later, Admiral Gherardi arrived aboard his flagship, *Philadelphia*, with a special note from Secretary Blaine.

It seemed that Gherardi, rather than Douglass, had been given the authority to negotiate for the Mole. Douglass considered resigning in protest, but, as he later wrote, "I consoled myself with the thought that I was acting like a good soldier."[19]

Bassett and Douglass set up a meeting with Foreign Minister Firmin and President Hyppolite in late January 1891. But the paranoid Gherardi would not allow Douglass to bring Bassett with him. Instead he brought his young staff lieutenant, fluent in French, to act as an interpreter. It left Douglass at a distinct disadvantage. As he would later write of the occasion, "I have reason to regret the absence of Mr. Bassett for it left me at the mercy of men whom, I begin to think, have intentionally misrepresented me."[20]

During the meeting, Gherardi took the lead, pressing hard on the fact that Hyppolite had promised the Mole during the rebellion after gaining U.S. support. The ham-handed manner with which Gherardi was conducting the negotiations not only disturbed the Haytians but also disturbed Douglass—and Bassett, when he heard. Of greatest difficulty was Gherardi's assertion that Haytians were not allowed to make similar leases to any other country. It was an attempt to block out European influence, but it was also clearly interference with Haytian sovereignty. Douglass tried to calm the waters, but the damage of indelicately forcing Hyppolite's hand was already done.

"It was alleged that, though our government did not authorize Rear Admiral Gherardi to overthrow Legitime and to set up Hyppolite as President of Hayti, it gave him a wink, and left him to assume the responsibility," Douglass later wrote. "I did not accept this as a foundation upon which I could base my diplomacy."[21]

Foreign Minister Firmin asked to see Gherardi's authority, which he noticed had only been signed by Secretary Blaine. The wily Haytian thought this insufficient and asked for President Harrison's signature on a similar document and for the proposal in writing. Gherardi left in a huff, promising the new credential in just days. But strangely, that letter was not forthcoming.

Afterwards, the foreign minister sought Bassett out and let him know their true concerns. Despite the support from the United States, Hyppolite's government felt it could not withstand the domestic pressure if it turned over any land to foreigners. "Why, if this government were to do that even, it could not stand three month," Firmin told him.[22]

Meanwhile it also seemed a policy fight had broken out in Washington on just how hard to push the Haytians. Gherardi was ready for war, and Blaine seemed to be in his corner. Gherardi had even written Blaine saying that Douglass supported the forceful taking of the Mole. Taking the undiplomatic counterattack, Douglass wrote his boss saying that the Admiral had been "amazingly inaccurate" and it was of "startling injustice" to say he supported war.[23]

Cooler heads finally prevailed and Harrison's letter months later granted joint authority to both Douglass and Gherardi to negotiate for the lease. As these new negotiations stalled, the admiral even threatened the Haytians by bringing a squadron of seven warships into territorial waters. But Hayti held firm. Douglass was left to write back to Blaine simply a one-sentence telegram: "Hayti has declined lease of Mole."[24]

Furious, Gherardi left. To Douglass and Bassett it was clear that the admiral had done more harm than good in the negotiations: "What wisdom was there in confronting Haiti at such a moment with a squadron of large ships of war with a hundred cannon and two thousand men? . . . We appeared before the Haitians, and before the world, with the pen in one hand and the sword in the other . . . We should have known that, whatever else the Haitian people may be, they are not cowards, and hence not easily scared."[25]

Adding to the confusion, a new battle began in Port-au-Prince with forces rising against President Hyppolite just as the Mole talks collapsed. During the celebration of the Feast of Corpus Christi, an angry rebellion began against the government. It seemed that Hyppolite's fears were right, but he brutally crushed the uprising, personally leading the charge.

During the battles, Douglass was trapped at a café. Bassett, who had joined him for dinner, took Douglass by the arm, rushing him toward safety. A reign of terror overtook the small capital, and the U.S. Legation was forced to take refugees for a time until a sense of calm returned.

Between his continuing health problems, the collapse of the Mole negotiation, and now this latest uprising, it was clear that Douglass no longer had the diplomatic stomach for it all. A few weeks later he packed his belongings, sold a good deal of his other items, and left Port-au-Prince to return to Washington.

Newspaper reports soon depicted the scenario as one where Douglass had been run out of town, fleeing for his life. Returning to the United States, he was forced to deny those charges. He also had to knock down stories that he had been recalled, as well as a worse rumor: that diplomatic relations had been broken between the two countries.[26]

In reality Douglass had left under threat of violence and with the Mole negotiations in tatters. Making matters worse, he also found new ire with the failure to help secure the Clyde concession. William P. Clyde and Co. wanted that concession from the Haytian government to establish a route of steamers between New York and Port-au-Prince. When Haiti demurred on this, just as they had with the Mole, Clyde and the New York shippers howled that Douglass had botched those talks as well.

As a result of these perceived failures, pressure began to build on Douglass to resign. The *Chicago Tribune* was among the first to make this call: "If all reports from Hayti be correct, there does not seem to be any way out of the present unfortunate complications in which Minister Frederick Douglass has involved American interests in that country except by his prompt resignation." The paper went on to add "there is no question in department circles at Washington that Mr. Douglass's administration of our interests has been a failure and that he is incompetent to hold the position." Giving further insult to the abolitionist leader, the paper said that it would be preferable to have a white man as the next minister.[27]

Back in New Haven on leave, Bassett read the flurry of newspaper articles on all sides of the debate. The majority in the media were harshly opposed to Douglass returning, saying he was acting more as a representative of the "negroes" than of the United States.

In the face of growing pressure, Bassett told his friend to remain strong: "I think you owe it to Hayti and to our race to hold right where you are. No other man of our race could fill just the breach that you now fill. You hold the fort. You stand between a handful of our people . . . and the devouring wolves gnashing their teeth in all the panoply of racial hatred to get at them. . . . Don't stir, don't move even an inch from where you now stand. Don't even whisper about resigning, for the moment you do that, the jig is up for Haiti."[28]

Bassett had also moved beyond simply toeing the line as the good soldier for American policy. He understood the effects that a takeover of the Mole would have on long-term Haytian relations, and most importantly, he feared, on their very autonomy. This issue was important for him not simply because of his obvious tie to Hayti as a country, but also for what that nation represented as the Black Republic. American control of the Mole would certainly not be in the best interest of Hayti, and he feared not in the best long-term interest of the United States either. He thought American racism would surely grind at Haytians' autonomy, provoking further violence and the loss of American lives. Just as he had been willing to stand up to the politicians in Washington on issues of asylum, again he urged a course of integrity and courage.

However, Douglass was not the only one to come under withering attack from the media. The *New York Sun* ran an interview with a "Haytian refugee" who had supposedly fled the island with the latest wave of violence. This unnamed source charged that Bassett was the man actually responsible for all of the calamity.

"The private secretary is Mr. Bassett, a mulatto, who has won the distrust of the whole population of Port-au-Prince," charged this refugee. The source further claimed that Bassett's return to the island as a "secretary" had aroused suspicion among the Haytians. His position led some to question Douglass' competence and suspect that Bassett was manipulating him. Most damning, however, was the charge leveled against Bassett that he had actually accepted the job only to enrich himself, even pocketing $15,000 in the process. "It was owing to his incompetence or fraudulent practices that the United States was deprived of the opportunity of purchasing this important coaling station," concluded the refugee.[29]

A man normally reluctant to engage in a public fight, Bassett was enraged with these charges. The very next day he went to the papers to deny the accusations. "They say that Mr. Douglass is completely at my mercy?" Bassett shot back at the paper. "He is a man thoroughly capable of acting for himself and does so act." Bassett went on to deny that he had enriched himself through Haytian dealings. This was especially ironic given his dire financial state, but he made no mention of that matter.[30]

The personal attacks also forced Douglass to speak out, defending himself and his secretary. Douglass denied that Bassett was hated by anyone in Hayti. "I can say with emphasis that it is not true that Mr. Bassett is an object of distrust in the eyes of the honest people of Port-au-Prince. On the contrary, I was daily surprised and gratified by the evidences of esteem in which he was held by the people of Port-au-Prince."[31]

Douglass, however, was old, tired, and had been unwell for much of his time in Port-au-Prince. Returning to the States expecting to recover, he had found that the attacks only continued, no matter what he said or did. In addition, he felt he did as much as humanly possible to walk the fine line between faithfully carrying out orders and truly protecting U.S. and Haytian interests.

Because it was obvious that these critics and "refugees" were actually those with financial ties to shipping interests, and undoubtedly white men, remaining the target for months longer simply made no sense. He wrote to Bassett on July 28 to break the news; he would resign as minister resident.

Bassett immediately wrote back expressing his regret. "Of my life with you in the West Indies, I can on my part most sincerely say to you just what you say to me, namely, our relations during the past two years have been intimate, confidential, and every way pleasant. No shadow that I know of has fallen between us. We joined hands as friends. I trust we part the same . . . And we ought both of us to find a crowning satisfaction in the renewed assurance which you give me that 'our work at the State Department is approved.'"

Always angling, Bassett concluded by asking for additional support in his own quest to gain another posting and requested that Douglass speak personally with President Harrison.[32]

Douglass, who had held his tongue for months while he had been excoriated in the media, finally lashed out after resigning by writing two articles in the *North American Review,* placing blame squarely with Gherardi. It created quite a stir in Washington, and any chance Bassett may have once had for gaining a posting went up in smoke with the burning words of Douglass.

"Thus we had Admiral Gherardi at every turn of Haitian affairs. It was his suggestion that a new minister was appointed. It was he who made American influence paramount in Haiti. It was he who was to conduct the negotiations for the naval station. It was he who counseled the State Department at Washington. It was he who decided the question of the fitness of the American Ministers at Haiti . . . no better way could have been devised to arouse the suspicion of Haitian statesmen and lead them to reject our application for a naval station than to make such representations as these coming from the decks of the flag-ship of Rear-Admiral Gherardi."[33]

Bassett said little further publicly about the breakdown over the Mole, taking the high road a few years later in a book he authored for the State Department on Hayti. "The importance which Haiti attached to these negotiations, all friendly as they were on the part of the United States, grew partly out of the unmistakable national sensitiveness which permeates all classes there about the most jealous conservation of her autonomy."[34]

But in spite of his reticence, Bassett continued to be the target of scurrilous attacks, even accused of being a Haytian agent. But Douglass always defended the man that had faithfully served at his side.

Douglass later wrote: "It is true that Mr. E.D. Bassett is my private secretary and interpreter and usually attended me whenever I held interview with the government of Haiti. It is true that his knowledge of the French language, as well as his experience in diplomacy having held the office of Minister to Haiti nine years made him very important to me. It is true that in the way of gaining important information by writing with the people as well as his knowledge of the form of diplomatic correspondence, I was much indebted to him. It is true that I have deemed myself fortunate in having a secretary so well qualified for the position he fills. All this is true. But it is not true that Mr. Bassett did override the Minister. What he did, was well done, but done as my private secretary. He spoke and wrote subject to my supervision and I am responsible for every word spoken or written in my name by him. . . . I owe it to Mr. Bassett to state that I have never found him other than a truthful and faithful man. If he ever gained much or lost heavily by gaming or lived luxuriously, it never came to my knowledge. So much I deem it due to say for a man whom I consider shamefully abused."[35]

In fact, Bassett was still desperately hoping against all odds that he would receive another diplomatic posting. He failed to realize that in spite of the strongest defense Douglass could muster, no one was in any mood to reward the man that had failed to deliver the Mole St. Nicholas into American hands.

14

Final Homecoming

Ebenezer Bassett was dejected at not being able to obtain a posting again with the State Department. After Douglass resigned, President Harrison named John Durham to Port-au-Prince. Durham was an alumnus of the Institute for Colored Youth, graduating there in 1876. Bassett knew that at the very least this was a young man who would be well educated to solidly represent the United States.[1]

Though the bureaucrats in Washington would not give Ebenezer Basset a foreign assignment, they recognized the expertise that he possessed when it came to Hayti. The Bureau of the American Republics was updating material that their own diplomats used to understand other countries. When they needed someone to write a new book on Hayti, they turned to Bassett as their author. He spent the next year completing a revised edition of *Hayti: State Department Bulletin Number 62*, which was over two hundred pages long and provided an overview of historical events leading up to those of the present day.

Sticking largely with facts, Bassett's narrative included descriptions of topography and climate, flora and fauna, social and educational structures, as well as the lives of the political figures. He also peppered the book with his first-hand recollections of life on the island. "It is said that no city, in proportion to extent and population, has more dogs than Port-au-Prince except Constantinople, but they are mostly of the 'cur' species, and they never fail to announce their presence on the slightest provocation, especially at night time," he wrote, adding flavor to what might have otherwise been a dry synopsis.

In another amusing passage, Bassett described an image he must have witnessed on numerous occasions: "The donkey is very common and

very useful everywhere in the country, and his proverbial docility, relia-
bility, and enduring strength there reach their height. He seems, besides,
to have acquired an understanding of the creole intonations on the word
la, which would puzzle even the intelligent foreigner for weeks, for his
mountaineer master cries out to him *la, la* when he is to go ahead, or back,
or stop, or turn to the right or the left, and he appears to know what is
expected of him by the intonation."

His telling of Haytian history was straightforward, doing little to veer
into controversy. When he wrote about the current regime, he noted that
"in spite of the criticism passed upon President Hyppolite, he is, nevertheless, a man of experience in the public affairs of his country, and has
shown capacity and dignity in office."

He assiduously avoided a prolonged discussion of the Mole St. Nicholas,
however, which was remarkable given the amount of time and interest that
the State Department had just spent on the issue. Only two paragraphs in
passing were written on the subject in which he understatedly noted:
"Great stress was laid on the recent negotiations for the cession or lease to
the Mole St. Nicholas for a naval station."

Rather than rehash those painful events, he obliquely quoted the
President of the Dominican Republic, who said: "I know very well that
what the great powers think they need, they must sooner or later have.
But if they take time to decide about making the initial request, they
must give us time to decide whether we can grant it. It will be found
that in reference to all matters of international moment, the people of
Hayti are not altogether insensible to or incognizant of the tendency of
things, the march of events, the spirit of the times."[2]

While Bassett was working on the book, he had also settled at home
again in New Haven and became reengaged in Republican politics. The
1892 presidential election was an important one as Lincoln's party hoped
to retain control of the White House, and black voters were an important
part of that equation. In May of 1892, the Republican State Convention
met in Hartford to discuss support for the reelection of President Harrison.
Though local politics was dominated by white leaders, they made a special effort to include Ebenezer Bassett as a spokesman for "the colored
race."[3] Harrison would go on to win the nomination but lost in his
rematch to Democrat Grover Cleveland, further removing Bassett from
the halls of power.

Since returning to the United States he also remained in touch with
Frederick Douglass. By 1893, Eliza and Ebenezer would frequently stay
with their daughter Charlotte in Philadelphia, and it was at her 29th
Street address that they learned of the death of Douglass's own grand-
daughter. The couple sent a simple note expressing their heartfelt

sympathies and asked that "Heaven help you to bear up with fortitude under this great trial."[4]

The final correspondence between the great civil rights leader and Ebenezer Bassett passed a few months later, in January of 1894. Douglass had written wishing him well over the holidays. In response, Bassett again poured his heart out to his close friend.

"I certainly join you with all my heart in the wish that our lifelong friendship may continue to the end. For my part I have no idea that it can be otherwise," Bassett promised. He also confided that his finances were weighing heavily on them, having amassed a debt that he was still hopeful of getting off his back. Unlike in previous letters, Bassett did not ask for any political support from Douglass to help secure him a job, but clearly the family was struggling to make ends meet. Almost too embarrassed to discuss the problem, Bassett continued, "Indeed I feel that it would pain you if I were here to go into details of the situation as it has all along been with me since I saw you and as it is with me today. Promises of returns made from investments made years ago, and from money lent to individuals when I was consul in New York, and worse of all promises of employment, have all failed me. But I am far from giving up the race of life."

Ebenezer also wanted to address concerns that had resurfaced after the failure of the Mole negotiations. Responding to rumors that sought to blame Bassett and discredit his work, critics charged that he duped both Douglass and the Haytians by mistranslating material and receiving money under the table. How someone who remained as financially strapped as Bassett was supposed to have been rolling in illicit profits was irrelevant to his enemies; he was simply a convenient scapegoat. But Bassett wanted to reassure his friend that there was never any truth to those malicious lies.

"I was under the impression that almost every gross misinterpretation possible had already been made concerning me while I was with you in Haiti. But this one that I received $5000 for keeping you friendly with Hyppolite's government is entirely new to me, and I think that, like others of its kind, it carries on its face its own contradiction. Just look at it," he told Douglass.

"And least of all could anyone who knows General Hyppolite and his advisors believe that they or men like them could possible be duped on facts before their eyes in the manner alleged for one moment, much less from day to day through nearly two years?" he incredulously asked.

It was a cathartic letter, and though neither of the two men knew it would be the last communication between them, Bassett concluded by reiterating his admiration and commitment to the icon whom he had followed over four decades: "No my dear friend, there never was one man more faithful and devoted to the interests of another than I was to you in Haiti in every respect and without exception."[5] A year later, Douglass died.

Tragedy continued in 1895 when he lost the woman who had been his companion, confidant, and greatest supporter over those same years. Eliza Bassett died that August. No records of her illness, and little information about her life, were available aside from brief references made to her graciousness and excellence as a hostess for diplomatic events. She was a selfless woman, accompanying her husband amidst danger and disease in the Caribbean, giving birth to eight children, five of whom survived into adulthood.

Eliza was buried in the Grove Street Cemetery in New Haven, leaving her husband at home with sixteen-year-old Wendell. Their other children had all grown by that point. Charlotte continued teaching at the Institute of Colored Youth, and Ulysses had just graduated from Yale University when their mother passed away. Pulling together for a time, much of the family united once again upon Eliza's passing and moved temporarily into the house in Philadelphia.[6]

Douglass' death, also, marked the end of an era. His absence from the scene finally passed the torch to the next generation, those who had not lived through the final years of slavery or the bloody Civil War. Although many of the new African American leaders of the day had seen the Reconstruction period, most were only witness to the declining years of federal protection that the end of the nineteenth century brought.

Since then, black Americans had seen their rights eroded to almost nil in many parts of the country, and ironically this erosion occurred in those areas where numerically they were strongest. The 1896 *Plessey v. Ferguson* case by the Supreme Court seemingly put the final nail in the coffin of efforts toward racial equality and harmony. That decision, which legalized state and local efforts of segregation, accompanied an uptick in violence against blacks across the country. White racists now felt they could act with impunity when the highest court in the land ruled in favor of "separate but equal" facilities.

In spite of his personal pain at the loss of his wife and close friend, Bassett did not give up his activism. Now speaking as an elder, he lent his voice to those protesting this disturbing trend of racial violence. In 1898, when race riots broke out in Indiana and the Carolinas, Bassett was among those that organized a meeting in New York City to seek solutions. Gathering at the Cooper Union in November of that year, Bassett presided as chairman to a group of over six hundred concerned citizens that sought ways to address this spread of racial warfare.

Local ministers and community leaders urged the crowd to maintain a nonviolent position, but several members of the audience shouted their disapproval. The largely black assembly grew agitated and demanded action. However, a hush fell over the group when sixty year old Ebenezer Bassett called the meeting to order. He understood the audience's impatience and shared their concerns about being taken for granted by a government that had left them vulnerable. The long-time diplomat brought a sense of calm to the proceedings by announcing that in the interest of friendship, he hoped that they could proceed to discuss the issues in peace and without violent or provocative language. In fact, numerous New York City police officers were there gauging the sentiments and acting as a buffer against the angry people in the crowd.

The first speaker, Thomas Fortune continued in this tone, saying: "We don't come here with dynamite up our sleeves or Winchesters on our shoulders, although we are people who are never shot in the back. We appeal to white Caesar drunk, to white Caesar sober. Shall we get our rights?"

When the crowd yelled in support, many shouted that they must fight for those rights. Fortune tried to bring them back to the point, imploring the crowd, "it doesn't do to butt your head against a brick wall."

Bassett stepped in once again to control the situation. "This meeting is called in the interest of civilization and good citizenship," he exhorted them. "We are here to warn our fellow citizens that the disregard of law and the resort to violence will lead to destruction. It is not the purpose of this meeting to indulge in violent language, but to make recommendations that will appeal to the judgment and good sense of the American people."

In the end he succeeded in swaying the emotional group and gained agreement on a resolution demanding that Southern states obey the law and ensure the full franchise for black citizens. "Resolved: That we recommend such Amendment to the Constitution as will enable the President to use the federal authority to protect the life and property of citizens of the United States from organized or mob conspiracy whenever the Governor of any state, from fear of collusion, neglects to afford such protections or to call upon the federal government to afford it." Similar meetings were held in Boston, Philadelphia, Chicago, and Washington.[7]

In the end, however, Bassett must have been frustrated that he and fellow black leaders were swimming against a racial tide. Arguments in favor of protecting black voters were all too similar to ones he had made in the 1850s as a young leader in the Convention of Colored Men. Now, here he was pleading the same case years after a civil war and constitutional amendments should have resolved the issue. Making matters worse, the level of violence against black communities in the country left few with a sense of hope for better relations. And in light of the *Plessey* decision, it must have been hard to maintain a sense of optimism about equality.

But the United States of 1898 was more consumed with other issues aside from its own domestic racial strife. A war broke out with Spain over problems that had been brewing for decades. Spanish dominance over its remaining Caribbean colonies, particularly Cuba, had been an open wound since Bassett's time in Port-au-Prince as minister resident. He had even been forced to confront a Spanish man-of-war as it blockaded the American-flagged *Hornet*. Cubans remained steadfast in their fight for independence since that time, and while America had stayed on the sideline until the 1890s, it was clear that they would remain neutral no longer. With work underway for an isthmus canal, and so much at stake for American dominance in the Caribbean, the two sides would finally come to blows after the destruction of the USS *Maine* in the harbor of Havana.

The United States went on to quickly rout the Spanish navy, and by the end of the conflict, the U.S. had gained control of several important parts of the decaying Spanish empire. Puerto Rico, the Philippines, Guam, and Cuba were among the major prizes. Hayti, fearful the United States was attempting to take over the entire Caribbean, asked Bassett back to serve as vice consul in New York City in 1898. It would be a position he held until his death.[8]

Unlike during his previous stints, Bassett remained out of the spotlight, providing quiet support to the office and the new leadership of President Tiresias Simon Sam in Port-au-Prince. But the events in that always turbulent country roiled out of control yet again in 1899. Uprisings there forced several Haytians to seek asylum in foreign legations, including that of the United States. When one local journalist came to the American Legation seeking help, he was dragged out and arrested by the police, in violation of the sovereignty of a U.S. diplomatic mission.

Bassett seemed perplexed when he was quoted in the papers as to what was happening down there. "I cannot understand it," he told reporters. "I have always understood that [the asylees] were favorable to the President. Mr. Fouchard, the former Minister of Finance, has always been of an eminently amiable and peaceable disposition. . . . Mr. Menos, former Minister of Foreign Affairs, who is said to have taken refuge in the American Legation, is one of the most distinguished lawyers of the republic, and a man of high intellectual and social attainments."

Seeming almost out of touch with the reality on the ground, Bassett told the media: "President Sam has always enjoyed the confidence of the country. He was Minister of War and Marine when President Hyppolite died suddenly of apoplexy while on horseback in 1896. He was not a candidate for the Presidency, but everybody turned to him instinctively as the one most fitted for the Presidency. He is a kind-hearted man of generous impulses, moderation, and sound common sense. He is naturally opposed to govern by arbitrary means and his Administration has been just and lenient."[9]

In reality President Sam followed in the long line of Haytian rulers who brutally put down all challengers. He had his own record of going against authority when he served under President Hyppolite, who later exiled him for his insurgent activities. Now he controlled the country with ferocity, but not in a manner out of the norm for Hayti. Serving as a vice consul, Bassett was responsible for offering defenses of the government, but his statements clearly indicated that his "elder" status put him more out of the loop internationally than as a real player.

If the dawn of the new century did not offer much more than hope of racial improvement, it brought a tremendous growth for the United States as a world power. As work proceeded on the canal, then underway in the newly established country of Panama, some Americans were looking for additional outposts in the Caribbean. Bassett, however, remained steadfast as a champion of independence for Hayti. In 1904 he authored an article in *Voice of the Negro* replying to the efforts by Idaho Senator Weldon Heyburn's resolution that Hayti be annexed to the United States. The resolution did not proceed beyond the Senate Foreign Relations Committee, but its proposal brought to the fore those old fears of outsiders taking over.

"It can be safely set down as positive fact that Haiti does not now and in all probability never will desire or consent to share her sovereignty with any other power whatsoever," Bassett wrote in the article. "Furthermore, Haiti is by far the most advanced the most important and the best established of the only three Republics in the world, where alone the Negro race has full and untrammeled liberty to develop its faculties and its possibilities." Bassett concluded his examination by simply asking, "Should Haiti be annexed to the United States?" His answer was definite and resounding: "Why, no, no. Let Haiti alone; let her alone to work out her mission for the children of Africa in the New World and to fulfill her destiny among the Nations of the Earth."[10]

Even if Haytians were disposed toward putting themselves under American control, as Puerto Ricans had been, the "race question" would obviate any perceived benefits of potential citizenship, Bassett argued. Turn-of-the-century America, while perhaps not more racist than during the time of the Civil War, had still not come to terms with its social inequities. Jim Crow segregation was now commonly practiced through much of the country and was legally sanctioned in all of the states of the old Confederacy as well as in the border states.

Ebenezer Bassett also maintained his interest and involvement in his first professional field—education. Although he had been out of this profession for several years, his daughter and son would both work in this field.

Bassett himself clearly stressed the need for the growing population of black students to meet high standards and for black teachers to be given the opportunities to teach. Although he was not an advocate of segregation, he felt that black teachers were uniquely qualified to instruct black students. He wrote on this matter in one piece on education in the city of Philadelphia: "I will, however, say this, that I wish that colored teachers might be employed wherever there is any considerable number of our own pupils; for there is no doubt in my mind that our own young women and young men are better adapted to governing, inspiring and teaching our children than white teachers, who cannot in the actual condition of things have much individual or social sympathy with them."

He noted with disdain the tendency in Philadelphia schools that teachers tended to seat black students together in groups, away from white students. Although segregation was not the law in most northern localities, social pressures raised an ugly specter for these children. Bassett was also angered by the tendency to push black students into technical programs, not allowing many to get the broader, classical education that colleges demanded. It relegated these students to menial jobs—and even these were often closed to them because of racial prejudice.

"For my part I insist that all this prevalent idea of teaching the Afro-American only how to work or to learn trades that he is systemically and shamefully kept from working at, is a fair off-shoot to the un-American untenable theory that somehow he is essentially different from other people and in inevitable tendency of the idea cannot be anything less than the building of a stone wall separating him from the great body of his fellow-citizens and consigning him to a station of inferiority, and if carried out it cannot fail to tend to the perpetuation of distinctions that are odious and repugnant to the true American idea which covers the equality of opportunity and the equality of citizenship and rejects privileged classes, all of which our own free government guarantee to every man under its flag."[11]

Bassett had not been one to quietly settle in his old age. He was sickened by the deterioration of racial progress since the end of Reconstruction. Although the twentieth century offered so many opportunities for economic progress for the United States, political problems would plague the country unless it developed a true rule of law that protected all citizens, regardless of color. Bassett was among those few voices still struggling to be heard about that necessity, and he applied the sample principle to perceptions of race overseas as well.

Remaining the tireless defender of the Caribbean and its blackness, when he read an interview with a Robert Hill in 1901 that claimed cannibalism was prevalent in Hayti, he was quick to attack that rumor. Writing in the *New York Sun* on March 24, 1901, Bassett argued that such claims were based on animus and were merely efforts to "pander to the widespread sentiment of contempt toward the negro race." He argued that in all his time in Hayti he never once saw a true case of cannibalism, stating: "I solemnly declare my unqualified conviction that the whole story about cannibalism in Haiti is nothing more than a myth."[12]

One of the last surviving pieces of correspondence by Bassett was written in 1904. He replied to a letter by Robert Adger of Philadelphia, who had sent him several copies of an image of the radical abolitionist John Brown. Writing from his desk at the Haytian Consulate in New York, Bassett said he would send a copy to the Haytian president, where the image would undoubtedly hang on the palace wall. "Surely you have rendered a real service to our people by placing so perfect a likeness of John Brown within the reach of us all."[13] In spite of his concern at the time of Brown's capture so many years earlier, he remained a true admirer of Brown's legacy and of his dedicated opposition to racial oppression.

The remaining years of his life passed with his children, now all adults. It must have pained him that none had borne him any grandchildren, but because many of their careers had led them to the education of children, it was a gratifying consolation even as he slipped finally from the public eye.

His obituary was simple when it ran on November 15 of 1908. The *New York Times* had over one hundred names of those in the city that had recently passed away. Listed only in alphabetical order, his read simply: "Bassett—146 Fulton St., Brooklyn, Nov 14, Ebenezer D. Bassett."[14]

15 ───────────────────────────────────────

Conclusion

By the end of his life, Ebenezer D. Bassett had been forgotten to history. The early part of the twentieth century would see further struggles against the evils of racism in the United States. However, it would not be until the latter half of the century and the Civil Rights movement that greater racial progress for which Bassett labored would really be made. The nation celebrated the work of contemporary heroes such as Martin Luther King Jr., Thurgood Marshall, and Jackie Robinson. And the United States also looked back at the leaders who paved the way for those giants. Frederick Douglass, Booker T. Washington, and Sojourner Truth were lifted up as examples of great African Americans who had made an impact and whose lives were worthy of celebration. Men and women that had first broken ground in their respective fields were hailed and popularized in stories about their lives.

But for the man who had broken the color barrier in diplomacy, there was an almost complete absence of interest.

It was not until the late 1960s that anyone wrote at length about Bassett. A graduate student in Nebraska, Robert Plante, recorded Bassett's work during his time as minister resident for his master's thesis. Bemoaning a lack of earlier information, Plante sadly noted that Bassett "provides solid achievements as a diplomat for the United States and a representative of the Negro race. . . . [but he] did his job, did it well and was promptly forgotten."[1]

Indeed, a few other small magazine articles later appeared and Bassett's name would be mentioned in encyclopedias of African American history, but nowhere would his full story be told.

Another disadvantage leading to the demise of information was the fact that he had no surviving grandchildren. His oldest daughter Charlotte died suddenly in 1912. His youngest son Wendell passed away in 1916. Lizzie's death occurred in 1920, while his remaining son Ebenezer Junior died in 1922, and Ulysses died in 1942. None of them apparently bore any living children, and with no one to carry on the family legacy, Ebenezer D. Bassett simply faded from view.

I came upon the incredible Bassett story during my first overseas assignment as a U.S. Foreign Service Officer in the Dominican Republic in 1999. Along the walls of the embassy leading to the ambassadorial suite were the photos and images of the former ambassadors and chiefs of mission. To my surprise, several faces among those earliest leaders were black. Equally surprising was the almost complete lack of information about that first black man.

It was Bassett's work that made it possible for Frederick Douglass to become minister resident twenty years after him in 1889. Haiti and Liberia, however, remained as the only locations where black political appointees could be assigned as chief of mission. Though only halting racial progress was made, black Americans slowly began making inroads across the service. The year 1897 saw George Jackson become the first black consul to pass the Consular Service exam; he was later appointed as consul in Cognac, France. By 1908, eleven African Americans were members of the Diplomatic and Consular Services.

The 1924 Rogers Act radically transformed the diplomatic service, combining the Consular and Diplomatic Corps into one unified professional career, requiring an examination for entrance. Although it did not do away with political appointees receiving ambassadorships, it brought in a cadre of professionals with international experience that would become the backbone of the Department of State.

The same year as the Rogers Act began, Clifton Wharton took the first Foreign Service exam, being one of only twenty people who passed, and making him the first African American Foreign Service Officer (FSO). Shockingly, it would take another twenty years for a second black American to hold the position.

Subsequently the most well-known African American diplomat was Ralph Bunche. His work during the Second World War at the Department of State, as well as his work in establishing the United Nations, made him one of the most prominent black officials of his day. It would not be until 1949, however, that the first African American would hold the title "Ambassador" while serving as chief of a foreign mission. That honor went to Edward Dudley, who was an outstanding lawyer with the NAACP, and appointed by President Harry Truman to serve in Liberia.

The first African American FSO to hold an ambassadorship would be Clifton Wharton, when President Dwight Eisenhower elevated him to head the U.S. Mission in Romania in 1958.

The first African American woman to become an ambassador was Patricia Harris, as President Lyndon Johnson's nominee to serve in 1965 in Luxembourg. New ground was broken again when FSO Terence Todman became the first African American Assistant Secretary of State in 1977, overseeing the Western Hemisphere Bureau. That final barrier would fall in 2001 with the appointment of Colin Powell to be the first African American Secretary of State.

The latest statistics for employment in the Department of State indicate that approximately 31 percent of Civil Service and another 6 percent of FSOs are black. But the Department also noted that 7.4 percent of all new Foreign Service hires are African American as of 2005.[2]

With the wave of immigration from Latin America, Asia, and other parts of the world, the racial dialogue in the United States is no longer simply black and white. And the diplomatic corps represents this diversity as well. But regardless of skin color or national origin, it is important to remember the man that first broke this new ground.

Bassett was not only important as a symbol, however. He also possessed other important qualities that set him apart from his contemporaries, such as his bravery in the face of violence, his humanity and concern for others, and his skill in negotiating. He was gifted at establishing personal relationships with foreign leaders. He also had a tremendous sense of political acumen and his reporting was superb.

His remarkable stance in the Boisrond Canal crisis was one of the most riveting aspects of his life. He vividly reported events to Secretary Hamilton Fish when the events first broke: "Hundreds of ignorant soldiers were posted all around us. They were in a state of excitement and were armed with Henry rifles which they did not know how to use properly. It was no uncommon experience for us to hear these deadly weapons firing off during night time, and we both believed, as I believe yet, that truly it required only one indiscrete word from an under officer even to have caused us all to disappear." Yet in spite of the pressure that a thousand armed soldiers at his doorstep posed, Bassett refused to relent and turn over a man to mob justice.

As he withstood the stress and assisted the Haitian leader in gaining his freedom, he also experienced personal loss. "I do not feel that I ought to trouble you with any further recital of details as to the never to be forgotten experiences through which I and my family have passed here on account of the presence of refugees under our roof . . . It has been a terrible trial for me," he wrote to Secretary Fish.[3] In the days before post traumatic stress syndrome was recognized, that and other experiences must have had a lasting impact on all of the Bassett family.

He would also face the displeasure of the politicians in Washington, actions which undoubtedly cost him additional appointments in the diplomatic corps. This courage to stand up for what he believed in was not just limited to human rights issues. He was also a strong proponent of protecting the independence and sovereignty of other nations against a tide of neocolonialism. When the United States made efforts to take over Haiti or the Dominican Republic, he was there on the scene to argue on behalf of their rights as well. Not one to dissent publicly, Bassett was always faithful in his duties. Yet his understanding of the sentiments and politics of those countries enabled him to advise his superiors about the best course of action, which at times ran counter to policy of the time.

Frederick Douglass, the man who had befriended the young student in 1855 in New Haven, and continued to maintain a relationship with him through the rest of his life, had nothing but positive words about this "gentleman and scholar." Writing in his autobiography, Douglass noted, "It is with a certain degree of pride that I am able to say that my opinion of the wisdom of sending Mr. Bassett to Hayti has been fully justified by the credible manner in which, for eight years, he has discharged the difficult duties of that position, for I have the assurance of Hon. Hamilton Fish, Secretary of State of the United States, that Mr. Bassett was a good minister. In so many words the ex-Secretary told me that he 'wished that one-half of his ministers abroad performed their duties as well as Mr. Bassett.' To those who know Hon. Hamilton Fish, this compliment will not be deemed slight, for few men are less given to exaggerate and act more scrupulously exact in the observance of law and in the use of language than is that gentleman."[4]

History has shown the wisdom of Douglass' support and Fish's sentiments. With 2008 marking the one-hundredth anniversary of his death, it seems only fitting that the world look once again upon the life of this great patriot and diplomat and celebrate.

Notes

Chapter 1

1. "Hayti." *Foreign Relations of the United States (FRUS)*. Washington DC, Government Printing Office, 1875, pp. 686–731.

Chapter 2

1. Valentina Peguero and Danilo de los Santos. *Vision General de la Historia Dominicana*. Universidad Católica Madre y Maestra, 1977, p. 112.

2. H. P. Davis, *Black Democracy,* New York: Dodge Publishing, 1936, p. 23.

3. Bryan Edwards. "An Historical Survey of the Island of Saint Domingo, and Account of the Revolt of Negroes in 1791, and a Detail of the Military Transactions of the British Army in that Island in 1793 and 1794." London, 1796, as cited in Davis, *Black Democracy*, p. 36.

4. Tim Matthewson. *A Proslavery Foreign Policy*. Westport Connecticut: Praeger, 2003, p. 1.

5. Rayford Logan. *The Diplomatic Relations of the United States with Haiti: 1776–1891*. Chapel Hill: University of North Carolina Press, 1941, p. 34.

6. "George Washington to Alexander Hamilton, September 24, 1791." *The Writings of George Washington from the Original Manuscript Sources, 1745–1799*. John C. Fitzpatrick, Editor.—Vol. 31, Mount Vernon, September 24, 1791.

7. "Government of Hayti Arrete." *United States Gazette*, March 29, 1804, Vol. XXV, issue 3579, p. 3.

8. Ludwell Lee Montague. *Haiti and the United States: 1714–1938*, Durham: Duke University Press, 1940, p. 52.

9. "Hayti." *Niles Weekly Register*. September 27, 1823, Baltimore, MD, p. 1.

10. Ludwell Lee Montague, pp. 68–69.

11. Rayford Logan, pp. 216–217.

12. Tim Matthewson, p. 144.

13. Ludwell Lee Montague, p. 53.

14. Ludwell Lee Montague, p. 54.

15. Ludwell Lee Montague, p. 59.

Chapter 3

1. *Congressional Globe*, 37th Congress, 2nd Session, 1862, p. 1773.

2. *Congressional Globe*, 37th Congress, 2nd Session, 1862, p. 1774.

3. *Congressional Globe*, 37th Congress, 2nd Session, 1862, p. 1806.

4. *Congressional Globe*, 37th Congress, 2nd Session, 1862, p. 1806.

5. *Congressional Globe*, 37th Congress, 2nd Session, 1862, p. 1815.

6. *Congressional Globe*, 37th Congress, 2nd Session, 1862, p. 2504.

7. *The Collected Works of Abraham Lincoln*. Vol. 5, Address on Colonization to a Deputation of Negroes, Aug. 14, 1862, New Brunswick, NJ: Rutgers University Press, 1953, pp. 372–375.

8. James Lockett, "Abraham Lincoln and Colonization," *Journal of Black Studies*, Vol. 21, No. 4 (1991), pp. 428–444.

Chapter 4

1. Litchfield Historical Society, "A Brief History of Litchfield," http://www.litchfieldct.com/twn/history.html.

2. Mattatuck Historical Society, "Timeline of Connecticut Slavery," http://www.fortunestory.org/resources/timeline.asp.

3. Israel P. Warren, *Chauncey Judd*, (Naugatuck, CT: The Perry Press, 1874), ch. 20.

4. Nancy O. Phillips, comp., *Town Records of Derby Connecticut, 1655–1710* (Derby, CT: Daughters of the American Revolution, Sarah Riggs Humphreys Chapter, 1901), p. 472.

5. Warren, *Chauncey,* ch. 20.

6. W. C. Sharpe, *History of Oxford* (Seymore, CT: Record Print, 1885).

7. Warren, *Chauncey,* ch. 20.

8. Samuel Orcutt, *The History of the Old Town of Derby, Connecticut, 1641–1880: With Biographies and Genealogies* (Springfield, MA: unknown, 1880), p. 193.

9. David O. White, *Connecticut's Black Soldiers: 1875–1883* (Chester, CT: Pequot Press, 1973), pp. 7, 31–33. White's research indicated a "Tobias Pero" as a troop of the Continental Army, and he mistakenly refers to him as Ebenezer Bassett's father.

10. White, p. 44, citing "To Whom Concern'd, 3/27/1787, in Pay Rolls, Commissary Papers and Miscellaneous Papers Connected with the War of American Revolution, 1776–1833, Shadrach Osborn, comp., Unbound Mss., Connecticut State Library."

11. W. D. Piersen, *Black Yankees: The Development of an Afro-American Subculture in Eighteenth-Century New England* (Amherst: University of Massachusetts Press, 1988), p. 133.

12. Orville Platt, "Negro Governors," *Papers of the New Haven Colony Historical Society* 6 (1900), p. 331.

13. 1800 census record of Amos Bassett, Derby, CT, listed one unnamed slave in the household.

14. Discussions with Bassett family genealogist Jeffrey Bassett have proved enlightening, but at this point, the direct connection between this branch of the family tree and Tobiah cannot be fully drawn through documentation. According to census records, Amos Bassett did own at least one slave in 1800. Amos was also a deacon at the Great Hill Congregational Church, and it could be that "Deacon" Bassett and "Squire" Bassett were one and the same. His brother, Lt. John Bassett, was married to Naomi Wooster (a cousin of Capt. John Wooster, one-time owner of Tobiah). So it is possible to see a slave such as Rachel changing hands from John Wooster, perhaps through his cousin Naomi, to her in-laws, Amos Bassett and family. What is certain is that by the 1840 census, records clearly list the senior Ebenezer as a "free colored person." And Ebenezer does remain living down the street from several of the white Bassett families in Derby during the 1840s.

15. Warren, *Chauncey,* ch. 28.

16. Platt, "Negro Governors," p. 332.

17. The 1850 census listed Susan Bassett as black, along with the rest of her family.

18. "Pequot History," http://www.dickshovel.com/peq.html.

19. According to the 1850 census, she would have been born in 1833, but in the 1860 census, she would have been born in 1832.

20. The 1850 census indicates that Eben Bassett with his wife and three children resided with the family of white Martin B. Bassett and his family. The two heads of household were roughly the same age and must certainly have grown up together.

21. Platt, "Negro Governors," p. 332.

22. Orcutt, *Old Town of Derby*, p. 352.

23. As cited in Orville Platt, "Negro Governors," *Papers of the New Haven Colony Historical Society* 6 (1900), p. 330.

24. George Clark, *A History of Connecticut* (New York: G. P. Putnam's Sons, 1914), pp. 161–163.

25. Robert A. Gibson, "A Deferred Dream: The Proposal for a Negro College in New Haven," *Journal of the New Haven Colony Historical Society, Spring 1991*, p. 2.

26. School records for Ebenezer D. Bassett, Central Connecticut State University Library, Special Collections.

27. Marriage record of Ambrose Beardsley and Mary Bassett, 1837, International Genealogical Index.

28. Orcutt, *Old Town of Derby*, pp. 677–678.

29. School records for Ebenezer D. Bassett, Central Connecticut State University Library, Special Collections.

30. Program for the "Order of Exercises at the Fifth Anniversary of the State Normal School of Connecticut," Central Connecticut State University Library, Special Collections.

31. Howard Bell, "Some Reform Interests of the Negro during the 1850s as Reflected in State Conventions," *Phylon* 21 (Summer 1960): p. 179.

32. James W. C. Pennington is credited with being the first black to study at Yale in the 1830s. *Yale Bulletin and Calendar* 29(19) (February 16, 2001).

33. "Proceedings of the Connecticut State Convention of Colored Men," (New Haven, CT: William H. Stanley Printer, 1849), Samuel J. May Anti-Slavery Collection, Cornell University Library.

34. Charles Wynes, "Ebenezer Don Carlos Bassett, America's First Black Diplomat," *Pennsylvania History* 51 (July 1984): pp. 232–233.

Chapter 5

1. Roger Lane, *Roots of Violence in Black Philadelphia: 1860–1900* (Cambridge, MA: Harvard University Press, 1986), p. 7.

2. Margaret Hope Bacon, "The Pennsylvania Abolition Society's Mission for Black Education," *Pennsylvania Legacies* Vol. 5, No. 2 (November 2005): pp. 21–22.

3. "Memorial of Thirty Thousand Disfranchised Citizens of Philadelphia to the Honorable Senate and House of Representatives," Pamphlets from the Daniel A. P. Murray Collection, 1818–1907, Library of Congress.

4. Benjamin Bacon, "Statistics of the Colored People of Philadelphia," (Philadelphia, PA: Philadelphia Board of Education, 1859), Daniel A. P. Murray Collection, Library of Congress, p. 9.

5. Fanny Jackson-Coppin, *Reminiscences of School Life, and Hints on Teaching* (Philadelphia, PA: L. J. Coppin, 1913), p. 21.

6. Ibid., p. 21.

7. Octavius V. Catto, "Our Alma Mater: An Address Delivered at Concert Hall on the Occasion of the Twelfth Annual Commencement of the Institute for Colored Youth, May 10th, 1864," (Philadelphia, PA: Philadelphia Press, 1864), Pamphlets from the Daniel A. P. Murray Collection, 1818–1907, Library of Congress.

8. C. Peter Ripley, Roy Finkenine, Michael Hembree, and Donald Yacovone, eds., *The Black Abolitionist Papers, Vol. IV: The United States, 1847–1858* (Chapel Hill: University of North Carolina Press, 1991), p. 354.

9. 1860 census, Philadelphia, PA, Ward 7, p. 3.

10. Harry C. Silcox, "Nineteenth Century Philadelphia Black Militant: Octavius V. Catto (1839–1871)," *Pennsylvania History* Vol. 44 (January 1977): pp. 56–57.

11. Benjamin Bacon, "Statistics of the Colored People of Philadelphia," (Philadelphia, PA: Philadelphia Board of Education, 1859), Daniel A. P. Murray Collection, Library of Congress, p. 6.

12. Franklin Sanborn, *The Life and Letters of John Brown* (Boston, MA: Roberts Brothers, 1891), p. 521.

13. Adger to McKinley, October 21, 1904, Carter Woodson Collection, Library of Congress, reel 1.

14. Silcox, "Philadelphia Black Militant," pp. 59–61.

15. "Addresses of the Hon. W. D. Kelley, Miss Anna E. Dickinson, and Mr. Frederick Douglass, at a mass meeting, held at National Hall, Philadelphia, July 6, 1863, for the promotion of colored enlistments," (Philadelphia, PA, 1863), African American Pamphlet Collection, Library of Congress.

16. "Addresses of the Hon. W. D. Kelley, Miss Anna E. Dickinson, and Mr. Frederick Douglass, at a mass meeting, held at National Hall, Philadelphia, July 6, 1863, for the promotion of colored enlistments," (Philadelphia, PA, 1863), African American Pamphlet Collection, Library of Congress.

17. *Mark Lardas, African American Soldier in the Civil War* (Oxford, UK: Osprey Publishing, 2006), p. 66.

18. Minutes of the Pennsylvania State Equal Rights League 1864–1872, October 10, 1864, Gardiner Papers, Historical Society of Pennsylvania.

19. Lane, *Roots of Violence*, p. 50.

20. Board of Managers Minutes, 1855–1866, Institute of Colored Youth, Friends Historical Library, Swarthmore College.

21. Catto, "Our Alma Mater."

22. Bacon, Margaret Hope, p. 24.

23. Harry Ashmore, *The Negro and the Schools* (Chapel Hill: University of North Carolina Press, 1954), pp. 6–7.

24. Ripley et al., eds., *The Black Abolitionist Papers*, p. 354.

25. "Speech of Ebenezer Bassett," Misc. Monographs and Pamphlets, microform 41431, Library of Congress.

26. Homer Calkin, "First Black U.S. Diplomat Was Consul General in Haiti," *Department of State Newsletter* (February 1980): 42.

27. Letters of Application and Recommendation (Andrew Johnson), Bassett to Seward, M 650, National Archives.

Chapter 6

1. United States Department of State, "Frequently Asked Historical Questions," http://www.state.gov/r/pa/ho/faq/.

2. As cited in "The Haytian Mission," unknown newspaper clipping, Charlotte Brown personal archives. Lincoln University no longer has the record of Bassett's honorary degree in a Master of Arts, according to an e-mail from Lincoln University's Susan Pevar, 5/7/2007.

3. Frederick Douglass, *Life and Times of Frederick Douglass: His Early Life as a Slave, His Escape from Bondage, and His Complete History to the Present Time* (Hartford, CT: Park Publishing Co., 1881), p. 425.

4. Letters of Application and Recommendations (Ulysses S. Grant), Bassett to Grant, March 17, 1869, M 968, National Archives.

5. "Hayti," New York Times, May 12, 1869, p. 4.

6. "Hayti," *New York Times*, May 12, 1869, p. 4.

7. *Journal of the Executive Proceedings of the Senate of the United States of America, 1869–1871*, Monday, April 12, 1869, p. 123.

8. "Washington," *New York Times*, April 13, 1869, p. 1.

9. "President Grant's Administration," *Chicago Tribune*, April 16, 1869, p. 2.

10. "Ebenezer D. Bassett," *Harper's Weekly*, May 1, 1869, p. 285.

11. *Journal of the Executive Proceedings of the Senate of the United States of America, 1869–1871*, Friday, April 16, 1869, p. 199.

12. Homer Calkin, "First Black U.S. Diplomat Was Consul General in Haiti," *Department of State Newsletter* (February 1980): 43.

13. E. D. Bassett, "Reminiscence of General Grant," *The Independent* XLVI (August 30, 1894), p. 6.

14. Douglass to Bassett, April 13, 1869, Series: General Correspondence 1869, The Frederick Douglass Papers, Library of Congress.

15. Spenser St. John, *Hayti, or the Black Republic* (London: Smith, Elder & Co., 1884), p. 113.

16. "Outrages in Hayti," *New York Times*, March 27, 1869, p. 6.

17. "Public Reception of the Hon. Ebenezer D. Bassett, Minister and Consul General to Hayti, at Shiloh Church New York," *National Anti-Slavery Standard* XXX(7) (June 19, 1869): p. 1.

18. Bassett to Douglass, July 3, 1869, Series: General Correspondence 1869, The Frederick Douglass Papers, Library of Congress.

19. "The Attack on Ex-Minister Hollister at Port-au-Prince Mr. Bassett.," *New York Times*, September 17, 1869, p. 2.

20. "Hayti," unknown newspaper, as cited in Wilma Dockett-McLeod, *Ebenezer Don Carlos Bassett* (Bloomington, IN: AuthorHouse, 2005), p. 53.

21. Hayti. Bassett to Fish, September 16, 1869, M 82, Roll 3, Department of State Despatches, National Archives.

22. Hayti, Crosswell to Fish, January 19, 1870, M 9, Roll 10, Despatches from Consul in Cap Hatien, Department of State Correspondence, National Archives.

23. Hayti, Bassett to Fish, July 24, 1869, M 82, Roll 3, Department of State Despatches, National Archives.

24. Hayti, Bassett to Fish, September 16, 1869, M 82, Roll 3, Department of State Despatches, National Archives.

25. Hayti, Fish to Bassett, October 13, 1869, File 77, Roll 95, Diplomatic Instructions of the Department of States, National Archives.

26. Hayti, Bassett to Fish, November 2, 1869, M 82, Roll 3, Department of State Despatches, National Archives.

27. Hayti, Fish to Bassett, December 16, 1869, File 77, Roll 95, Diplomatic Instructions of the Department of States, National Archives.

28. Hayti, Fish to Bassett, January 2, 1870, File 77, Roll 95, Diplomatic Instructions of the Department of States, National Archives.

29. Hayti, Bassett to Fish, January 15, 1870, M 82, Roll 3, Department of State Despatches, National Archives.

30. H. P. Davis, *Black Democracy*, New York: Dodge Publishing, 1936, pp. 128–129.

Chapter 7

1. "The Mania for Expansion: The St. Domingo Negotiations," *New York Times*, February 8, 1869, p. 4.

2. "Secretaries Travel Abroad," http://www.state.gov/r/pa/ho/trvl/ls/12993.htm.

3. Hayti, Bassett to Rameau, February 15, 1870, M 82, Roll 3, Department of State Despatches, National Archives.

4 Hayti, Bassett to Fish, January 15, 1870, M 82, Roll 3, Department of State Despatches, National Archives.

5. Hayti, Fish to Bassett, December 22, 1869, File 77, Roll 95, Diplomatic Instructions of the Department of States, National Archives.

6. Homer Calkin, "First Black U.S. Diplomat Was Consul General in Haiti." Department of State Newsletter, February 1980, p. 44.

7. Hayti, Bassett to Fish, February 17, 1870, M 82, Roll 3, Department of State Despatches, National Archives.

8. Hayti, Bassett to Fish, January 15, 1870, M 82, Roll 3, Department of State Despatches, National Archives.

9. Hayti, Bassett to Fish, February 17, 1870, M 82, Roll 3, Department of State Despatches, National Archives.

10. It was not until years later that Bassett revealed those sentiments in an article he wrote entitled "Should Haiti be Annexed to the United States?" *Voice of the Negro*, May 1904, 191–198.

11. Hayti, Fish to Bassett, February 4, 1870, File 77, Roll 95, Diplomatic Instructions of the Department of States, National Archives.

12. Hayti, Bassett to Lallemand, April 1, 1870, M 82, Roll 3, Department of State Despatches, National Archives.

13. "Hayti and San Domingo," *New York Times*, March 3, 1870, p. 4.

14. "Hayti," in *Foreign Relations of the United States (FRUS)*, (Washington, D.C.: Government Printing Office, 1870), p. 8.

15. Hayti, Fish to Bassett, February 9, 1871, File 77, Roll 95, Diplomatic Instructions of the Department of States, National Archives.

16. Frederick Douglass, *Life and Times of Frederick Douglass: His Early Life as a Slave, His Escape from Bondage, and His Complete History to the Present Time* (Hartford, CT: Park Publishing Co., 1881), pp. 416–418.

17. "Hayti," *New York Times,* September 7, 1870, p. 5.

18. Records have not been found to indicate her exact date of death, and it is unknown if Susan Bassett died around the time of this trip.

19. "Reception of Hon. E.D. Bassett, the Colored Minister to Hayti," *New York Times,* September 23, 1870, p. 8.

20. Hayti, Fish to Bassett, February 9, 1871, File 77, Roll 95, Diplomatic Instructions of the Department of States, National Archives.

21. Hayti, Bassett to Denis, September 19, 1871, M 82, Roll 4, State Department Despatches, National Archives.

22. "The West Indies," *New York Times,* February 5, 1871, p. 1.

23. Hayti, Fish to Bassett, March, 24, 1871, File 77, Roll 95, Diplomatic Instructions of the Department of States, National Archives.

24. "USS Hornet (1865–1869)," http://www.history.navy.mil/photos/sh-usn/usnsh-h/hornet5.htm.

25. Hayti, Bassett to Fish, December 8, 1871, M 82, Roll 4, State Department Despatches, National Archives.

26. "Hayti," *New York Times,* February 8, 1872, p. 5.

27. Hayti, Bassett to Fish, May 27, 1871, M 82, Roll 4, State Department Despatches, National Archives.

Chapter 8

1. *Hayti,* Bulletin No. 62, Bureau of the American Republics, Department of State (Washington, D.C.: Government Printing Office, 1892), p. 10. This work is written by Ebenezer Bassett, but he is not credited as author.

2. Hayti, Bassett to Fish, February 17, 1873, M 82, Roll 5, State Department Despatches, National Archives.

3. "Cannibalism in Hayti," *New York Times,* November 8, 1871, p. 8.

4. "Revolutionary Hayti," *New York Times,* March 17, 1872, p. 3.

5. Hayti, Bassett to Fish, March, 25, 1872, in *FRUS* (Washington, D.C.: Government Printing Office, 1872), p. 264.

6. "Hayti, Bassett to Fish, March 25, 1872, M 82 Roll 4, State Department Despatches, National Archives.

7. Hayti, Bassett to Etheart, May 31, 1872, in *FRUS* (Washington, D.C.: Government Printing Office, 1872), p. 283.

8. "Hayti Claims an Outrage," *New York Times,* May 21, 1872, p. 1.

9. Hayti, Etheart to Bassett, June 5, 1872, in *FRUS* (Washington, D.C.: Government Printing Office, 1872), p. 283.

10. Hayti, Fish to Bassett, June 26, 1872, File 77, Roll 95, Diplomatic Instructions of the Department of States, National Archives.

11. Hayti, Bassett to Fish, July 27, 1872, in *FRUS* (Washington, D.C.: Government Printing Office, 1872), p. 285.

12. Hayti, Bassett to Fish, February 17, 1873, M 82, Roll 5, Department of State Despatches, National Archives.

13. Hayti, Fish to Bassett, October 5, 1872, in *FRUS* (Washington, D.C.: Government Printing Office, 1872), p. 300.

14. Hayti, Bassett to Fish, February 17, 1873, M 82, Roll 5, Department of State Despatches, National Archives.

15. Hayti, Bassett to Fish, May 24, 1873, M 82, Roll 6, Department of State Despatches, National Archives.

16. Hayti, Fish to Bassett, June 7, 1873, File 77, Roll 96, Diplomatic Instructions of the Department of States, National Archives.

17. Hayti, Fish to Bassett, August 31, 1872, File 77, Roll 95, Diplomatic Instructions of the Department of States, National Archives.

18. Hayti, Bassett to Fish, October 3, 1872, M 82, Roll 5, Department of State Despatches, National Archives.

19. Hayti, Fish to Bassett, December 11, 1872, File 77, Roll 95, Diplomatic Instructions of the Department of States, National Archives.

Chapter 9

1. Hayti, Bassett to Fish, February 17, 1873, M 82, Roll 5, Department of State Despatches, National Archives.

2. Hayti, Bassett to Ames, June 4, 1873, M 82, Roll 6, Department of State Despatches, National Archives.

3. "Hayti," *New York Times,* May 26, 1873, p. 8.

4. Hayti, Bassett to Fish, January 18, 1870, M 82, Roll 3, Department of State Despatches, National Archives.

5. Hayti, Bassett to Fish, April 12, 1871, M 82, Roll 4, Department of State Despatches, National Archives.

6. Hayti, Bassett to Fish, March 25, 1872, M 82, Roll 4, Department of State Despatches, National Archives.

7. Hayti, Bassett to Fish, November 6, 1872, M 82, Roll 4, Department of State Despatches, National Archives.

8. Hayti, Bassett to Fish, February 17, 1873, M 82, Roll 5, Department of State Despatches, National Archives.

9. "Hayti," May, 6, 1873, in *FRUS* (Washington, D.C.: Government Printing Office, 1873).

10. Hayti, Bassett to Fish, February 17, 1873, M 82, Roll 5, Department of State Despatches, National Archives.

11. Hayti, Bassett to Fish, October 29, 1873, M 82, Roll 5, Department of State Despatches, National Archives.

12. "Hayti," October 16, 1873, in *FRUS* (Washington D.C.: Government Printing Office, 1873).

13. Hayti, Bassett to Fish February 17, 1873, M 82, Roll 5, Department of State Despatches, National Archives.

14. Hayti, Bassett to Fish, March 11, 1873, M 82, Roll 5, Department of State Despatches, National Archives.

15. Hayti, Bassett to Fish, May 16, 1873, M 82, Roll 6, Department of State Despatches, National Archives.

16. Hayti, Bassett to Fish, May 16, 1873, M 82, Roll 6, Department of State Despatches, National Archives.

17. "Hayti," *New York Times,* May 26, 1873, p. 8.

18. Hayti, Fish to Bassett, June 27, 1873, File 77, Roll 96, Diplomatic Instructions of the Department of States, National Archives.

19. Hayti, Bassett to Fish, April 16, 1873, M 82, Roll 6, Department of State Despatches, National Archives.

20. Hayti, Fish to Bassett, May 3, 1873, File 77, Roll 95, Department of State Despatches, National Archives.

21. Hayti, Bassett to Fish, August 11, 1873, M 82, Roll 6 Department of State Despatches, National Archives.

22. Hayti, Bassett to Fish, September 15, 1873, M 82, Roll 6, Department of State Despatches, National Archives.

23. "Latest News by Cable," *New York Times,* October 15, 1873, p. 1.

24. Hayti, Bassett to Fish, January 23, 1874, M 82, Roll 7, Department of State Despatches, National Archives.

25. Hayti, Bassett to Fish, January 15, 1870, M 82, Roll 3, Department of State Despatches, National Archives.

26. Hayti, Bassett to Fish, March 22, 1870, M 82, Roll 3, Department of State Despatches, National Archives.

27. Hayti, Bassett to Fish, February 23, 1874, M 82, Roll 7, Department of State Despatches, National Archives.

28. Hayti, Bassett to Fish, February 23, 1874, M 82, Roll 7, Department of State Despatches, National Archives.

29. Hayti, Bassett to Fish, April 17, 1874, M 82, Roll 7, Department of State Despatches, National Archives.

30. "Hayti," *New York Times*, April 26, 1874, p. 1.

31. *Hayti,* Bulletin No. 62, Bureau of the American Republics, Department of State (Washington, D.C.: Government Printing Office, 1892), p. 25.

32. Hayti, Fish to Bassett, April 20, 1874, File 77, Roll 95, Diplomatic Instructions of the Department of States, National Archives.

33. Tuttle, Roger, *Quarter Century Record of the Class of Ninety-Five, Yale College,* Yale University Archives (New Haven, CT: Tuttle, Morehouse, and Taylor Company, 1922), p. 106.

34. Hayti, Bassett to Consulates, May 2, 1874, M 82, Roll 7, Department of State Despatches, National Archives.

35. Hayti, Bassett to Fish, May 21, 1874, M 82, Roll 7, Department of State Despatches, National Archives.

36. Hayti, Bassett to Fish, June 23, 1874, M 82, Roll 7, Department of State Despatches, National Archives.

37. Hayti, Bassett to Fish, May 21, 1874, M 82, Roll 7, Department of State Despatches, National Archives.

Chapter 10

1. Hayti, Bassett to Fish, June 6, 1874, File 77, Roll 96, Diplomatic Instruction of the Department of State, National Archives.

2. Hayti, Bassett to Fish, June 6, 1874, File 77, Roll 96, Diplomatic Instruction of the Department of State, National Archives.

3. "Hayti," *New York Times*, November 3, 1874, p. 5.

4. Hayti, Bassett to Fish, June 22, 1874, M 82, Roll 7, Department of State Despatches, National Archives.

5. Hayti, Bassett to Fish, September 9, 1874, M 82, Roll 7, Department of State Despatches, National Archives.

6. Hayti, Bassett to Fish, October 28, 1874, M 82, Roll 7, Department of State Despatches, National Archives.

7. Hayti, Bassett to Fish, January 28, 1875, M 82, Roll 7, Department of State Despatches, National Archives.

8. Hayti, Bassett to Fish, June 6, 1874, M 82, Roll 7, Department of State Despatches, National Archives.

9. St. John, Spenser, p. 118.

10. Hayti, Bassett to Fish, February 3, 1875, M 82, Roll 7, Department of State Despatches, National Archives.

11. Heinl, Robert and Nancy, *Written in Blood* (Lanham, MD: University Press of America, 1996), p. 245. British Consul St. John referred to Domingue as a Papaloi, or head priest of one of the sects, in St. John, p. 124.

12. "Hayti," *New York Times,* February 12, 1875, p. 1.

13. Hayti, Bassett to Fish, February 24, 1875, M 82, Roll 7, Department of State Despatches, National Archives.

14. Hayti, Bassett to Fish, April 9, 1875, M 82, Roll 7, Department of State Despatches, National Archives.

15. Hayti, Fish to Bassett, May 3, 1875, File 77, Roll 96, Diplomatic Instruction of the Department of State, National Archives.

16. "Revolution in Hayti," *New York Times,* May 6, 1875, p. 1.

17. Hayti, Bassett to Fish, May 8, 1875, M 82, Roll 7, Department of State Despatches, National Archives.

18. Hayti, Fish to Bassett, June 4, 1875, File 77, Roll 96, Diplomatic Instruction of the Department of State, National Archives.

19. Hayti, Bassett to Fish, May 19, 1875, M 82, Roll 8, Department of State Despatches, National Archives.

20. Hayti, Bassett to Fish, May 19, 1875, M 82, Roll 8, Department of State Despatches, National Archives.

21. Hayti, Bassett to Fish, May 8, 1875, M 82, Roll 8, Department of State Despatches, National Archives.

22. Hayti, Bassett to Fish, July 16, 1875, M 82, Roll 8, Department of State Despatches, National Archives.

23. Hayti, Bassett to Fish, July 16, 1875, M 82, Roll 8, Department of State Despatches, National Archives.

24. Hayti, Bassett to Fish, June 8, 1875, M 82, Roll 8, Department of State Despatches, National Archives.

25. Bassett to Cadwalader, Consular Despatches, Port au Prince, September 9, 1875, T 346, Roll 5, National Archives.

26. Bassett to Cadwalader, Consular Despatches, Port au Prince, September 9, 1875, T 346, Roll 5, National Archives.

27. Hayti and Santo Domingo, Fish to Bassett, September 7, 1875, File 77, Roll 96, Diplomatic Instruction of the Department of State, National Archives.

28. "The Haytien Difficulty," *New York Times,* September 21, 1875, p. 1.

29. Hayti, Bassett to Fish, October 12, 1875, M 82, roll 8, Department of State Despatches, National Archives.

30. Hayti, Bassett to Fish, October 5, 1875, M 82, Roll 8, Department of State Despatches, National Archives.

31. Hayti and Santo Domingo, Fish to Bassett, November 10, 1875, File 77, Roll 96, Diplomatic Instruction of the Department of State, National Archives.

32. Bassett to Cadwalader, Consular Despatches, Port au Prince, November 30, 1875, T 346, Roll 5, National Archives.

Chapter 11

1. Hayti, Bassett to Fish, January 19, 1876, M 82, Roll 8, Department of State Despatches, National Archives.

2. "Discontent with the Government Increasing—Symptoms of Another Revolution," *New York Times*, January 24, 1876, p. 1.

3. "Hayti," *New York Times*, January 29, 1876, p. 1.

4. Hayti, Bassett to Fish, February 17, 1876, M 82, Roll 8, Department of State Despatches, National Archives.

5. Hayti, Bassett to Fish, January 19, 1876, M 82, Roll 8, Department of State Despatches, National Archives.

6. Hayti, Fish to Bassett, April 27, 1876, File 77, Roll 96, Diplomatic Instruction of the Department of State, National Archives.

7. Hayti, Bassett to Fish, June 26, 1875, M 82, Roll 8, Department of State Despatches, National Archives.

8. Bassett to Cadwalader, Consular Despatches, Port au Prince, January 18, 1877, T 346, Roll 5, National Archives.

9. Hayti, Bassett to Fish, February 17, 1876, M 82, Roll 8, Department of State Despatches, National Archives.

10. Hayti, Bassett to Fish, March 13, 1876, M 82, Roll 9, Department of State Despatches, National Archives.

11. Hayti, Bassett to Fish, March 11, 1876, M 82, Roll 9, Department of State Despatches, National Archives.

12. Hayti, Bassett to Fish, March 25, 1876, M 82, Roll 9, Department of State Despatches, National Archives.

13. Hayti, Bassett to Fish, April 10, 1876, M 82, Roll 9, Department of State Despatches, National Archives.

14. St. John, Spenser, p. 123.

15. Hayti, Bassett to Fish, April 27, 1876, M 82, Roll 9, Department of State Despatches, National Archives.

16. "The West Indies," *New York Times,* May 4, 1876, p. 5, and Robert and Nancy Heinl, p. 246.

17. Hayti, Fish to Bassett, June 6, 1876, File 77, Roll 96, Diplomatic Instruction of the Department of State, National Archives.

18. Hayti, Bassett to Fish, April 27, 1876, M 82, Roll 9, Department of State Despatches, National Archives.

19. Fanny Jackson-Coppin, p. 140. Unfortunately, Yale records no longer show any record of Ebenezer Bassett lecturing at the school.

20. *FRUS* (Washington, D.C.: Government Printing Office, 1875), p. iii.

21. "The Disputed Election of 1876," The Rutherford B. Hayes Presidential Center, http://www.rbhayes.org/hayes/president/display.asp?id=511&subj=president.

22. "Voter turnout in Presidential Elections," The American Presidency Project, University of California, Santa Barbara, http://www.presidency.ucsb.edu/data/turnout.php.

23. Hayti, Bassett to Fish, May 31, 1876, M 82, Roll 9, Department of State Despatches, National Archives.

24. "The United States and Hayti," *New York Times,* January 12, 1877, p. 2.

25. Hayti, Bassett to Fish, January 30, 1877, M 82, Roll 9, Department of State Despatches, National Archives.

26. "The West Indies," *New York Times,* March 24, 1877, p. 2.

27. Hayti, Bassett to Evarts, July 25, 1877, M 82, Roll 10, Department of State Despatches, National Archives.

28. Letters of Application and Recommendation (Andrew Johnson), Langston to Seward, M 650, National Archives.

29. Langston, John M., *From the Virginia Plantation to the National Capitol* (New York: Arno Press, 1996), p. 276. Langston claimed that he was actually offered the position in Port-au-Prince first by President Johnson in 1867 but turned it down. There is no record that indicates this, however.

30. Hayti, Evarts to Bassett, July 23, 1877, File 77, Roll 95, Diplomatic Instructions of the Department of States, National Archives.

31. Hayti, Bassett to Evarts, August 23, 1877, M 82, Roll 10, Department of State Despatches, National Archives.

32. Roger Tuttle, p. 106.

33. Hayti, Evarts to Bassett, October 5, 1877, File 77, Roll 96, Diplomatic Instruction of the Department of State, National Archives.

34. Langston, *From the Virginia Plantation to the National Capitol* (New York: Arno Press, 1996), p. 362.

35. Hayti, Langston to Evarts, November 29, 1877, M 82, Roll 10, Department of State Despatches, National Archives.

Chapter 12

1. 1880 Census, Philadelphia, PA, p. 135B, National Archives.

2. E-mail from Yale University Archivist Rebecca Hatcher indicating that Ebenezer D. C. Bassett attended classes from 1881–1882 but he did not graduate from Yale.

3. "History," http://www.hopkins.edu/who/history/.

4. 1880 Census, New Haven, CT, p. 218A.

5. "Wrongs of the Colored Race," *New York Times*, April 5, 1880, p. 8; and "The Arkansas Refugees," *New York Times*, April 25, 1880, p. 11.

6. "Hayti," in *FRUS* (Washington, D.C.: Government Printing Office, 1879), p. 567.

7. "Hayti," in *FRUS* (Washington, D.C.: Government Printing Office, 1879), p. 572.

8. Preston to Evarts, December 20, 1879, Notes from the Haytian Legation, T 803, Roll 3, National Archives.

9. "E. D. Bassett's New Position," *People's Advocate*, January 3, 1880, personal archives of James and Charlotte Brown.

10. "Hayti," in *FRUS* (Washington, DC: Government Printing Office, 1878), p. 411.

11. "Hayti," in *FRUS* (Washington, DC: Government Printing Office, 1879), p. 547.

12. "Hayti," in *FRUS* (Washington, DC: Government Printing Office, 1881), p. 645

13. "The Old Guard Reception," *New York Times*, January 15, 1882, p. 7.

14. "Lincoln Birthday Banquet," *New York Times*, February 15, 1882, p. 5.

15. "The Princess Soulouque," *Bulletin*, July 8, 1882, personal archives of James and Charlotte Brown.

16. "Hayti," in FRUS 1882 (Washington, DC: Government Printing Office, 1882), pp. 361–362.

17. "The Trouble in Hayti," *New York Times*, September 15, 1883, p. 2.

18. "A Suspected Cargo Detained," *New York Times*, November 20, 1883, p. 5.

19. "Washington Notes," *New York Times,* November 25, 1883, p. 7.

20. Langston, John M., p. 393.

21. "Hayti," in *FRUS* 1883 (Washington, D.C.: Government Printing Office, 1883), p. 586.

22. "The Haytian Minister," *New York Times,* February 3, 1884, p. 6.

23. Notes from Haitian Legation, Preston to Frelinghuysen, February 29, 1884, T 803, Roll 3, National Archives.

24. "Expressions of Sympathy," *New York Times,* July 21, 1885, p. 1.

25. "A Nation at a Tomb," *New York Times,* August 9, 1885, p. 1.

26. "The General's First Name," *New York Times,* August 4, 1885, p. 1.

27. Notes from Haitian Legation, Bassett to Frelinghuysen, October 22, 1884, T 803, Roll 4, National Archives.

28. Notes from Haitian Legation, Bassett to Davis, January 13, 1885, T 803, Roll 4, National Archives.

29. "Chiefs of Mission by Country, 1778-2005," Hayti, http://www.state.gov/r/pa/ho/po/com/10876.htm. In fact, another black man, George Washington Williams, had been nominated by the lame-duck Arthur administration, but Williams never took the posting.

30. "Hayti," in *FRUS* (Washington, D.C.: Government Printing Office, 1885), p. 521.

31. James Padgett, "Diplomats to Haiti and Their Diplomacy," *Journal of Negro History* Vol. XXV, No. 3, (July 1940), p. 289.

32. "Hayti," in FRUS (Washington, DC: Government Printing Office, 1885), p. 543. Van Bokkelen's representatives were later awarded $60,000 by the arbitrator in the claim. Hayti, in *FRUS* (Washington, D.C.: Government Printing Office, 1888), p. 1036.

33. "Hayti," in *FRUS* (Washington, D.C.: Government Printing Office, 1886), pp. 543–545.

34. "The Black Republic," *Chicago Daily,* December 16, 1888, p. 27.

35. "Hayti," in *FRUS* (Washington, D.C.: Government Printing Office, 1888), p. 942.

36. "Condition of Affairs in Hayti," *New York Times,* November 9, 1888, p. 8.

37. "Prospect of Peace in Hayti," *Chicago Daily Tribune,* November 23, 1888, p. 6.

38. "Hayti," in *FRUS* (Washington, DC: Government Printing Office, 1888), p. 936.

39. "Badly Treated in Hayti," *New York Times,* November 30, 1888, p. 5.

40. "On the Bounding Billow," *New York Times*, December 13, 1888, p. 5.

41. "The Black Republic," *Chicago Daily*, December 16, 1888, p. 27.

42. "Hayti," in *FRUS* (Washington, D.C.: Government Printing Office, 1888), p. 990.

43. Notes from Haitian Legation, Haustedt to Bayard, December 7, 1888, T 803, Roll 4, National Archives.

44. "The Black Republic," *Chicago Daily*, December 16, 1888, p. 27.

Chapter 13

1. "Wants to be Minister," *New York Times*, May 22, 1889, p. 1.

2. Bassett to Douglass, November 21, 1888, Series: *General Correspondence 1888, The Frederick Douglass Papers*, Library of Congress.

3. Bassett to Douglass, March 6, 1889, Series: *General Correspondence 1889, The Frederick Douglass Papers*, Library of Congress.

4. Bassett to Douglass, June 27, 1889, *Series: General Correspondence 1889, The Frederick Douglass Papers*, Library of Congress.

5. Bassett to Douglass, July 11, 1889, Series: *General Correspondence 1889, The Frederick Douglass Papers*, Library of Congress.

6. Bassett to Douglass, July 24, 1889, Series: *General Correspondence 1889, The Frederick Douglass Papers*, Library of Congress.

7. Ludwell Lee Montague, *Haiti and the United States: 1714–1938* (Durham, NC: Duke University Press, 1940), pp. 129–143.

8. Bassett to Douglass, September 2, 1889, Series: *General Correspondence 1889, The Frederick Douglass Papers*, Library of Congress.

9. Bassett to Douglass, September 9, 1889, Series: *General Correspondence 1889, The Frederick Douglass Papers*, Library of Congress.

10. David Healy, *James. G. Blaine and Latin America* (Columbia: University of Missouri Press, 2001), p. 189.

11. "Douglass Trip to Hayti," *New York Times*, September 30, 1889, p. 5.

12. "Hayti," in *FRUS* (Washington, D.C.: Government Printing Office, 1890), p. 521.

13. "Hayti," in *FRUS* (Washington, D.C.: Government Printing Office, 1890), p. 532.

14. Bassett to Douglass, July 27, 1890, Series: *General Correspondence 1890, The Frederick Douglass Papers*, Library of Congress.

15. Bassett to Douglass, August 30, 1890, Series: *General Correspondence 1890, The Frederick Douglass Papers,* Library of Congress.

16. "About Diplomats," *New York Times,* January 13, 1890, p. 2.

17. Bassett to Douglass, October 10, 1890, Series: *General Correspondence 1890, The Frederick Douglass Papers,* Library of Congress.

18. Douglass to Blaine, January 6, 1891, Series: *General Correspondence 1891, The Frederick Douglass Papers,* Library of Congress.

19. Frederick Douglass, *Life and Times of Frederick Douglass* (Boston, MA: De Wolfe and Fisk Co., 1892), p. 735.

20. Mole St. Nicholas, Folder 1 of 4, Speech, Article, and Book File, 1846–1894 and Undated. The Frederick Douglass Papers, Library of Congress.

21. Douglass, Frederick, *Life and Times,* p. 738.

22. E. Bassett, "Should Haiti be Annexed to the United States?" *The Voice of the Negro,* May 1904, p. 193.

23. Douglass to Blaine, April 20, 1890, M 82, Roll 25, Department of State Despatches, National Archives.

24. William McFeely, *Frederick Douglass* (New York: W.W. Norton and Company, 1991), p. 359.

25. Douglass, *Life and Times,* p. 745.

26. "Minister Douglass at Home," *The New York Times,* July 4, 1891, p. 8.

27. "The Haytian Complication," *Chicago Tribune,* April 18, 1891, p. 4.

28. Bassett to Douglass, July 14, 1891, Series: *General Correspondence 1891, The Frederick Douglass Papers,* Library of Congress.

29. "A Haytian Refugee's Story," *New York Sun,* June 7, 1891, p. 4.

30. "Bassett Denies It All," *New York Sun,* June 8, 1891, p. 4.

31. "Douglass's Own Story," *New York World,* July 13, 1891, p. 2.

32. Bassett to Douglass, August 1, 1891, Series: *General Correspondence 1891, The Frederick Douglass Papers,* Library of Congress.

33. Douglass, *Life and Times,* p. 726.

34. *Hayti,* Bulletin No. 62, Bureau of the American Republics, Department of State (Washington, D.C.: Government Printing Office, 1892), p. 68. Although this work was written by Ebenezer Bassett, he is not credited as author.

35. Hayti, Speech, Article, and Book File, 1846–1894 and Undated. The Frederick Douglass Papers, Library of Congress.

Chapter 14

1. Padgett, James, "Diplomats to Haiti and Their Diplomacy," *Journal of Negro History* XXV(3) (July 1940): p. 297.

2. *Hayti,* Bulletin No. 62, Bureau of the American Republics (Washington, D.C.: Government Printing Office, 1892), 11, 12, 23, and 68.

3. "Bulkeley to Head the List," *New York Times,* May 4, 1892, p. 5.

4. Bassett to Douglass, November 26, 1893, Series: *General Correspondence 1893, The Frederick Douglass Papers,* Library of Congress.

5. Bassett to Douglass, January 18, 1894, Series: *General Correspondence 1894, The Frederick Douglass Papers,* Library of Congress.

6. Archives of Hopkins Academy. E-mail from archivist Thom Peters, July 2007.

7. "Negroes in the North Protest," *Chicago Tribune,* November 18, 1898, p. 5.

8. Fanny Jackson-Coppin, *Reminiscences of School Life, and Hints on Teaching.* (Philadelphia, PA: L. J. Coppin, 1913), pp. 140–141.

9. "The Haytian Consul's View," *New York Times,* August 4, 1899, p. 7.

10. Bassett, E., "Should Haiti be Annexed to the United States," *The Voice of the Negro,* May 1904, p. 198.

11. Bassett, E. D., "Education and Schools in Philadelphia," *African Methodist Episcopal Church Review* 15(3) (January 1899): p. 728.

12. Bassett, E. D., "No Cannibalism in Haiti," *New York Sun,* March 24, 1901.

13. Bassett to Adger, September 22, 1904, Carter Woodson Collection, Library of Congress, Reel 7.

14. Obituary, *New York Times,* November 15, 1908, p. 9.

Chapter 15

1. Robert Plante, *Ebenezer Don Carlos Bassett: United States Minister to Haiti 1869–1877* (Master's Thesis, Omaha: University of Nebraska at Omaha, 1969), p. 122.

2. Marc Susser and Kathleen Rasmussen, "The African American Heritage." U.S. Department of State Career Newsletter, March/April 2006.

3. Hayti, Bassett to Fish, October 12, 1875, M 82, Roll 8, Department of State Despatches, National Archives.

4. Frederick Douglass, *The Life and Times of Frederick Douglass* (Hartford, CT: Park Publishing, 1883), p. 510.

Bibliography

Books

Ashmore, Harry. *The Negro and the Schools*. Chapel Hill: University of North Carolina Press, 1954.

Clark, George. *A History of Connecticut*. G. P. Putman and Sons, 1914.

The Collected Works of Abraham Lincoln, vol. 5, New Brunswick, NJ: Rutgers University Press, 1953.

Davis, H. P. *Black Democracy*, New York: Dodge Publishing, 1936.

Dockett-McLeod, Wilma. *Ebenezer Don Carlos Bassett*. Bloomington, Indiana: AuthorHouse, 2005.

Douglass, Frederick. *Life and Times of Frederick Douglass: His Early Life as a Slave, His Escape from Bondage, and His Complete History to the Present Time*. Hartford, CT: Park Publishing Co., 1881.

Douglass, Frederick. *Life and Times of Frederick Douglass*. Boston: De Wolfe and Fisk Co., 1892.

Edwards, Bryan. *An Historical Survey of the Island of Saint Domingo, and Account of the Revolt of Negroes in 1791, and a Detail of the Military Transactions of the British Army in that Island in 1793 and 1794*. London, 1796.

Foreign Relations of the United States (FRUS). Washington D.C.: Government Printing Office, editions from 1869–1891.

Hayti, Bulletin No. 62, Bureau of the American Republics. Department of State, Washington, D.C.: Government Printing Office, 1892, p. 68. (This work was written by Ebenezer Bassett, but he is not credited as author).

Healy, David. *James G. Blaine and Latin America*. Columbia: University of Missouri Press, 2001.

Heinl, Robert and Nancy. *Written in Blood*. Lanham: University Press of America, 1996.

Jackson-Coppin, Fanny. *Reminiscences of School Life, and Hints on Teaching*. Philadelphia: L. J. Coppin, 1913.

Lane, Roger. *Roots of Violence in Black Philadelphia: 1860–1900*. Cambridge, MA: Harvard University Press, 1986.

Langston, John Mercer. *From the Virginia Plantation to the National Capitol*. New York: Arno Press, 1996.

Lardas, Mark. *African American Solider in the Civil War*, Oxford: Osprey Publishing, 2006.

Logan, Rayford. *The Diplomatic Relations of the United States with Haiti: 1776–1891*. Chapel Hill: University of North Carolina Press, 1941.

Matthewson, Tim. *A Proslavery Foreign Policy*. Westport, CT: Praeger, 2003.

McFeely, William. *Frederick Douglass*. New York: W.W. Norton and Company, 1991.

Montague, Ludwell Lee. *Haiti and the United States: 1714–1938*, Durham, NC: Duke University Press, 1940.

Orcutt, Samuel. *The History of the Old Town of Derby, Connecticut, 1641–1880: With Biographies and Genealogies*. Springfield, MA: unknown, 1880.

Peguero, Valentina, and de los Santos, Danilo. *Vision General de la Historia Dominicana*. Universidad Catolica Madre y Maestra, 1977.

Piersen, W. D. *Black Yankees: The Development of an Afro-American Subculture in Eighteenth-Century New England*. Amherst: University of Massachusetts Press, 1988.

Plante, Robert, *Ebenezer Don Carlos Bassett: United States Minister to Haiti 1869–1877*. Master's Thesis, Omaha: University of Nebraska at Omaha, 1969.

Platt, Orville, "Negro Governors." *Papers of the New Haven Colony Historical Society*, vol. 6 (1900), New Haven, CT: Tuttle, Morehouse and Taylor Co. Printers, 1900.

Ripley, C. Peter, Roy Finkenine, Michael Hembree, and Donald Yacovone, eds. *The Black Abolitionist Papers: Vol. IV: The United States, 1847–1858*, Chapel Hill: University of North Carolina Press, 1991.

Sanborn, Franklin. *The Life and Letters of John Brown*, Boston: Roberts Brothers, 1891.

Sharpe, W. C. *History of Oxford*, Seymore, CT: Record Print, 1885.

St John, Spenser. *Hayti, or the Black Republic*. London: Smith, Elder, 1884.

Town Records of Derby Connecticut, 1655–1710, Sarah Rigg Humphreys Chapter, Daughters of the American Revolution, Derby, 1901.

Warren, Israel P. *Chauncey Judd*. Naugatuck, CT: The Perry Press, 1874.

White, David O. *Connecticut's Black Soldiers: 1875–1883*. Chester, CT: Pequot Press, 1973.

Newspapers and magazines

Bacon, Margaret Hope. "The Pennsylvania Abolition Society's Mission for Black Education." *Pennsylvania Legacies*, November 2005.

Bassett, E. D. "Reminiscence of General Grant." *The Independent*, XLVI, August 30, 1894.

Bassett, E. "Should Haiti be Annexed to the United States?" *The Voice of the Negro*, May 1904.

Bell, Howard. "Some Reform Interests of the Negro During the 1850s as Reflected in State Conventions." *Phylon* Vol. 21 (Summer 1960).

Bulletin, 1882.

Calkin, Homer. "First Black U.S. Diplomat Was Consul General in Haiti." Department of State Newsletter, February 1980.

Chicago Daily, 1888.

Chicago Tribune, 1869.

Congressional Globe. 37th Congress, 2nd Session, 1862.

Gibson, Robert A. "A Deferred Dream: The Proposal for a Negro College in New Haven," *Journal of the New Haven Colony Historical Society* 37:2 (Spring 1991).

Harper's Weekly, 1869.

Journal of the executive proceedings of the Senate of the United States of America, 1869–1871, Monday, April 12, 1869.

Journal of the executive proceedings of the Senate of the United States of America, 1869–1871, Friday, April 16, 1869.

Lockett, James. "Abraham Lincoln and Colonization." *Journal of Black Studies*, Vol. 21, No. 4, 1991, pp. 428–444.

National Anti-Slavery Standard, 1869.

New York Sun, 1875–1891.

New York Times, 1869–1908.

New York World 1889–1891.

Niles Weekly Register. Baltimore, MD, 1823.

Padgett, James. "Diplomats to Haiti and Their Diplomacy." *The Journal of Negro History*, Vol. XXV, No. 3, July 1940.

The People's Advocate, 1880.

"Public Reception of the Hon. Ebenezer D. Bassett, Minister and Consul General to Hayti, at Shiloh Church New York." *National Anti-Slavery Standard*, Vol. XXX, No. 7, June 19, 1869.

Silcox, Harry C. "Nineteenth Century Philadelphia Black Militant: Octavius V. Catto (1839–1871)." *Pennsylvania History*, Vol. 44 (January 1977).

Susser, Marc, and Kathleen Rasmussen. "The African American Heritage." U.S. Department of State Career Newsletter, March/April 2006.

Tuttle, Roger. *Quarter Century Record of the Class of Ninety-Five, Yale College*, New Haven, CT: Tuttle, Morehouse, and Taylor Company, 1922.

United States Gazette, March 29, 1804, Vol. XXV, Issue 3579.

The Voice of the Negro, May 1904.

Wynes, Charles. "Ebenezer Don Carlos Bassett, America's First Black Diplomat." *Pennsylvania History* Vol. 51 (July 1984).

Yale Bulletin and Calendar, February 16, 2001, Vol. 29, No. 19.

Archives

African American Pamphlet Collection, Library of Congress.

Carter Woodson Collection, Library of Congress.

Charlotte Brown personal archives.

Census Records, 1800–1910, National Archives.

Congressional Globe. 37th Congress, 2nd Session, 1862, State Department Library.

Consular Despatches, Port au Prince, National Archives.

Daniel A. P. Murray Collection, Library of Congress.

Frederick Douglass Papers, Library of Congress.

Friends Historical Library, Swarthmore College.

Gardiner Papers, Historical Society of Pennsylvania.

Hayti. 1869–1891, Department of State Despatches, National Archives.

Hayti. 1869–1891, Diplomatic Instructions of the Department of States, National Archives.

Letters of Application and Recommendation (Andrew Johnson) Bassett to Seward, M 650, National Archives.

Letters of Application and Recommendations (Ulysses S. Grant) Bassett to Grant, March 17, 1869, M 968, National Archives.

Samuel J. May Anti-Slavery Collection, Cornell University Library.

School Records for Ebenezer D. Bassett, Central Connecticut State University Library, Special Collections.

Web sites

"A Brief History of Litchfield." Litchfield Historical Society, http://www.litchfieldct.com/twn/history.html

"Chiefs of Mission by Country, 1778–2005: Haiti," http://www.state.gov/r/pa/ho/po/com/10876.htm

"The Disputed Election of 1876." The Rutherford B. Hayes Presidential Center, http://www.rbhayes.org/hayes/president/display.asp?id=511&subj=president

"Frequently Asked Historical Questions." United States Department of State, http://www.state.gov/r/pa/ho/faq/

"History." http://www.hopkins.edu/who/history/

"Pequot History." http://www.dickshovel.com/peq.html

"Timeline of Connecticut Slavery." Mattatuck Historical Society, http://www.fortunestory.org/resources/timeline.asp

"USS *Hornet* (1865–1869)." http://www.history.navy.mil/photos/sh-usn/usnsh-h/hornet5.htm

"Voter turnout in Presidential Elections." The American Presidency Project, University of California Santa Barbara. http://www.presidency.ucsb.edu/data/turnout.php

Index

About the Author

CHRISTOPHER TEAL has extensive foreign policy experience as a consultant for the Department of Defense and Senate aide, as well as at the U.S. State Department. Fluent in Spanish, he served five years in Latin America on diplomatic assignments. He has also written on topics ranging from election monitoring to anti-Americanism and is currently a member of the editorial board of the Foreign Service Journal. Prior to his government service, he collaborated with journalist Juan Williams on the award-winning biography *Thurgood Marshall: American Revolutionary*.